THE CONCERT TRADITION

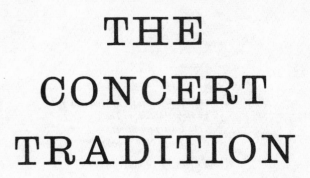

THE CONCERT TRADITION

*From the Middle Ages to the
Twentieth Century*

PERCY M. YOUNG

ROY PUBLISHERS, INC.
NEW YORK 10021

First published 1965

Published in the United States of America 1969
by Roy Publishers Inc.
30 East 74th Street,
New York, N.Y. 10021

© *Percy M. Young, 1965*

Library of Congress Catalog No. 69–15420

Printed in Great Britain

Contents

Plates

Preface

MUSICAL HISTORY IS THE SUM TOTAL OF the biographies of individual composers, of the record of the changes in expression that are collected into the category of 'forms', of the long list of mechanical refinements that have produced various kinds of instruments, and of the classification of functions which have required music. Function leads to patronage, to the direct association of a musician with a public, and to the tensions that stimulate both action and reaction.

Up to a point the patron is a familiar figure: the traditional demon king in the literature of music. Yet, being indispensable, he deserves a closer scrutiny. Thereafter he often turns out to be more agreeable than had previously been thought. But the patron is a changing figure. Pope, Emperor, King, Count, and Cardinal are certainly at the one end of the scale of patronage, but at the other are the butcher, the baker, and the candlestick-maker. In a democratic age the patron is everybody — or nobody; or the answer is the same as it was before.

The most convenient way of describing the history of patronage is by making the institution of the concert the centre-piece of an extended study. A concert, after all, is the focal point of general musical experience. Here prejudice meets enthusiasm, taste is moulded through a communal process, and the living composer is fed to the lions. The concert-life of a community is the result of local and national conventions, of attitudes to politics, to morality, to economics, to education. In this book the growth of such conventions and their relevance to each other are outlined. At the same time the manner in which different forms of organisation have affected the lives of composers and performers, and the character of musical forms, is shown. This, then, is a history of music—secular music excluding opera, that is—but with more emphasis on the audience than is normally allowed. The main part of this story lies between the seventeenth and the early twentieth centuries, the period in which the public concert as we now know it was shaped. So far as is possible the origins of the world's major musical organisations are described, but to have continued each in detail quite to the present time would have been impracticable. It seemed prudent, then, to end the book at the point at which, one day, another might begin.

There are in some societies (not for the first time) various crises to overcome; these concern the economics of music; the content of programmes; the relationship between audience and composer. All of these issues are part of a larger one (which requires no further definition), and all are at least shown to the reader. The hope is that he, now understanding his function in the partnership of music, may feel himself to be a directly interested party. The welfare of music, as a creative activity, depends not on 'them' but on 'us': if it does not, it should.

I wish to acknowledge the courtesy of the Public Trustee and the Society of Authors in permitting quotation from *The Tyranny of Ancoats* and *London Music in 1888/9* (George Bernard Shaw), and of the Oxford University Press in respect of a translation by C. S Terry taken from his *Bach: A Biography*. For assistance in the selection of illustrations I am grateful to Dr W. Eisen, Mr Charles Cudworth, Dr Konrad Sasse, Mr Edouard Robbins, the Trustees of the British Museum, and the Bärenreiter-Verlag, of Kassel.

P.M.Y.

A Process of Secularisation

INTRODUCTION

*T*HE NECESSARY COMPONENTS OF A CONCERT are these—composer(s), composition(s), performer(s), and audience. In general the occasion of a concert is accepted as secular, though this is by no means obligatory, and instrumental music tends to preponderate. In relation to the whole history of music the record of the concert, as such, is brief, covering hardly more than two and a half centuries. That this is so is due to philosophical, social, and economic factors, which have contrived to leave instrumental music in particular with a large starting handicap in relation to organised vocal music and to the other arts.

It may appear that during the last two hundred years instrumental music has more than made up for lost time; but it may be seen that not all the privileges granted to the other arts have been accorded to this form of music. It is, for example, still a subject of debate in some societies as to whether, or how, musical performances should be subsidised from public funds; and for whom, and in what form, they should be available. A good deal of this book demonstrates the virtues of self-help, of private or corporate determination. It is an account of social change, and of the effect of such change on the function of the composer and, therefore, of the constitution of music. It is also a partial answer to the abiding question as to what music 'does', or 'is'. Since the answer is given in human terms—of relationship between composer and patron (audience)—it may be described as humanistic. The derivation of this term from humanism suggests a point of departure: that at which humanism became a positive ideal. This ideal centred on present, and

1

worldly, attractions, rather than on possible eschatological penalties or rewards, and was, therefore, fundamentally opposed to the conclusions of most medieval theologians in respect of the purposes of music.

The operative word in respect of concert is organisation, and the application of this to music in a social environment depends on the principles of organisation which underlie society itself. This being so one element of musical expression, that contained within the broad limits of folk-music, is largely excluded from consideration. For folk-music is essentially a spontaneous, improvisatory, form of expression. If the threads are picked up in the middle ages it is to show that the desire to view music in the light of somewhat freer impulses than those officially defined was at least latent. The progress of medieval church music is normally considered as one of development from monody to polyphony, across a number of hazards put in its way by an authority that would appear to have been as philistine as most authorities. At the end of a long vocal tradition it is often suggested that orchestral instruments made their first effective appearance, in Venice, in the sixteenth century.

INSTRUMENTS IN CHURCH

The Establishment, insofar as musical history may be said to have one, has tended to be prejudiced against nascent instrumental music (as were the earliest theoreticians), probably because, its written evidence having largely disappeared, there is little that can directly be written about. In fact there is ample evidence to show that instruments played a considerable part in medieval church music. The English Bishop Aldhelm, who lived in the eighth century, was a well-known enthusiast for the organ, but he also described in some detail how the psalms were accompanied by a miscellany of wind and stringed instruments; while many pictorial records, from those which illuminate the Utrecht Psalter of the ninth century to the Bible of Olmütz of the fifteenth century give vivid, and realistic, suggestions as to the nature of the orchestral resources of those times. The conclusion to be drawn from allusion to instrumental *cum* vocal music by a large number of writers—John Cotton, the anonymous scribe of the *Chronicle of Ailnoth*, Adelard of Bath, and so on—is that instrumental music was not ungenerously promoted by the Church. The liveliest of the illustrators put in what the chroniclers left out or deplored—that music gave a great deal of pleasure. There is no doubt, for instance, that this infected the 'Young Musicians' of the Bible of Olmütz; nor that the rather more idealised, and angelic, ensemble of Piero della Francesca's *Nativity* were also enjoying themselves. Presuming that some of the faithful were also present on such occasions their interest and delight may reasonably be inferred. As to the nature of the music, that is largely a matter for speculation. The deduction that plainsong, accompanied by an instrumental group largely dominated by percussion, may have resembled Javanese Gamelan music[1] and may have had its associations with oriental practice leaves one standing somewhere near the neo-primitivism of some parts of contemporary popular music. But medieval church music, whatever it sounded like, was inflexibly dedicated to the attention of God rather than to the sensuous instincts of man. That the latter were probably stimulated was irrelevant, or, if not, to be condemned.

BARDIC MUSIC

Bardic music was also purposeful. This, growing from folk art, had its own *rationale*. It was instructive, and a source of valour. The conditions of bardic life are relatively familiar, but a later, somewhat anachronistic, display of the tradition shows its function in engaging terms. Sir Philip Sidney, as plenipotentiary, visited Hungary on behalf of Elizabeth I, of England, in 1573. There, in a country all but destroyed by the Turks at the time of the Battle of Mohács, he discovered the art of Sebestyén Tinódi, whose *Cronica* (1554) related national accomplishments in a melodic idiom that comprehended Turkish, ecclesiastical, and folk idioms. In that part of his *An Apologie for Poetrie* concerning 'lyric Poetry' Sidney observes on the effectiveness of Tinódi's works at 'All Feasts, and other such meetings'. By the time of Tinódi, however, the greater part of Europe had moved forward to a different, less committed, acceptance of music.

INFLUENCE OF THE TROUBADOURS

That music, together with poetry, should exist for its own sake was an idea promoted by the troubadours, the trouvères, and

[1] See W. Krüger: *Die authentische Klangform des primitiven Organum*, p. 62.

their German counterparts the Minnesänger. The music of this tradition—more relaxed and rhythmic than that of the Church, to which, however, it was bound by the general principles of tonality that then prevailed—was centred on the general theme of earthly rather than heavenly love. If the two sometimes became confused it was not altogether surprising, but the principal theme set the atmosphere for more or less uninhibited enjoyment of music. Instrumental music also played its part, and a splendid illustration of a poem by Meister Heinrich Frauenlob (of Meissen) in the thirteenth century[1] shows a viol player—watched by the Meister, who seems to be conducting the performance, and an admiring group of colleagues—apparently midway through a cadenza.

Among the trouvères these were the most important—Adam de la Halle, Guiraut d'Espanha de Toloza, and Guillaume d'Amiens; and among the Minnesänger Walther von der Vogelweide and Neidhart von Reuental. Pioneers in musical humanism, they necessarily confirmed the independent status of the active and practical musician, and in so doing began to mark a division between the performer and the audience. At the same time humanistic considerations led to the institution of standard-raising get-togethers such as the French competition known as *Le Puy* (which lasted until the seventeenth century) and the Festival of Song of the Wartburg, immortalised in *Tannhäuser*. The competitive musical festival extended its scope in Germany through the taking over of the Minnesänger tradition by the Meistersänger. Heinrich Frauenlob was the last of the Minnesänger and the first of the Meistersänger[2].

NEW IDEALS

By the time of Dante (1265–1321) through the intercourse between music and poetry, the influence of the spreading humanism that, together with intellectual and cultural activities that began to distinguish courtly society, and the acceptability of secular music, listening to and taking part in musical performances was a valuable adjunct to social life. By reference to

[1] *Manessische Handschrift*, University of Heidelberg Library.

[2] Recordings of music by these composers are issued in conjunction with *Das Orbis-Lexikon*, Ring der Musikfreunde, Cologne, 1960.

Pietro Casella, his friend and the author of songs and so-called madrigals, Dante goes some way towards establishing the special position of the composer as an individual artist. In the Second Canto of *Purgatory* Dante recognises Casella, who, exercising his art, is delaying his fellow-travellers on the way to Purgatory.

The fourteenth century in Italy was the age of the *Ars Nova*, that movement, associated with Florence, and the composer Giovanni da Cascia (Johannes de Florentia) which aimed at the future emancipation of music from the constricting influence of an increasingly rebarbative ecclesiastical science. Another notable exponent of the *Ars Nova* was the blind composer Francesco Landino, who, skilled as a performer on the organ, the lute, the rebec, and the recorder, wrote *ballate* (dance-songs), *madrigale, caccie*, and *canzone*. In such works voices and instruments met on equal terms. Landino was patronised by the ruler of Verona and applauded by the King of Cyprus, whose interest in music thus shows the place it was by now beginning to occupy among the diversions of the court.

Boccaccio does not omit to give due regard to Florentine music in the *Decameron*. After dinner on the first day the elected Queen of the assembly, Pampinea, called for musical instruments,

> for that all the ladies know how to dance, as also the young men, and some of them could both play and sing excellently. Dioneo and Fiammetta, having so been ordained, respectively took lute and viol and began, softly, to play a dance. Then the queen and the other ladies and the two other young men (the servants having been sent out to eat) danced a brawl, and when this was finished they sang a number of quaint and cheerful songs. This went on until bed-time.

So, this being at a time of plague,

> music was not silenced even in the midst of horror and despair: the Florentines thinking with Euripides, who, in his *Medea*, complains that the exquisite pleasure arising from this charming art is usually lavished on the happy at convivial festivals: whereas it should be administered to the afflicted and miserable, as a balm and cordial to mitigate the ills of life[1].

[1] A. Burgh: *Anecdotes of Music*, London 1814, I, p. 255.

In fourteenth- and fifteenth-century Florence ideals of grace in living (contrasting with theological obsession with grace in dying) were progressively established by Dante, Boccaccio, Petrarch, by Giotto, Fra Angelico, Fra Lippo Lippi, Paolo Vecello, Piero della Francesca, Botticelli, and by their princely patrons. In the process of relaxation of medieval strictness music played an increasingly important part; often in conjunction with spectacle and pageantry. Russian delegates to the Council of Florence in 1439 were captivated by the trumpets and tambours that accompanied the great procession on the Feast-day of St. John, by the multitude of instruments—trumpets, tambours, shawms, stringed instruments, and organs, that were laid on for the reception of the Pope: all this, they emphasised, was in accordance with general, local practice[1]. Whatever the occasion the Florentines celebrated it with the vivid colours of instrumental music—the acoustical counterpart of their pictorial art; and the whole of Italy was affected[2]. The influence, moreover, spread beyond Italy.

OPEN-AIR MUSIC

In England and France new and old manners met, and the musicians of the Chapels Royal found themselves associating with the minstrels in pageants, masquerades, and moresquos, in which music, impelled by visual forces, the fantasies and allegorical allusions of descriptive poetry, and the movements of the ceremonial dance, moved towards its own apotheosis. When Henry VI, of England, returned from France in 1431 he was welcomed by a fine display in the City of London, in which some token respect was paid to the spiritual values. At one point 'seven virgins' offered up the seven gifts of grace, and then sang a 'roundell with a hevynly melodye'; at another a representation of the Trinity was set up, 'with a multytude of aungellys playinge and syngynge upon all instruments of musyk'[3]. When

---

[1] Vladimir Fédorov, 'Des Russes au Concile de Florence 1438-9', in *Hans Albrecht Gedenkschrift*, pp. 27–33.

[2] See *A Concert* (School of Palma Vecchio), *The Virgin of the Girdle* (Matteo di Giovanni), and *The Virgin and Child Enthroned* (Cosimo Tura), all illustrating this point, in the National Gallery, London.

[3] Robert Fabyan: *Chronicles*, ed. H. Ellis, London, 1811, pp. 603 ff.

(a)   Church musicians, woodcut, Wittenberg, 1556.

(b)   A village concert, engraving by Jan Theodor (?) de Bry

1.   Music in Germany in the sixteenth century

2.   Collegium Musicum, Frankfurt; Members' book.

John Lydgate, the probable author of the previous piece, was requested to make a Christmas entertainment for the King and Queen at Eltham he went entirely pagan in a show, incentive to productivity, of which the climax was the offering of wine, wheat, and oil as emblems of peace, plenty, and gladness[1].

In the Mediterranean climate music in the open-air was a regular part of life, whether for the reception of some religious object of devotion (as when the supposed skull of St. Andrew reached Rome in 1462), the signification of conquest—and defeat (as in Florence in 1492 and Naples in 1494), or for some merely Bacchanalian festival. Music stretched from the lyrical *laudes* of the Church, to the *canzoni a ballo* and the *canti carnascieleschi* in which poets and musicians met on equal terms, and, further, to the lewd Carnival *burlescas* that caught the full blast of Savonarola's fulminations[2].

CITY AND COURT

In Bologna the city's fifers were well organised by 1422 and on all public occasions played to the citizens from the Palazzo della Signoria. A little more than sixty years later the bridal procession of Lucrezia d'Este was led by a lusty company of '100 trombite e 70 piferi e trombuni e chorni e flauti e tamburini e zamamele'. Municipal patronage of wind music was, by this time, common throughout Europe. In Halle, for instance, the town pipers (sometimes loaned to nearby Leipzig) were officially recognised by a Council resolution on May 9, 1461; while the *Instrumentalkapelle* of Weimar was founded, nine years before a *Vokalkapelle*, in 1482. The duties of such players —who enjoyed a privileged status—ranged from the provision of ducal chamber-music to confirming the hours of day, and blowing alarms in the case of outbreaks of fire[3]. It was from the ranks of town musicians that the Bach family sprang into prominence, and Johann Sebastian, the Leipziger, in his civic

[1] Enid Welsford, *The Court Masque*, Cambridge, 1927, p. 54.

[2] Nanie Bridgman, 'Fêtes italiennes de plein air au Quattrocento' in *Hans Albrecht Gedenkschrift*, pp. 34–38.

[3] *Halle als Musikstadt*, p. 9; Hans Pischner, *Musik und Musikerziehung in der Geschichte Weimars*, p. 7.

role maintained a long tradition[1]. As for the aristocratic leaders of fashion they were vying with each other, as they were to do for a long time to come, in pursuit of cultural ends. The Medici, whom Dufay the great Burgundian master of ecclesiastical polyphony and the secular *chanson* (he wrote 59 to French texts and 7 to Italian) visited during his Italian travels, esteemed music highly, and Lucrezia Tornatuoni, mother of Lorenzo the Magnificent, was not disinclined to interrupt a court ball in order to sing a song. At the Ferrarese Court the instrumental ensemble included lutes, viols, lyres, cornets, trombones, bagpipes, organs, and cembalo. As for the Court of Mantua, where the Gonzagas reigned and where Alberto Ripi was chief lutenist until accepting an appointment from Francis I of France, the musical activities were memorialised by Teofilo Folengo in his *Maccaroneide*.

THE VIRTUES OF MUSIC, AND THE ACCADEMIA

The scientific aspect of the Renaissance, insofar as music was concerned, met the aesthetic in the 'Academies' that were instituted, on literary models, during the fifteenth century. The first was formed in Bologna in 1482, and Milan followed suit two years later. By the middle of the sixteenth century Bologna had four such societies, as also had Siena, while in Florence there were five. The Academies varied their functions. Some were for performance and discussion, some for instruction, and some for joint endeavours in music and drama.

By these means music became established as a necessary accomplishment, and Baldassare Castiglione could write as follows in *Il Cortegiano* (1528), a text-book of gallantry that affected England through Thomas Hoby's translation, and the derivative writings of Surrey, Sidney, and Spenser.

'My Lords', said the Count, 'you must think I am not pleased with the Courtier if he be not also a musician, and besides his understanding and cunning upon the book, have skill in like

[1] His grandfather, 'Hans der Spielmann', of Wechmar, who died in the Plague of 1626 was a merry character, in his association with his more modest fellow-citizens not far removed from the minstrel. Underneath his portrait was inscribed:
Hier siehst du Geigen Hansen Bachen,
Wenn du es hörst, so mustu lachen.
Er geigt gleichwohl nach seiner Art
Und trägt ein hübschen Hans Bachen's Bart.

manner on sundry instruments. For if one weighs it well, there is no ease of the labours and medicines of feeble minds to be found more honest and more praiseworthy in time of leisure than it. And principally in courts, where (beside the refreshing of vexations that music bringeth unto each man) many things are taken in hand to please women withal, whose tender and soft hearts are soon pierced with melody and filled with sweetness. Therefore no marvel that in the old days and nowadays they have always been inclined to musicians, and counted this a most acceptable food of the mind[1].'

A hundred years later Henry Peacham wrote in similar vein in *The Compleat Gentleman* (p. 104):

... But to conclude, if all Arts hold their esteeme and value according to their Effects, account this goodly Science not among the number of those which *Lucian* places without the gates of Hell as vaine and unprofitable: but of such which are ... the fountaines of our lives good and happinesse. Since it is a principall meanes of glorifying our mercifull Creator it heighthens our devotion, it gives delight and ear to our travailes, it expelleth sadnesse and heavinesse of Spirit, preserveth people in concord and amity, allayeth fiercenesse and anger; and lastly, is the best Phisicke for many melancholy diseases.

MUSICAL FORMS AND PRACTICES

In the period between Castiglione and Peacham polyphonic music reached its peak of development. Vocal in origin, and inspired by a verbal background[2], it produced a cohesive, all-purposes, Italianate style, with regional inflections from Flanders, England, Germany, and Spain, and a vast literature of masses, motets, and madrigals accrued—the latter, especially in northern Europe, reaching out to the simplicities inherent in the *chanson* and the folk-song. Through the madrigal, and its allied forms, domestic music-making spread into the middle reaches of society, as the dedications of the English and northern European madrigals especially demonstrate. Through such music, in which instrumental ensembles played a supporting role of greater or lesser significance according to the ability and numerical adequacy of the singers, technical advances led to the expressive potentiality of chromatic harmony and towards a tonal structure, based on major and

[1] Quoted from Strunk, *Source Readings in Musical History*, pp. 281-2.
[2] The pattern at first being set by the poems of Petrarch, Tasso, and Ariosto.

9

minor scales, that was rationalised in the course of the seventeenth century. In Venice the expansive experimentation of Adrian Willaert, Andrea and Giovanni Gabrieli, Baldassare Donato, and Gioseffe Zarlino (whose *Institutioni armoniche*, of 1588, hinted at adoption of major–minor tonality) led to an increased appreciation of dynamic and colour effects both in vocal and instrumental music. Venetian influence spread outwards through the sometime pupillage in that city of such composers as Schütz, Hassler, and Sweelinck. By enlarging the expressive properties of music these (and other) composers were also, unconsciously, revealing its own semantic possibilities, and were thus preparing the way for a form of music released from dependence on verbal associations, to be defined as 'abstract'.

At this point instrumental musicians reached towards independence by moving from the familiar practices of vocal music to develop the canzona, the fantasia, the ricercar, the sonata, all of which appear in the output of Giovanni Gabrieli; and from the court and the popular dance towards the rudimentary suites, or sets of contrasting pieces, that may be encountered in the collections for virginals and in the consort publications of the late sixteenth and early seventeenth centuries. Except for those who were distinguished in the field of vocal polyphony, or as keyboard virtuosi, composers, or arrangers, of instrumental ensemble music received less than their adequate share of commendation. Yet it was composers like John Adson (fl. 1600–1620) and William Brade (c. 1560–1630), to name only two from among a large body of English chamber-music exponents, who were in large measure responsible for laying the foundations of a broadly-based concert tradition. Adson, sometime a member of the musical establishment of the Duke of Lorraine and, later, a member of the English court band, published, in 1611, his *Courtly Masquing Ayres* (in five and six parts), and in so doing introduced into bourgeois house-music the most attractive pieces from the repertoire of Jacobean music-drama. Brade, neither the first nor the last Englishman to be more applauded abroad than at home, was in court service, as chamber-musician in Denmark and in Brandenburg, and in civic employment in Hamburg. Among his publications were *Newe Ausserlesene liebliche Branden, Intraden, Mascharaden,*

10

Balletten, All'manden, Couranten, Volten . . . (five parts), 1609 (Hamburg); *Melodieuses Paduanes, Chansons, Galliardes*, 1619 (Antwerp); and *Newe lustige Volten, Couranten, Balletten, Paduanen, Galliarden, Masqueraden, auch allerley Arth neuer französische Täntze*, 1621 (Berlin). These, which introduced to Germany for the first time the 'Branden' or 'Branles', the Masquerade, and the Volta, played an important part in helping to establish the pattern of German chamber-music, and, indirectly, the character of the German audience.

A German contemporary, and acquaintance, of Brade was Samuel Scheidt—one of the notable company of German provincial musicians who prepared the climate in which Bach and Handel were to be nurtured. In his *Concertus Sacrae*, his *Ludi musici*, his *Tabulatura nova*, and his *Newe geistliche Konzerte* he presented works for every occasion, sacred and secular, embracing techniques from Venice, from Holland (he studied in Amsterdam), and (he wrote variations on a theme of John Dowland) from England. With a taste for folk-song and an aptitude for making effective instrumental arrangements therefrom he built up a general and high appreciation of music in Halle, where he was both town and court musician. In that city the Margraf of Brandenburg maintained a modest musical establishment, consisting of two violins, two viols, two gambas, two lutes, cornet, and organ on the instrumental side, and two male sopranos, two tenors (one an Italian), and one bass in the choir. Additionally two trumpets were available.

THE COLLEGIUM MUSICUM

The *Accademie* of Italy and their derivatives in France were aristocratic. In Germany the late flowering of the Renaissance ran into an upsurge of middle-class prosperity, symbolised by the effective powers of the municipalities (who arranged their affairs in conjunction with, sometimes in despite of, the local princes), and the growing importance of the Universities. Music well-established in the towns, as has been seen, practised in the home and the Church (Lutheranism bringing the ecclesiastical and secular together into a prosperous partnership[1]), and cultivated in the great houses was, and has so remained to the

[1] See Arno Werner 'Die Kantoreigesellschaften', in *Freie Musikgemeinschaften alter Zeit im mitteldeutschen Raum*, 1940, pp. 7–18.

11

present day, an essential, unquestioned, unexceptional, part of social intercourse. An effective means of guaranteeing its standing was the *Collegium Musicum*.

The *Collegium Musicum*, essentially German in its seriousness, its thoroughness, and its sociability, was in effect a society, middle-class and more often than not comprising university students, dedicated, like the Italian *Accademia*, to the general cultivation of music. The early trend was towards polyphony and philosophy, so that about the year 1530 a dissertation could appear in Frankfurt-am-Oder entitled *Convivia Musica seu philosophica*. In the next few years societies favoured practice rather than theory, *convivia* rather than *philosophica*: hence the foundation of a *Musik-Kränzlein* in Worms in 1561, *Convivia* in Görlitz in 1570—which became a *Collegium Musicum* a hundred years later—and in Wernigerode in 1587. In Nürnberg there were both a *Musik-Kränzlein* and a *Musikgesellschaft* between 1568 and 1585, while the *Convivium Musicum* founded in Weida in 1583 also became a *Collegium Musicum* in 1651. The *Collegium Musicum* of Frankfurt, of which the title page of the members' book is illustrated on Plate 2, was established in 1588. Mühlhausen had a *Musikalische Societät* in 1617 and in the same year Friedland a *Musikalische Gilde*. By the middle of the seventeenth century there were further *Collegia Musica* in Bremen and Delitzsch, the latter giving a notable out-of-doors performance, by the town church, at the delayed Peace Celebrations of 1650.

The institution was adopted in neighbouring countries. In 1597 Johannes (Jan) Tollius dedicated a set of Madrigals[1], and Sweelinck his Second Book of Psalms to that in Amsterdam, and the Minutes of the *Collegium Musicum* in Prague, for the inaugural year of 1616, stated:

soll dieses Collegium principaliter und allein auf das Exercitium der Musica in quellen Motteten, Madrigalien . . . angesehen sein[2].

[1] 'Inclito Amsterdamensium Musicorum Collegio Optime de se Merito, L.M.Q.D.D., Johannes Tollius, Amorfortius'.

[2] Cf. another Dutch dedication: 'A l'honorable compagnie des nourrisons, disciples, fauteurs et amateurs de la dance et sainte musique, à Amsterdam en Hollande, Louis Mongart dédie d'humble affection ce premier livre de Psaumes de David, pour témoignage de fraternelle coniunction et gage d'amitié pardonable en Christ. L'an 1597 au mois de Mars.'

In Switzerland similar important bodies were instituted in Zürich, in 1613, in St. Gallen in 1620, and in Berne in 1674. By this time the original, private intention had been modified in some cases so that the *Collegium Musicum* in Hamburg, under the direction of Matthias Weckmann, a Thuringian, and Christoph Bernhard, of Danzig, both former pupils of Schütz in Dresden, gave weekly public performances in the cathedral. These were somewhat similar to the seasonal *Abendmusik* given in Lübeck since 1641. The origins of the Hamburg occasions, however, were slightly different in that the aims were ambitious and the honour of being associated with the Hamburg *Collegium* was sought after, so that Mattheson could later note how—

die grössesten Componisten ihre Namen demselben einzuverleiben suchten.

Music in Germany pursued its individual and moderately conservative course during the first half of the seventeenth century, in spite of the Thirty Years' War, but the development of oratorio, and of instrumental music, was strongly affected by Italian practice. Schütz was a disciple of the Venetian School and brought its influence to bear on his pupils at Dresden. Michael Praetorius, organist and court musician at Wolfenbüttel, whose *Syntagma Musicum* (1615–1620) is the most comprehensive of guides to early baroque method and practice, was a strong supporter of Venetian influence. As for Christoph Bernhard, he was not only a pupil of Schütz, but, through the Elector of Saxony's generosity, a student of Roman method at first hand in that he had worked with Carissimi. Since, however, he lost his appointment at Dresden through the machinations of Italian musicians who came to work at that court his enthusiasm may have been somewhat modified. At this juncture, however, it is necessary to consider the Italian situation again, because, while organisation of music for the general benefit was thus proceeding in Germany, music itself was undergoing further revolution.

Musical Entertainments
in Seventeenth Century Italy

MUSIC AND AN AUDIENCE

THE CONCEPT OF ART FOR ART'S SAKE was a by-product of Renaissance humanism and nowhere was it put into practice more thoroughly and effectively than in sixteenth- and seventeenth-century Italy. Having spent some frustrating years in Spain the priest–musician Pietro Cerone gave five reasons in his *El Melopeo y Maestro* (published in 1613), one of a flood of theoretical works of music of that period, for the particular excellence of Italian music. They form a good recipe for general adoption, not least on account of their simple logic.

There were in Italy, he said, good teachers and industrious pupils. This was not altogether surprising, since the Italians as a race entertained 'a general affection for music'. The nobility were lacking neither in enthusiasm nor in skill, and among those distinguished as composers or theoreticians he named five counts and two dukes, of whom the only one to retain a firm place in the annals of composition was Carlo Gesualdo. Cerone stressed the importance of the *Accademie*, of which there were none in Spain, and 'the continual exercise of the Italian masters in the art of practical composition'.

The five reasons of Cerone being brought together at a particular point, and under favourable conditions, went far towards investing music with a more public character; to be appreciated from without as by an audience, and not solely from within as by a participant. Vocal polyphon and instrumental music derived from it were essentially for the benefit of the

14

performer—and, in the first case, God; while the more extravert works for solo instruments were as yet necessarily limited to an intimate company. On the other hand the cult of large-scale choral and instrumental music, as in the Cathedral of Venice, that of the solo voice, as in Florence, and of the violin, in all parts of Italy, were directed at a listening public.

Thomas Coryate, an English traveller, visited St. Mark's in Venice, in 1608, where he was captivated by the virtuosity of a treble viol player. It was, he declared, 'so excellent that no man could surpass it'. On the Festival of St. Roche the ecclesiastical celebration

> consisted principally of music, which was both vocal and instrumental, so good, so delectable, so rare, so admirable, so superexcellent, that it did even ravish and stupify all those strangers that never heard the like ... Sometimes there sang sixteen or twenty men together, having their master or moderator to keep them in order; and when they sang, the instrumental musicians played also. Sometimes sixteen played together upon their instruments, ten sackbuts, four cornets, and two viol da gambas of an extraordinary greatness; sometimes ten, six sackbuts and four cornets; sometimes two, a cornet and a treble viol ... Those that played upon the treble viols, sung and played together, and sometimes two singular fellows played together upon theorbos, to which they sung also, who yielded admirable sweet music, but so still that they could scarce be heard but by those that were very near them. These two theorbists concluded that night's music, which continued three whole hours at the least. For they began about five of the clock, and ended not before eight[1].

The following morning there was another three-hour session (in which a male singer particularly distinguished himself in Coryate's ears, the more so because he was not a *castrato*), at the end of which the company made a collection for the musicians, bestowing on them the sum of 100 ducats.

At that time Giovanni Gabrieli (1557–1612) was in charge of the music at St. Mark's (Heinrich Schütz becoming his pupil during the next year) and the kind of music Coryate heard is contained in his *Concerti a 6–16 voci* (1587), his *Sacrae symphoniae* (I, 1597), and his *Canzoni e sonate a 3–22* (1615).

---

[1] *Coryate's Crudities*, 1611, p. 250.

Gabrieli exploited large masses of choral tone; explored possibilities of dynamic and—insofar as he set off wind against string groups—tone-colour contrast; and, following the lead of Viadana in establishing the continuo (with figured-bass) in the instrumental sonata, went a long way towards the full emancipation of instrumental music. Two terms by now in use were *symphony* and *concerto*, not as yet with the particular definitive significance later assumed but effective in suggesting new intentions. As has already been seen these terms were quickly taken over by those German musicians acquainted with Venetian practice. It may be argued that Gabrieli was concerned with church music and that his influence on the 'concert' was at best indirect. Church music in Venice, however, was not as it had been, nor how it should have been if the prescriptions of the Council of Trent had been followed: it was, in fact, as secular as the outlook of the gentlemen who then comprised the Sacred College.

NUOVE MUSICHE

In Florence, in 1589, Ferdinando dei Medici married Christina of Lorraine in the Church of Santo Spirito. During the ceremony Giulio Caccini, a protégé of Giovanni Bardi, Count of Vernio, and the principal of a *Camerata* (or *Accademia*), sang a song entitled 'O Benedetto Giorno'. This, said Caccini's pupil, Severo Bonini, was the first public presentation of the new monodic style of singing, which was then a topic for frequent consideration at the meetings at Bardi's establishment. The audience, said Bonini, was shocked, but also delighted at Caccini's singing, and they conferred on him the temporary title of 'Benedetto Giorno'. During the festivities consequent on the wedding, and held at the Medici court, Caccini helped other composers— Peri, Marenzio, Malvezzi, and Cavalieri, and Bardi—who assumed general responsibility for the musico-dramatic diversions. Except for Caccini the composers followed polyphonic practice. Caccini, however, persisted in putting into practice what was frequently discussed at the *Camerata*, and a second example of monody, a song accompanied by lute, was added to the first[1]. This was the point in musical history nicely summarised by Domenico Corri: 'In process of time', he wrote,

[1] Contained in Florence, Bibl. Naz., Magl. 66.

when music was emancipated from the tyranny of the cloisters, and cultivated for the theatre and other public entertainment, it began to take a different turn. The subjects on which it was now employed requiring a much greater variety of expression and effect than those to which it had been hitherto confined, melody, the great vehicle of expression, became of necessity a principal object of attention and study; of consequence it received great improvements, though it still remained fettered by the strict adherence which the composers of those times deemed indispensable to the laws of *contrapunto*. The singers, on the other hand, in proportion as they saw their efforts please, took occasion to add new graces to what they sung . . . But although the composer could not avoid approving of their ornaments, yet, wedded to the forms of the school in which he had been educated, he continued still to write down nothing but the notes which were essential to the completion of the harmonic parts, leaving the singer to decorate them as his taste should direct[1].

The great break-through, towards the audience, was achieved by Caccini and his companions.

It was agreed by the members of the *Camerata* that fresh theories concerning the relationship between words and music were a valid foundation for a new style which should be consonant with the rational ideas of the Renaissance and, more importantly, with the demands of contemporary drama. However hard the polyphonic composer tried (as did both the Italian and English madrigalists) to accommodate musical to verbal rhythms, the result, from the dramatic point of view, was unwieldy. On the one hand clarity in narrative was obscured, on the other the individual talent of the singer was restricted. Caccini was primarily a singer. He was a close student of singing method. Monody, he urged, would make for better singing. Supported by Bardi, for whom he also acted as secretary, Caccini did the social rounds, giving examples of new-style song; and not only in Florence, for in 1592 he sang in Rome at a house-party given by Pietro Nenni. In 1601, after monody had established itself through the famous operas of *Dafne* and *Euridice*, by Peri and with Caccini's assistance, the latter published the *Nuove Musiche*, an anthology of madrigals and solo songs distinguished by a prefatory discourse on music.

[1] *'Explanation'* to *Select Collection* etc. Edinburgh, 1779? pp. 4–5.

Herein the author gave instructions for the performance of *trilli*, *gruppi*, *passagi*, and *exclamazioni*. 'I am', he wrote, 'never satisfied with the ordinary and usual devices of others; I am given to investigate all the new effects possible for me, because it is through what is new that we can realise the true foundation of music, which is to delight and move the spirit.'

THE VIRTUOSO ELEMENT

That the spirit was ready to be, and was, so delighted is evident from the approbation of Venetian music by Coryate. The initial *Dramma per musica* became fashionable, and, under the inspiration of Monteverdi, expanded into opera, in which monody bifurcated into recitative and aria; in which instrumental music was valued for its capacity to underline drama or sentiment; and in which a non-religious musical art for the first time gained parity in esteem. In the first place the pioneer operas were presented *in camera*, before select audiences. By 1637 Italian secular music had broken out of its aristocratic containment and wider interests were appealed to when a public theatre, that of San Cassiano, was opened in Venice. Collaterally, at first through the endeavours of Cavalieri, later through those of Landi, Mazzocchi, Rossi, and Carissimi, oratorio took the new style into church, where it united with the independent *concerto sacro* to furnish the basis of that form of oratorio that was to reach its fullest form of expression in the English works of Handel. By the side of opera and oratorio the smaller cantata flourished, and *sonata* developed.

At this point the special place of the violin should be noticed. This instrument, in tentative use during the sixteenth century, was used by Giovanni Gabrieli and Monteverdi (the latter demanding a technique that was then exceptional), and by the 1620's solo pieces by Marini and Quagliati had appeared, while Carlo Farini, a Mantuan who became violinist to the Court at Dresden, included in his *Capriccio Stravagante* (Dresden, 1627) a whole range of realistic and virtuoso effects that demonstrated the claim to public appeal inherent in the instrument. Another virtuoso of the period was Giovanni Battista Fontana, whose three-movement sonatas (six for violin solo and continuo, and twelve for violin, cornet, bassoon, lute, and violoncello) moved

18

in the direction of a specifically string idiom, which also distinguished the so-called symphonies of Bartolomeo Montalbano, of Palermo and Bologna[1], and the sonatas of Uccellini and Merula. The latter, the first to exploit the G string, by his work in Bologna helped to gain for that city a high reputation for violinists and violin music. In Bologna sonatas divided into the *Sonata da Camera* on the one hand, and the *Sonata da Chiesa* on the other. Among the early composers of sonatas of both kinds was Biagio Marini, whose works, thus titled, were published in Venice in 1655. Like many of his contemporaries Marini was much travelled. He worked in Venice and in Brescia before joining the musical staff of the Gonzagas at Parma. He moved on to Munich, as *maestro della musica* to the Duke of Bavaria. After being in Düsseldorf for some time he returned to Italy, to Ferrara, where he was attached to the *Accademia della Morte*, and to Milan. In the third quarter of the seventeenth century Vitali and Bassani, both of Bologna, were the acknowledged masters of sonatas for violins and bass. The former was a member of the Bolognese *Accademia degli Unanimi*, the latter of the *Accademia dei Filarmonici*, of which he became principal and in which Arcangelo Corelli spent the years from 1666 to 1670 as a pupil of Benvenuti and Bragnoli.

EFFECTS OF PUBLICATION

In retrospect it may seem that stylistic changes in music took place with dramatic suddenness. In fact, of course, this was not the case. So far as the public is concerned what is accessible becomes accepted as satisfactory, even though there is an innate curiosity as to what is reported as new. Since, from the middle of the sixteenth century, printed music had become increasingly available (a further means of developing a wider appreciation) libraries of music were not uncommon. Among those well removed from the centre of affairs who possessed a considerable collection—comprising 300 items—was the Slovenian Prince-Bishop of Ljubljana. This was catalogued in 1620 to show a variety of masses, motets, madrigals, ricercari, fantasias, sonatas, canzoni, all representative of the late sixteenth century,

---

[1] Op. 1, *Sinfonie ad uno e doi violini, a doi, e Trombone, con il Partimento per l'Organo, con alcune a quattro viole.*

but also Caccini's *Euridice*, which had been published in 1601. Such a library (the Church had a long tradition in this respect, and an acquaintance with faculties other than theological becoming more or less obligatory, abbeys and cathedrals in Catholic countries continued to build up their musical stocks for a long time to come) was an important means of extending knowledge of musical progress, and in one way and another—as will be seen—the education of the commonalty was advanced.

VISITORS TO ROME AND VENICE

On one side Italian music was aristocratic, a subject for intellectual scrutiny and polite disputation, but invariably tested by direct, practical, personal experience; on the other it was popular. The two sides, however, complemented one another so that there was no great conscious distinction between what might now be considered the superior and the inferior. A picture of secular musical life in Italy in the mid-seventeenth century is drawn by John Evelyn, who, at the age of twenty-five, was fully disposed to enjoy the varied attractions of the Grand Tour. In Rome he contrived an invitation to the Palace of the Prince Galicano, where, in company with Cardinal Pamfili—the Pope's nephew and a noted patron of music—a variety of Cardinals, governors of the City, ambassadors, and miscellaneous nobility, he heard Colonna's *La Proserpina Rapita*. In Padua he savoured music in a more intimate environment, became a pupil of Dominico Bassano[1] and learned to play the theorbo. He also met Bassano's daughter, who was married to a lawyer but so far from allowing marriage to atrophy the talents implanted by her father sang, played some nine instruments as well as anybody Evelyn had ever heard, and composed. As a souvenir she presented the impressionable young Englishman with copies of two recitatives, all her own work.

He went to Venice for the Carnival:

the women, men, and persons of all conditions disguising themselves in antique dresses, with extravagant music and a thousand

[1] There were many musicians of this name in Italy and a number of Bassanos went from Italy to England, during the sixteenth and seventeenth centuries, to serve in the royal music.

gambols, traversing the streets from house to house, all places being then accessible and free to enter. Abroad, they fling eggs filled with sweet water, but sometimes not over sweet. They also have a barbarous habit of hunting bulls about the streets and piazzas, which is very dangerous, the passages being generally narrow. The youth of the several wards and parishes contend in other masteries and pastimes, so that it is impossible to recount the universal madness of this place during this time of licence. The great banks are set up for those who will play at bassett; the comedians have liberty, and the operas are open; witty pasquills are thrown about, and the mountebanks have their shops at every corner.

The diversion which chiefly took me up was three noble operas[1], there were excellent voices and music, the most celebrated of which was the famous Anna Renche, whom we invited to a fish supper after four days in Lent, when they had given over at the theatre. Accompanied with an eunuch whom she brought with her, she entertained us with rare music, both of them singing to an harpsichord. It growing late, a gentleman of Venice came for her to show her the galleys, now ready to sail for Candia. This entertainment produced a second, given us by the English Consul of the Merchants, inviting us to his house, where he had the Genoese, the most celebrated bass in Italy, who was one of the late opera band. This diversion held us so late at night, that conveying a gentlewoman who had supped with us to her gondola at the usual place of landing, we were shot at by two carbines from out another gondola in which was a noble venetian and his courtezan unwilling to be disturbed . . .

The pursuit of culture was, in some respects, a hazardous occupation.

A later appreciation of Venetian music and galanterie came from Limojon de St. Didier, who referred to the

extraordinary fine concerts of Musick, which the Gallants of the City have in Boats to serenade the Ladies and Nuns who are much pleased with these Diversions . . . the liberty of the Night, and sweetness of the Air equally inspires with desire both Sexes to pass away *en deshabille* the Evenings upon the Water: everyone endeavours to avoid being known, so you find a mighty silence in the midst of this great concourse, fully and quietly enjoying the

---

[1] Three acts of one opera; the opera being Rovetta's *Ercole in Lidia*. Rovetta was *Maestro di Cappella* at St. Mark's after Monteverdi and before Cavalli.

pleasure of the Music, and the most agreeable Delights of the cool Breezes[1].

VENETIAN CHARITIES

The provision of music throughout the Renaissance and the Baroque eras was, for a variety of reasons, regarded as obligatory. The strongest force, after the diminution of patristic austerities into a conventional 'ad majorem Dei gloriam', was that now represented by the term 'public relations'. The quality and power of a Court, of an institution, of a family, was symbolised in cultural displays that not infrequently were adroitly angled so as to make at least indirect reference to their supposed virtues. This was the case throughout Europe. It was, therefore, necessary to keep up a constant supply of performing musicians. These were nurtured in different ways: in ecclesiastical foundations, in grammar or charity schools, through various forms of apprenticeship, or through a combination of opportunities. The fortunate—those whose concern for music was most disinterested—were able to take advantage of private tuition. The under-privileged were put through a rigorous musical curriculum so that they might eventually combine their talents in this field with any that they could show in the execution of subordinate household duties. Reference to the biographies of seventeenth- and eighteenth-century composers adequately documents the main principles and methods of musical (and general) education. In Venice, however, certain exceptional charitable institutions played a significant part in the development of the concert.

Society being what it was, there was in the city a high rate of production of bastards. Illegitimate sons came off tolerably well and were often taken into the bosom of the family; their unfortunate sisters, on the other hand, were either farmed out or simply left on an unfamiliar doorstep. To ameliorate the situation hospitals were instituted for their reception and subsequent education. There were similar institutions in other parts of Europe—in London Christ's Hospital was founded in which considerable provision was made for musical training—but those of Venice developed music to a singularly high standard.

[1] *The City & Republick of Venice*, London 1699, I, pp. 71–72.

(a) Title-page of music by Johann Petzold.

(b) Students' serenade.

3. Music in Leipzig.

4. A performance in a German church.

In due course musicians of standing were content to take over the musical directorships of the Pietà, the Mendicanti, the Ospedaletto, and the Incurabili. Legrenzi, who was to re-organise the orchestra of St. Mark's in due course, was in charge of the music of the Mendicanti for a time, and from 1704 to 1740 Antonio Vivaldi (c. 1675–1741), a pupil of Legrenzi, was in charge of that at the Pietà.

The performances at the Pietà attracted general attention, and, when Vivaldi was there, no visitors to Venice missed the opportunity to attend. The music was enchanting, and so, it seems, were the girls.

'They sing like angels', wrote Charles de Brosses in 1739,

and play violin, flute, organ, hautboy, violoncello, bassoon; in short there is no instrument so large as to frighten them . . . I swear to you that there is nothing so agreeable as to see a gay and pretty nun, in white robes with a bouquet of pomegranate flowers behind her ear, conduct the orchestra and beat time with all grace and precision imaginable[1].

At a later date William Beckford recounted:

The sight of the orchestra still makes me smile. You know, I suppose, it is entirely of the feminine gender, and that nothing is more common than to see a delicate white hand journeying across an enormous double-bass, or a pair of roseate cheeks puffing, with all their efforts, at a French Horn. Some that are grown old and Amazonious, who have abandoned their Griddles and their lovers, take vigorously to the kettle-drum; and one poor limping lady, who had been crossed in love, now makes an admirable figure with the bassoon[2].

Richard Edgcumbe was another whose gratification at being able to attend performances of the Conservatorio dei Mendi-canti, in 1784, was conjoined with astonishment at the 'almost incredible sight of an entire orchestra of female performers'[3]. A more professional assessment of these Venetian conservatories in the latter part of the eighteenth century came from Charles Burney[4].

[1] *Lettres familières sur l'Italie*, Paris, 1931, Vol. I, p. 238.
[2] *The Travel-Diaries*, ed. Guy Chapman, Cambridge, 1928, I, pp. 108–9.
[3] *Musical Reminiscences of an old Amateur*, 1773–1823, London, 1827, p. 42.
[4] See *The Present State of Music in France and Italy*, 2nd ed. 1773, I, pp. 145–6 and p. 190.

ARISTOCRATIC PATRONAGE AND THE CAREER OF
ARCANGELO CORELLI

Among the notable Venetian families that of Ottoboni was outstanding. Three members of the family served in succession as Chancellors of the Republic of Venice, and in 1689 the son of the last of the Chancellors was elected Pope. Alexander VIII was not unmindful of the duties that were expected of him and all his younger relatives were elevated to posts of special honour and responsibility. Pietro Ottoboni, a great-nephew, had lived with his patron in St. Mark's Palace in Venice before he was installed, first as a prelate, and then as a Cardinal, in 'a magnificent Apartment' in Rome. Pietro was entrusted with the offices of Superintendent General of all Affairs in the Ecclesiastical State, Legate of Avignon, Chancellor of the Holy Church, and sufficient rents, pensions, and other emoluments to ensure him an annual income of 88,000 crowns a year.

He has,' wrote de Blainville, former Secretary to the Spanish States General,

> the natural quality of all Venetians, that is, he is a good politician. He has an exquisite sense of humour, and loves to appear and to make himself valued. He is liberal, obliging, well-behaved to everybody, and very affable to strangers, whom he receives with most complaisant manner at his house. He loves poetry, music, and men of learning; so that every fortnight he holds, in the palace of the Chancery where he lodges, an Academy of learned men, at which several prelates and other learned persons assist..... His Eminence likewise keeps in his pay the best musicians and performers in Rome, and amongst others the famous Arcangelo Corelli (1653–1713), and young Paolucci, who is reckoned the finest voice in Europe; so that every Wednesday[1] he has an excellent concert in his palace, and is assisted there this very day[2].

Ottoboni was so devoted to music that at the Papal Conclave of 1691 he was reported to have had his orchestra playing outside his cell—to the distraction of some of his fellow-Cardinals.

---

[1] According to Giovanni Mario Crescimbini the musical *Accademie* were held on Monday evenings—*The Harmonicon*, 1824, p. 79. Other musicians engaged were Tomaso Albinoni, Mascitti, and Adami da Bolsena.

[2] *Travels*, II, ed. D. Soyer, 1743, Chapter 40.

Such was the patron of the most influential instrumental composer of the late seventeenth and early eighteenth century. Corelli was a Bolognese, a pupil of Giovanni Benvenuti and Leonardo Bragnoli if not, as was formerly supposed, of Bassani. In 1675 Corelli was a member of the orchestra of the Church of St. Louis-des-Français in Rome and four years later leader of the orchestra of the Teatro Capranica. In 1681 he published his first set of trio sonatas. These, like the third set issued in 1689, were *sonate da chiesa*, whereas those of 1683, 1685, 1694, and 1700—these last being for solo violin and bass—were *sonate da camera*. These works, except for the earliest set, were dedicated to Corelli's patrons: to ex-Queen Christina of Sweden, then resident in Rome; to Cardinal Pamfili, patron of the society known as the Arcadians[1], in whose service Corelli was between 1687 and 1690; to the Duke of Modena; and to Ottoboni, who employed him from 1690 until his death. Betweenwhiles Corelli visited Florence, Germany, and Naples, where the King would have seduced him from his Roman allegiance.

Corelli made the weekly receptions at the Ottoboni palace famous, by the quality of his own playing, by the style he encouraged in his colleagues, by the care he lavished on his orchestra, and by the quality of his compositions. Of these the most important were his Opus 6 *Concerti Grossi*. This collection, posthumously published in 1714, represented the kind of music that had furnished the chief interest of the performances over the previous two decades. For Georg Muffat, the German composer who became a disciple of Corelli, said that he had heard his master's *concerti* in 1682. Like the sonatas the concertos represented the *chiesa* and *camera* traditions, the last four belonging to the latter, and providing successions of dance music in contrast to the severer counterpoint of the first eight. In these concertos Corelli rationalised the string ensemble and in so doing laid the foundations of all subsequent orchestral music; and also a style. Corelli's style was based both on a scientific attitude to the *materia musica* and on an appreciation

[1] Founded after the death of, and as a monument to, ex-Queen Christina, this was an *Accademia Poetico-Musicale*, of which membership in the first place was restricted to noblemen and to poets. Crescimbini was the Secretary. In 1706 Alessandro Scarlatti, Corelli, and Bernardo Pasquini were, exceptionally, admitted as members. Handel was a guest of this Academy, but never elected to membership.

25

of the particular, enlightened, but pleasure-seeking, character of his audience. His qualities were summarised by his pupil Geminiani, who wrote:

> His merit was not depth of learning like that of his contemporary Alessandro Scarlatti, nor great fancy nor an invention rich in melody and harmony; but a nice ear and very delicate taste, which led him to select the most pleasing melodies and harmonies, and to construct the part so as to produce the most delightful effect upon the ear[1].

Scarlatti confessed, 'I find nothing to admire in his composition, but am extremely struck with the manner in which he plays his concertos, and the nice management of his band, the uncommon accuracy of whose performance gives the concerto an amazing effect, even to the eye, as well as the ear[2].' It may be mentioned that Corelli had no purism in his make-up. On one occasion he directed a gala performance, in honour of the Pope and subsidised by Queen Christina, which involved a string band of 150 players: truly a *concerto grosso*. At Christmas, 1699, a nephew of Samuel Pepys wrote home that he had attended a concert at which Corelli played with 30 others; so that even a normal ensemble was of reasonably generous proportions.

As to the *Ospedale* in Venice, so foreign visitors engineered their entrance to the Ottoboni performances. Among them were English gentlemen prepared to guarantee the excellence of Corelli when they returned home. There were, for instance, Lord Castlemain, whose wife had been mistress to Charles II, and whose credentials as a connoisseur of art were higher than those in diplomacy which led James II to appoint him as Ambassador to the Court of Rome. There was also Lord Edgcumbe, lately down from Cambridge and Member of Parliament for Cornwall, who not only became Corelli's pupil, but also arranged for Hugh Howard to paint the master's portrait. In due course Corelli's favourite violin found its way to England to become, it was said, the property of Charles Avison[3], and his concertos became the main plank of the

---

[1] Quoted in *The Harmonicon*, 1824, p. 81.

[2] *Ibid.*, p. 82.

[3] Burney, *A General History of Music*, IV, p. 640.

English concert platform. 'His productions', it was written in *The Harmonicon* in 1824, 'continued longer in unfading favour in England—where they still retain a due portion of esteem— than even in his own country, or indeed in any other part of Europe.'

Corelli's reputation was assisted by fellow composers from abroad, who admired not only the music but the man. He was generous, modest, helpful. His supporters included Strungk, of the Courts of Hanover and Dresden (and the founder of the Leipzig opera-house), Muffat, and Handel (whose own *concerti* pay tribute to the style of Corelli) from Germany, and publishers in Amsterdam and London, who saw the prospects that were beginning to open up in the field of orchestral music now fully emancipated from the theatre and the Church. Muffat carried the hedonistic principle of the Italian seventeenth century into the Preface of his *Auserlesene Instrumental-Musik* (1701) and wrote that 'these concertos .... composed for the express refreshment of the ears, may be performed most appropriately in connection with entertainments given by great princes and lords, for receptions of distinguished guests, and at state banquets, serenades, and assemblies of musical amateurs and virtuosi'. The most effective missionary in the case of Corelli was, however, Francesco Geminiani, whose mature gifts were dedicated to the people of England and Ireland, and whose sonatas and concertos also helped to form the public musical taste of the British.

Concert Beginnings in England

VIOLIN VIRTUOSI AND THE EARLY CULT OF CORELLI

THE INSTITUTION OF PUBLIC MUSIC IN ENGLAND, in the seventeenth century, was stimulated by a number of factors. Among them the chief were the constant arrival of fortune-seeking virtuosi from the Continent; a general inclination—in due course—enthusiastically to adopt foreign fashions; the restoration of the monarchy, in 1660; the disposition of patronage; and the distribution of musical interest. From Tudor times instrumental performers had been imported into the royal music, but when Thomas Baltzar and Nicola Matteis came, the one from Germany, the other from Italy, they came as freelances. Baltzar arrived during the period of the Commonwealth, and even though, after six years, he joined the royal band he made his particular mark on the bourgeoisie.

In a country in which conservative habits in music were already strong, the consort of viols maintaining its popularity longer than elsewhere, Baltzar with his violin had prejudice to overcome. John Evelyn, whose musical opinions were assisted by his Italian experience, heard Baltzar play soon after his arrival in England. On March 4, 1656, he recorded:

This night I was invited by Mr Roger l'Estrange[1] to hear the

---

[1] Mr, later Sir, Roger l'Estrange (1616–1704) was a zealous Royalist, who became the Surveyor of Printing Presses at the time of the Restoration, from which office he was ejected after the Revolution of 1688; a linguistic scholar of considerable achievement; a keen amateur musician, who performed creditably on the bass viol. He was a pupil, as also was Roger North, of John Jenkins, composer of much viol music that was greatly esteemed and of an early set of sonatas for two violins and bass (1660). These latter have not survived.

incomparable Lubicer [i.e. native of Lübeck] on the violin. His variety on a few notes and plain ground with that wonderful dexterity, was admirable. Though a young man, yet so perfect and skilful, that there was nothing, however cross and perplexed, brought to him by our artists which he did not play off at sight with ravishing sweetness and improvements, to the astonishment of our best masters. In sum, he played on the single instrument a full concert, so as the rest flung down their instruments, acknowledging the victory. As to my own particular, I stand to this hour amazed that God should give so great perfection to so young a person.

Baltzar was, at the time, twenty-five or -six years of age, and living with Sir Antony Cope, near Oxford. It was thus that Anthony à Wood, the historian, was able to hear him play. Neither Wood, 'nor any in England saw the like before', and John Wilson, the then Professor of Music in the University, is said to have stooped 'down to Baltzar's feet, to see whether he had a huff [hoof] on'. A man of genial habits, Baltzar tried to keep up with English drinking habits, failed, and died in 1663, to be buried in the cloister of Westminster Abbey.

Matteis came to London nine years after Baltzar's untimely death, and once again Evelyn was afforded an opportunity to hear him. On November 19, 1674, he wrote:

I heard that stupendous violin, Sigr Nicholao (with other rare musicians), whom I never heard mortal man exceed on that instrument. He had a stroke so sweet, and made it speak like the voice of a man, and, when he pleased, like a consort of several instruments. He did wonders upon a note, and was an excellent composer. Here was also that rare lutenist Dr Wallgrave; but nothing approached the violin in Nicholao's hand. He played such ravishing things as astonished us all.

Less than a fortnight passed and Evelyn was invited to another musical evening, this time at the home of Henry Slingsby, Master of the Mint[1].

[1] See also Evelyn's entry for November 20, 1679: 'I dined with Mr Slingsby . . . with my wife, invited to hear music, which was excellently performed by four of the most renowned masters; Du Prue, a Frenchman, on the lute; Sigr Bartholomeo, an Italian, on the harpsichord; Nicholao on the violin . . . There was also a flute douce, now in much request for accompanying the voice. Mr Slingsby, whose son and daughter played skilfully, had these meetings frequently in his house.' Bartholomeo, alias Bartleme, alias Bartholomew, was much sought after as player (he appeared at Court in 1674) and as teacher, and Evelyn's daughter Mary was one of his pupils.

Heard Sigr Francisco on the harpsichord, esteemed one of the most excellent masters in Europe on that instrument; then came Nicholao with his violin and struck all mute but Mrs Knight[1], who sang incomparably, and doubtless has the greatest reach of any English woman; she had lately been roaming Italy, and was much improved in that quality.

It is possible that it was Matteis who introduced the works of Corelli to the English. Be that as it may, the works of this master began to appear, in printed form, in 1695. Even before this Thomas Shuttleworth, of Spitalfields, had been putting round manuscript copies and arranging semi-public performances by his talented family. On September 23 of that year the *London Gazette* announced 'Twelve Sonatas (newly come over from Rome) in three parts, composed by Signeur Archangelo Corelli, and dedicated to His Highness the Elector of Bavaria, this present year 1694, are to be had fairly pricked from the true original, at Mr Ralph Agutter's, Musical Instrument Maker, over against York Buildings in the Strand, London'.

A principal supporter of Corelli's cause in England was the Italo-German Niccola Haym, who not only edited Corelli's sonatas (for ultimate retailing in London) for Estienne Roger of Amsterdam but also recommended to him such English composers as could write in the authentic Corellian style. The works of the master and his disciples were played at the establishment of the second Duke of Bedford, a rare nobleman who, after his grand tour, set up a private musical academy of which Haym was, until 1711, the head. Under Bedford's patronage wide cultural interests were pursued, for his protégés included the scientist William Sherard and his botanist brother James—who between them founded the Professorship of Botany at Oxford. James, in addition to his scientific skills, was an excellent fiddler and a good enough composer to have his two sets of sonatas—published by Roger—favourably compared with those of Corelli; Sherard, sometimes designated Giacomo, was, perhaps, the only Fellow of the Royal Society to excel in music to this extent. His interest was symptomatic

---

[1] Maria Knight was in favour at Court and during that year took part in the royal masque, *Calisto*.

of the high esteem for music entertained at that time by the English intellectuals.

DISAGREEMENT AT COURT

The return of Charles II to the throne had a profound effect on both drama and music. Once again the theatres were open, and musicians were given scope within the manner of Restoration drama—though no incentive towards the Italian style of opera now generally prevalent in Europe, and in the intervals of plays. The Chapel Royal was reorganised and acquaintance with practice at the French Court induced the King to instal a string band. Evelyn was not pleased. On December 21, 1662, he described the new arrangement: 'One of His Majesty's Chaplains preached, after which, instead of the ancient grave, and solemn wind music accompanying the organ, was introduced a concert of twenty-four violins between every pause after the French fantastical light way, better suiting a tavern or playhouse than a church.' The King was of the intention that church music was none the worse for approximating to that of the tavern or the playhouse, and musicians, indifferent to questions of propriety of style, welcomed new opportunity.

During this year John Banister, back from a refresher course in France, was appointed to a place in the royal band, and was given special responsibility for a select group of twelve players— *la crème de la crème*. Banister was allowed £600 a year, to be shared among the twelve as extra emolument. Within two years, however, this payment became irregular. The protests of the musicians accumulated, and the French players found themselves at cross purposes with their English colleagues. An investigation was set up and Banister was deprived of his superior office, on the grounds that he had kept much of the money for himself. The complaint was laid against Banister by the Frenchman, Louis Grabu. On March 14, 1667, an official resolution read as follows:

> Whereas John Banister appointed to make choice of 12 of the 24 violins, to be a select band to wait upon His Majesty, was paid £600 for himself and the 12 violins in augmentation of their wages, His Majesty authorises the payment of £600 to Lewis Grabu, Master of His Majesty's Music, appointed in the place of John Banister, for himself and the 12 violins following:

John Singleton, William Young, William Clayton, Henry Comer, Philip Beckett, Symon Hopper, Isaac Staggins, Henry Smyth, Richard Hudson, John Strong, Robert Strong, Theophilus Fitz[1].

There were those—with a marked sense of patriotism—who averred that the charge of peculation was false and that the real reason for Banister's dismissal was his opinion, expressed to the King, that the English violinists were superior to the French. Grabu, whose lack of talent was remarked on to Samuel Pepys by Pelham Humfrey, lasted as leader of the band of twelve until 1674, throughout his period of office finding it as difficult to get funds out of the Treasury as previously had Banister.

English musical life differed from that of the Continent in that there was but one Court, and patronage, although not without enlightenment under the Stuarts, was limited: the nobility had, of course, used up much of their surplus funds in the Civil War, after which they had been inclined to sit on their reserves. Charles II, however, did invest in talent on his accession and his Francophile interests greatly widened the outlook of English musicians—however much they might resent the incursion of Frenchmen and Italians. Pelham Humfrey, like Banister, was sent abroad to study French style in composition and performance, and the results of such study were imparted to Henry Purcell when he came under the influence of Humfrey. The greatest difference between England and the Continent was in the slowness of the English to adopt opera. This being the case there was more chance of the development of other musical functions.

MIDDLE-CLASS INTEREST

Fundamentally the English were neither more nor less musical than other races, and the recreational activities of the Master of the Mint, of Evelyn, of Pepys, are sufficient evidence that the tradition of middle-class music established during the madrigal era[2] was healthily maintained. Private music—since

[1] *Lord Chamberlain's Records*, Vol. 742, p. 228.

[2] In the Preface to *Musica Transalpina* Nicholas Yonge described how he brought to his house 'a great number of Gentlemen and Merchants of good account (as well of this realm as of foreign nations) for the exercise of music daily'.

the social graces practised at Court inevitably set a pattern—was a status symbol. 'Up betimes', wrote Pepys on August 3, 1664, 'and set some joiners on work to new-lay my floor in our Wardrobe, which I intend to make a room for music.' The regular association of amateur musicians—with professional collaboration—had produced various English counterparts, of modest nature, to the Italian Academy. Sir Roger l'Estrange used to visit the house of John Hingston, Cromwell's musician-in-chief, and related how on one occasion Cromwell himself paid an unexpected visit. In Oxford William Ellis conducted a music club in his house, and Anthony à Wood mentioned other meetings in Exeter and Magdalen Colleges as well as one of mobile character which visited different Colleges in rotation. In London Pepys went on two occasions at least to musical meetings in the Post Office, that is, the Black Swan, in Bishopsgate, in 1664.

It was in this year, according to Roger North, that what he called the first public concert

> was given in a lane behind Paul's in the Mitre, where there was a chamber organ that one Philips [John] played upon, and some shopkeepers and foremen came weekly to sing in consort, and to hear and enjoy ale and tobacco; and after some time the audience grew strong, and one Ben Wallington got the reputation of a notable bass voice, who also set up for a composer, and has some songs in print . . . this showed an inclination of the citizens to follow music. And the same was confirmed by many little entertainments the masters made voluntarily for the scholars. In being known they were always crowded[1].

Of the music at these meetings and of the meetings themselves there is a memorial in a song by Pelham Humfrey, 'sung at a Music Feast':

Verse:

How well doth this Harmonious Meeting prove
A Feast of Music is a Feast of Love,
Where Kindness is our Tune, and we in parts
Do but sing forth the Consorts of our hearts.
For Friendship is nothing but concord of votes,
And Music is made by a friendship of notes.

[1] Roger North, *Memoirs*, ed. Rimbault, pp. 107–8.

Chorus à 3:
> Come then to the God of our Art let us quaff,
> For he once a year is reported to laugh[1].

The office of impresario was patently initiated by Edmund Chilmead, a Royalist scholar who was ejected from his chaplaincy in Oxford by the Puritan régime and compelled to scrape a living in the Black Horse, in Aldersgate Street, at which smoking and drinking were admitted to assist the better appreciation of music, and Chilmead's profits. Public houses were acknowledged centres of English culture, and a French traveller (translated by Evelyn) commented on the sacrilegious way in which the London publican had 'translated the organs out of the churches to set them up in taverns, chanting their dithyrambics and bestial bacchanalias to the tune of those instruments which were wont to assist them in the celebration of God's praises'.

JOHN BANISTER'S INITIATIVE

The Puritans indirectly aided the course of music in England by breaking for a time the pre-eminence of the Church, by giving opportunity to music teachers, and by fortuitously helping to democratise the art. Thrown out of his principal office (although he still held his place among the 24 violins) John Banister followed the example of Chilmead, but on a more ambitious scale. In the *London Gazette* of December 30, 1672, the following advertisement appeared:

> These are to give notice, that at Mr John Banister's house (now called the music school) over against the George Tavern, in White Friars, near the back of the Temple, this Monday, will be music performed by excellent masters, beginning precisely at 4 of the clock in the afternoon, and every afternoon for the future, precisely at the same hour.

Banister erected a dais for his players, and protected them by curtains. His audience, in which were many shopkeepers, was

---

[1] Playford, *Choice Ayres and Dialogues II . . . Most of the Newest Ayres and Songs, sung at Court, And at the Public Theatres,* 1679. Benjamin Wallington contributed to this as he had to Playford's *The Musical Companion* (1673), and *New Ayres and Dialogues [for] voices and viols Together with Lessons for Viols or Violins,* John Banister and Thomas Low (1678).

disposed 'ale-house' fashion around small tables, and for a shilling entitled to as much ale and tobacco as they might require. 'There was', said Roger North,

> very good music, for Banister found means to procure the best hands in the town and some voices to come and perform there, and there wanted no variety of humour, for Banister himself did wonders upon a flageolet to a thorough Bass, and the several masters had their solos. This continued full one winter, and more I remember not.

After a second season, in 1673, Banister moved to Chandos Street, Covent Garden, for the next series. Two years later he set up his Academy in Lincoln's Inn Field, and in 1678 in a house in Essex Street, off the Strand. Banister's concerts were advertised in the *London Gazette*, as also his intention to support novelty, which could take the form of rare instruments—such as the four 'trumpets marine' ('never heard of before in England') which were promised in the *London Gazette* of February 4, 1674[1], or of contemporary music. Matteis published his first set of Airs for the Violin 'at the desire and change of certain well-wishers to the work' at the end of 1676, and they found a ready market. There were publications by Banister himself, by Pietro Reggio, and by various 'sound excellent masters'. By 1681 the value of the concert to publishers was acknowledged by Brown & Benskin, who advertised 'A New Collection of the Choicest Songs, as they are sung at Court, both the Theatres, the Music-schools and Academies, etc.'[2] and to composers who, like Gerhard Diessener, could arrange concerts in their houses to demonstrate their new works[3]. Among the publishers the most prominent were John Playford and his son Henry, who issued various anthologies and instruction books. In 1683 John Playford published Henry Purcell's sonatas for two violins and bass, at which point the wheel came full circle; for herein was the influence of the Italian

---

[1] At the Fleece Tavern, St. James's.

[2] *The Domestick Intelligence*, December 8.

[3] *The Loyal Post*, October 28, 1682. Diessener, formerly a member of the court music at Kassel, had visited Paris in 1660, and his *Ouvertures, Ballets et Allemandes* were the first German works in the style of Lully. Diessener (called in England 'Diesineer') settled in London in 1663.

school, especially Corelli, but subdued to the genius of an English composer of individual character. These sonatas were the first-fruits of the public concert.

It was during Banister's operations that the idea of building a public music-room was first mooted, by Thomas Mace in his *Musick's Monument* (1676). He proposed that such a building should be erected at the public expense, that it should be raised off the ground, on stilts, to prevent the damage and discomfort caused by dampness, that the musicians should be accommodated in an area six yards square, and the audience in galleries partitioned off from the music room, but with aural access thereto through specially bored and conical apertures. But this idea was still-born.

THOMAS BRITTON (1644–1714)

Banister's concerts retained their club atmosphere, especially when, as North testifies, there were those patrons who went to sing as well as to listen. Half-a-dozen years after Banister had taken the initiative another society of some fame was founded, 'in a very obscure part of the town, viz. at Clerkenwell, in such a place, and under such circumstances, as tended to disgrace rather than recommend such an institution. In that it was in the house, or rather hovel, of one Thomas Britton, a man who for a livelihood sold small-coal about the streets . . .'[1]. Sir John Hawkins held views about class distinction that were stronger than those of Sir Roger l'Estrange, who, together with other gentlemen of similar standing, had the highest personal regard for Britton. The latter was distinguished by a general and remarkable culture that spread itself generously over the fields of literature and music. l'Estrange recommended that the long, low room above the coal-store was admirable for musical performances, and if access was by way of an unsteady staircase pinned to the outside of the building, that was no hindrance to genuine lovers of music.

Civil servants, representatives of the aristocracy, and a miscellany of writers and wits, made their way to Clerkenwell for the music meetings for a period of thirty years. For a long

[1] Hawkins, *General History of Music*, V, p. 1.

time Britton refused to countenance any charge on his guests, but was eventually persuaded to accept a nominal shilling per head. Among the musical eminences who were there to be encountered were Pepusch and Handel, while it was at Britton's that the youthful prodigy Matthew Dubourg made his debut with, it was suggested by Hawkins, a sonata by Corelli.

The concerts at Clerkenwell were described with robust humour, but in considerable detail, by Ned Ward in his *Satirical Reflections on Clubs*[1]. As for the music:

> We thrum the fam'd Corella's airs,
> Fine solos and sonnetos,
> New riggadoons and maidenfairs,
> Rare jigs and minuettos.
>
> Sometimes we've a song,
> Of an hour or two long,
> Very nicely performed
> By some beau that's so warmed
> With the charms of his Chloe's sweet face
> That he chooses out his love
> Like the amorous dove;
> Which the ladies approve,
> And would gladly remove
> All the cause of his sorrowful case.

Britton died in 1714, and at the end of that year his effects were sold by auction, some being acquired by Sir Hans Sloane. His music, the catalogue of which was printed by Hawkins, gives a record of the taste of an amateur musician of the period, and an index to the programmes of his Thursday evenings. Of the older composers he possessed church music by Tallis, Byrd, and Gibbons, and the first and second sets of madrigals by Wilbye, and 'six sets of books, most of Dowland, for many parts'. He had many works by Henry Lawes, airs by Ravenscroft, and companionable catches. On the instrumental side the classical English fantasy was represented by specimens of Coperario, Lupo, Ferrabosco, Jenkins, and Christopher Gibbons. The new Italian school contributed sonatas by Bassani, Corelli, Vitali,

---

[1] Reprinted in *The Romance of the Fiddle*, E. Van der Straeten, London 1911, pp. 115 ff.

Vecellini, and concertos by Corelli and Vivaldi, while Sherard's Op. 1 was in the collection. From the currently popular German instrumental school there were examples by Biber and Rosenmüller, as well as Baltzar. Britton cultivated Lully and Grabu, but was zealous in supporting his fellow-countrymen; thus he possessed what of Purcell was published, and works by Wilson, Locke, Child, Croft, Blow, and the anglicised Pepusch, Finger, and Paisible.

Britton's library clearly was one of the more remarkable features of English musical life. But it was essentially for practical service: music to be heard rather than seen, to be played and sung and not merely to be made the cause of earnest, academical disputation. It was from this source that Handel gained acquaintance with the long tradition of English music, and in that company that he learned to appreciate the qualities of English connoisseurship. The manner in which the music was dispensed established a precedent to be followed during the eighteenth century, and even beyond.

EXTENSION OF CONCERT PROMOTION IN LONDON

During this period the cultivation of the sociabilities of music was greatly assisted by those schools and dancing academies[1] which advertised music as part of the curriculum. If these were not exclusively for Young Ladies—in 1665 Samuel Turberville announced that he dispensed music in his boys' school in Kensington—for the most part they were; the most celebrated was that conducted by Josias Priest. It was for this establishment, moved from Leicester Fields to Chelsea in 1680, that Purcell wrote *Dido and Aeneas*. Mrs John Playford also maintained a school, and on November 23, 1685, the *London Gazette* advertised that

> Several Sonata's, composed after the Italian way, for one and two Bass Viols, with a Thorough Bass . . . are to be performed on Thursday next, and every Thursday following, at Six of the clock in the Evening, at the Dancing School in Walbrook, next door to the Bell Inn, and on Saturday next, and every Saturday following, at the Dancing School in York Buildings. At which place will be

[1] See p. 35 above.

also some performance upon the Baritone Viol da gamba by Mr August Keenell[1], the Author of this Music. Such as do not subscribe, are to pay their Half Crown, towards the discharge of performing it.

The proliferation of concert promotion[2] encouraged entrepreneurs from other than purely musical circles, and when the gentlemen who had previously run it resigned their organisation of a meeting in Fleet Street the publican whose premises were involved took over. He 'hired masters to play, and made a pecuniary concert of it, to which for the reputation of the music numbers of people of good fashion and quality repaired'[3].

A CORPORATE VENTURE BY MUSICIANS

At this juncture there was, temporarily, joint action by the musicians, who

finding that money was to be got in this way, determined to take the business into their own hands; and it proceeded so far, that in York buildings a fabric was reared and furnished on purpose for public music. And there was nothing of music valued in town, but was to be heard there. It was called the Music-Meeting; and all the quality and *beau monde* repaired to it, but the plan of this project was not so well laid as ought to have been, for the time of this beginning was inconsistent with the park and the play houses, which had a stronger attraction . . .

As time went on the musicians did their best to undermine their own undertaking, for 'every one was forward to advance his own talents', while the programme had no design or order,

for one master brings a consort with fugues, another shows his gifts in a solo upon the violin, another sings, and then a famous lutenist comes forward, and in this manner changes followed each other, with a full cessation of the music between every one, and a

---

[1] August Kühnel (1645–c. 1700) a famous German viol da gamba player, and composer, formerly of the Court of Zeitz, who became Kapellmeister at Kassel soon after his London visit. His gamba sonatas and partitas composed for the Landgraf Carl of Hesse, were among the best of works for this instrument.

[2] Cf. also the sale of a house near Lamb's Conduit, formerly known as 'Coleman's Musick House' (*The Loyal Post*, April 6, 1682).

[3] North, *op. cit.*, p. 112.

gabble and bustle while they changed places; whereas all entertainments of this kind ought to be projected as a drama, and having a true connexion, set off each other[1].

In the course of the eighteenth century concerts, with oratorio divisions principally in mind, were to be projected along the lines of drama, and arranged in Acts.

North's reference to a newly reared and furnished fabric represents another step forward. The building in which a music-room was thus designed was erected on property formerly belonging to the Archbishop of York (hence the name), transferred by him to the Duke of Buckingham, and then acquired for 'development'. In 1689 the concerts apparently initiated by Kühnel's visit combined with those that had been organised at the Two Golden Balls, in Bow Street, and took place on Mondays and Thursdays (except when interrupted by the King's Birthday celebrations). The season was from October to May, and the capacity of the music-room was sufficient for 200 persons. That a certain hardiness was required of the audience is indicated by an advertisement (January 2, 1690) by the Duke of Northumberland concerning his loss of a 'sable muff lost at the music-meeting in York Buildings', while at the end of the same month a reward was offered for the return of a 'Palatine of Russian Sable' lost at the same place.

OPPORTUNITIES FOR FOREIGN TALENT

After the early hazards described by North the York Buildings became the focal point for new music, both vocal and instrumental: the element of novelty reigned supreme, and rarely can London have been so generously supplied with contemporary works that did not cause disaffection among the concert-going public. So—from the *London Gazette*:

January 9, 1693: 'The Italian lady (that is lately come over that is so famous for her singing) has been reported that she will sing no more in the concert in York Buildings: This is to give notice that next Tuesday . . . she will sing in the Concert in York Buildings, and so continued during this season[2].'

[1] North, *op. cit.*, pp. 112 ff.

[2] Margarita de l'Épine (d. 1746) who having come to London stayed there for the rest of her life, singing in Handel's early operas and, in 1718, marrying John Christopher Pepusch.

October 26, 1693: 'Signor Tosi's[1] concert of music will begin on Monday the 30th instant in York-buildings, at 8 in the evening, to continue weekly all the winter.'

January 25, 1694: 'At the Concert-room in York-buildings, on this present Thursday, at the usual hour will be performed Mr Purcell's Song composed for St. Cecilia's Day[2] in the year 1692, together with some other compositions of his, both vocal and instrumental, for the entertainment of His Highness, Prince Lewis of Baden.'

During this year regular concerts in York Buildings were directed by Gottfried Finger, a German immigrant violinist and composer, and an old associate of John Banister, whose son was also among the performers at York Buildings. Other composers to display their latest works were Staggins, the Professor of Music at Cambridge and Master of the King's Music, Vaughan Richardson, former choir-boy of the Chapel Royal and organist of Winchester Cathedral, William Turner, singer at Westminster Abbey and a Doctor of Music of Cambridge, Blow, and Daniel Purcell, brother of Henry. The 'Chiefest masters in England' were well represented in the programmes, and there was no tariff against those of Italy, France, and Germany. York Buildings grew from its modest beginnings to be a fashionable obligation by the end of the century, and on more than one occasion it served as an annexe to the Court, for the entertainment of visiting princes: a change from the Jacobean and Caroline eras when guests of rank were diverted by the flatteries that belonged to the Masques at Whitehall.

After a season of collaboration the Bow Street promoters broke away from those at York Buildings and, removing to new premises, again specially adapted for the purpose, in Charles Street set up a lively competition. The organiser was Johann

---

[1] Pier Francesco Tosi (1646–1727), singer, teacher, and composer of cantatas, but principally remembered for a treatise on singing (Bologna 1723, London 1742).

[2] St. Cecilia's Day was celebrated in England from 1683, usually in the Hall of the Stationers' Company, which, in the early eighteenth century, was also used for other concerts. Odes by Finger, John Blow, and Nicola Matteis were performed at those in York Buildings.

Wolfgang Franck (who had murdered a subordinate musician at the Court of Ansbach, where Franck was Kapellmeister), a previously successful opera composer in Hamburg. The Charles Street room was known as the Vendu, because it was also used for the sale of pictures (additional revenues at York Buildings came through the letting of the room for dancing lessons and for lotteries). The programmes in the Vendu were a little more sensation-seeking than those of the other concerts. In 1694, for instance, 'a gentlewoman sings that hath one of the best voices in England, not before heard in public', and, on a later occasion, 'a young gentlewoman of twelve years of age'.

While clubbable concerts, after the Britton pattern, were maintained at the Castle Tavern, as well as at the Queen's Head, in Paternoster Row, and the Queen's Arms, near St. Paul's Cathedral, and went their informal way through the eighteenth century, to the delight of such musical worthies as Handel and Maurice Greene, the more or less formal occasions of the York Buildings and the Vendu were imitated elsewhere. Before the seventeenth century was out concerts took place at Richmond New and Old Wells, at Lambeth Wells (where up to thirty performers were engaged from time to time), at Sadler's Wells (morning concerts between 11 and 1, and at a cost only of sixpence per person), and at Hickford's Dancing School, where James Kremberg[1], 'lately come out of Italy', presented 'a New Concert of Music by very great Masters, of all sorts of instruments, with fine singing', and 'always with New Compositions'.

At the same time there was a tendency towards concert music in the theatre. Frequently entr'acte items took the form of violin sonatas by Corelli, or pieces by Banister, Paisible, Lully (Drury Lane, April 10, 1705): a habit that was to have some effect on Handel's design of his oratorios.

BENEFIT CONCERTS

The cult of the virtuoso had started when Baltzar and Matteis first astonished audiences that had previously rested in insular

---

[1] Jacob Kremberg, formerly of the University of Leipzig, the Courts at Halle, Stockholm, and Dresden, and the Hamburg Opera. The concert at Hickford's Dancing School was announced in *The Post Bag* for November 20, 1697.

contentment and the belief that Davis Mell was as good as any fiddler in any land. By the end of the century the leading performers were enjoying Benefit Concerts (an institution not even yet quite dead) and the range of instrumentalists was enlarged. The pride of London was, indeed, a trumpeter, John Shore, for whom Purcell wrote virtuoso parts and whose 'Trumpet Tune' was transformed as a top favourite to the harpsichord by Jeremiah Clarke. Shore was an artist. So he was noticed in *The Gentleman's Journal* of January 1692, after his performance at the St. Cecilia's Day Feast of the preceding November:

> Whilst the company is at table the hautboys and trumpets play successively. Mr Showers [i.e. Shore] hath taught the latter of late years to sound with all the softness imaginable; they played us some flat tunes in a flat key made by Mr Finger, with a general applause, it being a thing formerly thought impossible upon an instrument designed for a sharp key.

A 'SPIRITUAL' CONCERT

While these entertainments proliferated there were those who considered the proprieties of music. Thus, at the beginning of 1701, one Cavendish Weedon, a member of Lincoln's Inn, who had one laudable intention of endowing a school whose faculties should be 'religion, music, and accounts', and another 'for the relief of poor decayed gentlemen', inaugurated a kind of spiritual concert in the Hall of the Stationers' Company. After an oration written by himself, and two poems by the Laureate, Nahum Tate, the main part of the performance comprised anthems by Drs Blow and Turner. A year later another such occasion included an anthem and *Te Deum* by Dr Blow—the doyen of the 'cathedral school'. Weedon also subsidised Sunday morning vocal and instrumental services in the Chapel of Lincoln's Inn.

ACTIVITY IN SCOTLAND

In this flexible, and prolific, era of musical entertainment musicians came and went. Among those who did both was John Abell, an Aberdonian and sometime member of the Chapel Royal, whom Charles II had sent to Italy to develop his

43

talents. On his return from Italy Abell was heard and approved by Pepys, after which he remained in the Chapel Royal until 1688. Then dismissed on suspicion of Papist leanings he wandered adventurously around Europe until he became Intendant of the theatre in Kassel in 1698. A year or two later he was back in London, whence he undertook missionary work in his native Scotland. To this Allan Ramsay made allusion in 'Bagpipes no music: Being a Satire of Scots Poetry':

> Sooner shall China yield to earthenware
> Sooner shall Abel teach a singing bear,
> Than English bands let Scots torment their ear.

On September 26 the *Edinburgh Courant* printed the following announcement: 'Whereas Mr Abel hath had the Honour to pay his Humble Duty to the Nobility and Gentry, in several Parts of this Kingdom, i.e. Scotland, in four several Voyages from Foreign Parts; Does intend with the Help of God, to be at Aberdeen on Saturday the Third of November 1705.' In this northern city music was, indeed, flourishing, so that in 1713 Sir Samuel Forbes could write: 'Music here is much in vogue, and many citizens sing charmingly. The well-known Abel was a native of this place, and his kindred are known by the name of Eball; and, it's said, there are others [of this family] as good as he.'

In one way or another, then, there was much public music practised by the beginning of the eighteenth century in Britain. Performances were speculative, founded on the developing principle of making a profit in a free market, untidy in organisation, but both varied and vigorous. If a sense of purpose was missing—compare, for instance, the career of Purcell with those of, say, Corelli, or Lully—there was plenty of incentive to originality.

In 1710 Handel arrived in England and thereafter the pattern of musical life was more rigorously defined.

4

Concert Spirituel

THE ACADÉMIE

*J*T HAS ALREADY BEEN SEEN THAT the origin of the concert was in the Italian Accademia, and that the educational,
social, and aesthetic principles connected with that institution
were subject to adaptation to different environments. The
aristocratic ideal was maintained in Italy, whereas in Germany
it was modified by the intelligentsia, and in England by the
middle classes. In France, however, as in Italy, minority
interests were zealously protected. At the same time, rather
more than elsewhere, certain national considerations were taken
into account. In the reign of Louis XIV, indeed, music as a
whole was regulated (as much as music may ever be regulated)
according to the demands of interests of state. In terms of
musical entertainment these interests centred on the supremacy of French ideas on the one hand, and the engagement
(and indoctrination) of artists who would ensure this
supremacy on the other.

In fact the French Court was early in the field of concert
promotion, for Charles IX granted to J. A. de Baïf a patent to
establish an Academy (henceforth known as the Académie
Baïf) in 1570. According to the classical models this was to be
concerned primarily with poetry, but also with music insofar as
this was related to literary expression. This foundation did not
function for long, but while it did it established conditions
greatly superior to those which were to obtain elsewhere for
some time to come. There was, for instance, a separate place
marked out for the musicians, who were given further consideration in that people were not permitted to enter the
auditorium during a performance, while the audience was

45

instructed not to make a noise while music was in progress, and—somewhat superfluously one might think—'to be as still as possible'.

The Académie Baïf, however, failed to survive, and the next ventures were by ambitious professional musicians. The first of the great claveçin composers was Jacques Champion de Chambonnières (1602–1672), the titles of whose pieces reflected the general 'Academy' viewpoint that literature and music went best together, and in this respect set a precedent. About the year 1630 Chambonnières organised 'assemblées des honestes curieux', at which he mostly played his own works. A dozen years later Parisian society was occasionally entertained by the 'concert de la musique almérique', and by 1650 Pierre de Chambonceau de la Barre (d. 1656), organist to the Chapel Royal, was arranging performances under the patronage of the Duchesse de Liancour and her sister, the Duchesse de Schomberg. These concerts were of a serious nature—the element of seriousness thus established was maintained for a long time—and, described as *Concerts Spirituels*, were flippantly called by their noble patronesses their 'Second Vespers'.

THE COURT OF LOUIS XIV

At the Court Louis XIV insisted on music by La Lande[1] and by the Philidor brothers being played during supper. He also liked to listen to pieces by Chambonnières, Couperin, Marais, Gaultier, and to the airs and overtures of Lully (sometimes arranged for claveçin by d'Anglebert). As for performers he would engage the best in Europe: for instance, Anna Carriata, the Roman singer, Johann Paul von Westhoff, violinist to the Elector of Saxony, and an unnamed English trumpeter, who would play 'les plus beaux airs du monde'. The private concerts of Louis XIV were described by Jean de la Fontaine—in somewhat sceptical tones—in his Épître a M le Niert sur l'Opéra (1677):

---

[1] Some of La Lande's *Sinfonies pour les soupers du Roi*, edited by Roger Desormière, are in the modern orchestral repertoire. His *Concert de Trompettes pour les Festes sur le Canal de Versailles* was a pioneer work in the tradition best known through Handel's *Water Music* suites.

Grand in all ways he imbues everything with grandeur.
War stimulates his joy and his enthusiasm,
And a war-like feeling pervades all his entertainments.
His instrumental concerts sound like thunder,
While those for voices recall the noise
Of shouting soldiers on a day of battle.

Music of less heroic properties was promoted by Mme de Montespan and Mme de Maintenon, and noblemen's concerts became so general that Molière felt obliged to draw attention to the cult in *Le Bourgeois Gentilhomme*, where in Act II, the music-master says to M Jourdain:

Anyone like you—with a sense of what is fitting—who is accustomed to the best of everything—should hold a concert every Wednesday or Thursday ... You need three voices, one tenor, one soprano, and one bass, and these require the accompaniment of bass viol, theorbo, and harpsichord (for the figured bass), and two treble violins for the ritornelli.

PROFESSIONAL CONCERTS FOR THE NOBILITY

Among the professional concerts those given by the lutenists Dessanssonières and Gallot at their houses were especially celebrated, and in 1683 the Siamese ambassador was a guest at one of those arranged by Gallot. He was reported as thus appreciative:

The concert was found most attractive ... M Gallot played lute solos, and the ambassador again said that he thought nothing could have been added to the concert in the way of beauty. When he played solo there were delicate effects that could not have been appreciated had there been a group of instruments, where so much seems to be lost.

Composers of modest pretensions, as in England, took the opportunity to publicise their new publications by public demonstration. These were advertised in the *Mercure Galante* in this way:

You may, if you please, tell all your friends in the province who will be in Paris that they may attend a most agreeable guitar concert which is held at M Medard's house once a fortnight. He has issued a volume of his pieces, and those most qualified to express an opinion agree that he has explored the most attractive qualities of his instrument. The concert will have a contrasting work in a Dialogue for voices on the subject of Peace ... (December, 1678).

PROVINCIAL SOCIETIES

The proliferation of musical evenings in the capital was quickly followed by similar provincial activity, Rouen and Orléans being the first cities to establish Academies. At Rouen, in 1662, the guiding spirit was a priest. Elsewhere—at Troyes, Nancy, Nantes, Clermont-Ferrand, Moulins, Caen—the local gentry took the lead. The number of members varied but sometimes reached a hundred, and subscribers were permitted to introduce guests to performances. The regulations were drawn up with care, so that the right kind of visitor (especially lady visitors) was brought. In many cases the local garrison was allowed a small number of complimentary tickets. At Nancy, at the beginning of the eighteenth century, a minimum age limit was ordained: children under ten were excluded so that 'ils ne troublent la tranquilité du concert'.

ACADEMIE DE MUSIQUE

Over and above every musical activity in France in the later years of Louis XIV was the Académie de Musique, incorporated by the King in 1669 and entrusted to the Abbé Pierre Perrin, Cambert the composer, and the Marquis de Sourdéac. In 1672 the Académie passed under the direction of Lully, who obtained control through the influence of Mme de Montespan. The terms of his appointment were broadly stated in the letters Patent granted to him:

'The Arts and Sciences', said the King,

being the principal ornaments of States, our greatest pleasure has been, since we gave peace to our subjects, to revive them, by taking all those persons under our protection who have acquired reputation by excelling in them, not only within the extent of our kingdom, but likewise in foreign countries, and, in order to induce them the more to aspire to perfection, we have honoured them with marks of our esteem and benevolence; and as Music stands on the first rank in the list of liberal arts, with a view to encouraging its cultivation in the fullest extent, we thought proper to grant to the Sieur Perrin . . . a permission to establish in our good town of Paris, and other towns of our dominions, Musical Academies for the performance of operas as is practised in Italy, Germany, and England. But having since been informed that the care and pains which the aforesaid Perrin has taken relative to this establishment have not fully recorded our intention, nor raised music to that pitch of perfection in which we expected to have seen it; in order to ensure better success, we have been of opinion that it was expedient to give the direction of it to a person whose experience and capacity are known to us, and who is well able to perfect scholars for singing and acting in the theatre, as to prepare and regulate bands of violins, flutes, and other instruments[1].

Lully was given a free hand, and while the opera benefited in the first place orchestral music in general greatly appreciated.

Italian music inevitably invaded France but, as was noted in the *Mercure Galante*, November, 1713, not without difficulty:

It must be allowed, said one of them, that the majestic music of France deals with heroic subjects with greater nobility and more dramatic sense. In Italian music everything seems uniform; for joy, anger, grief, and the happiness and hopes of lovers are all described with the same musical gestures. Italian music is an everlasting gigue. It is brilliant and full of energy, but often expresses quite other things than the words suggest.

Seventeen years later Jacques Aubert sent out his *Concerts de symphonie* with this animadversion on current taste which explained some part of the reason for the opposition to Italian music:

Although the Italian concertos, in which justice has been done to Corelli, Vivaldi, and others who have done excellent things of the same kind, have been successful in France for a number of years, it has often been remarked that this kind of music is not to everybody's taste; particularly to that of the ladies, whose judgement has always determined the pleasures of the nation . . . The author's intention has been to unite the lively features and gaiety associated with French songs. He does not flatter himself

[1] See *A Universal Dictionary of Music*, appended to James Hook's *Lessons*, London, 1813.

49

that he has fully succeeded; but he provides opportunity for the most talented. The pieces are for large choir (as in the concerts) and should be useful for Academies, and for whatever is termed an 'Orchestra'.

ESTABLISHMENT OF THE CONCERT SPIRITUEL

By this time the Concert Spirituel of Anne Philidor, following the example of that of de la Barre, had, not without some difficulty, taken its place in French musical life. Philidor, one of a long line of Philidors attached to the royal music, obtained permission from Francine, manager of the Opera, to give concerts of appropriate music during Lent. On March 17, 1725, after a three-year contract had been signed, the first of such concerts took place, with the following programme:

Lalande	—	Suite
Lalande	—	Caprice
		Motet, 'Confitebor'[1]
Corelli	—	'Christmas' Concerto
Lalande	—	Motet

The concerts were soon transferred to the Salle des Suisses in the Tuileries, where Philidor took the opportunity to give adequate place to his own works in the programmes. Thereby he stimulated a jealousy not unusual in the history of concert promotion. At the same time, however, he included pieces by Lalande, Bernier, Gilles, Campra, Couperin, and Gaveau. Motets were prominent in the early Concert Spirituel (and so they remained for many years to come), but also included were prologues to, and excerpts from, operas, 'divertissements', cantatas, suites of airs, and fanfares—music, in fact, which formed the mainstay of the Chapel Royal and of the private *concerts du dimanche* of the King. For such performances Couperin composed his clavecin *Ordres*, and his *Concerts royaux*. These latter were suites of dances, based on those of the theatre and the ballet, but prefaced by an Italianate Prelude. The *Concerts royaux* of Couperin were published in two books, in 1722 and 1725. Foreign music, especially Italian, was gradually

---

[1] Composer not stated.

introduced into the Concert Spirituel, and Bononcini was the Italian composer most generally welcomed.

The social status conferred by musical interest is thus conveyed by J. C. Nemeitz, in his *Séjour de Paris*, 1727:

> If one has already made some progress in the art of singing, or if one can already play upon some instrument, one should not delay putting one's knowledge into practice in Paris also, if one takes pleasure in it and feels so disposed. This gives a young man the privilege of entry into the polite world, and one can take part in the best concerts, which are to be heard every day, and spend in this innocent pleasure many hours that might otherwise be disagreeable. There is no lack here of excellent masters for all kinds of instruments, and I greatly doubt whether one can ever find elsewhere so many highly qualified men as there are in Paris. Among composers there, I know of nearly thirty who have made themselves famous in all branches of music by the works that they have brought out[1].

Philidor managed the Concert Spirituel for three years, when he transferred his privilege to Simond, who appointed Jean Joseph Mouret musical director. Mouret, a protégé of the Duchesse de Maine, first distinguished himself as a composer of operas and ballets, but for the Concert Spirituel he wrote a number of motets (published in 1742). He also composed many 'Divertissements', 'Fanfares', 'Concerts de chambre', and—in this he was a pioneer—'Simphonies pour des violins, des hautbois et des cors de chasse'. In 1734 the Académie Royale took over the administration of the Concert Spirituel, appointing François Rébel, a member of the royal chamber music ensemble, to succeed Mouret. Under the direction of Mouret and Rébel Jean Marie Leclair was the outstanding musician to appear. As a violinist, who studied in Italy, Leclair took first place in the French school, but he was not less distinguished as a composer. His sonatas and concertos were in the Italian style, conservative in character, but also illuminated by a characteristic French charm, and melodic grace. Rébel also brought wind-players into higher esteem by his engagement of two of the celebrated Besozzi family, Antonio and Carlo, members of the royal orchestra in Dresden, the best ensemble of its period in

---

[1] Quoted in 'More about Marais', in *The Consort*, No. 10, 1953, p. 14.

Europe[1]. After Rébel came Joseph Royer, whose period of office was the longest in the history of the concerts, lasting until his death in 1755.

PRIVATE ORGANISATIONS

During the first fifty years of its existence the Concert Spirituel was affected by the progressive attributes of the private, and aristocratic, music meetings that were a distinguishing feature of French society until the Revolution.

Contemporary with the earliest meetings of the Concert Spirituel were those of the society known as the *Concert des Mélophilètes*, promoted by Louis-Armand de Bourbon, Prince de Conti. The music was provided for, and by, amateurs, and no one paid a subscription. The works of Lully were particularly cultivated here, a favourite item being the *passacaile* from *Armide*, but the sonatas of Corelli were also highly regarded. It was after the performance of a prelude in the style of this master that the shade of Corelli was made to appear, and to speak the following lines:

Ils ont embelli leur modelle
En prêtant à mes Avis une grace nouvelle
C'est nous rendre encore plus qu'ils n'ont reçu de nous
Mais bien loin d'en être jaloux
Nous rentrons satisfaits dans la Nuit éternelle[2].

The salons of Crozat, art-collector and patron of Watteau, and of the Duchesse de Maine were also fashionable centres of musical activity, but the most ambitious undertakings were those of le Riche de la Pouplinière, the *Fermier-général*. De la Pouplinière's receptions were on the grand scale, and comparable only with those of Ottoboni. At the town house, or at the Château at Passy, Vaucanson, the engineer, de la Tour and Vanloo, the artists, as well as Jean François Marmontel, Jean-Jacques Rousseau, and Voltaire were regularly entertained. Rameau was for many years a pensioner of the de la Pouplinière household, and he lived agreeably (except for differences of opinion with Rousseau over the latter's pretensions as composer),

[1] See p. 71.
[2] 'They have taken my advice and improved their model, adding to it a new grace. They give back to us what they received from us: without any sense of jealousy we return, satisfied, to the Eternal Night'.

with every encouragement being shown by his patron, and patroness, both being his pupils. Mme de la Pouplinière played the claveçin and sang, while her husband aspired to be a composer. On Rameau's advice de la Pouplinière also took under his protection François Joseph Gossec, who, shortly after leaving the choir of Antwerp Cathedral in 1757, became conductor of de la Pouplinière's private orchestra. With an ear for contemporary tonal values de la Pouplinière had developed the rarer instrumental colours. He was the first in France to use horns regularly at his concerts. This, it was said, was due to the advice of Johann Stamitz. His band also included two clarinets and three trombones. All these players—the horn-players were Syryneck and Steinmetz, and the clarinettists Proksch and Flieger—were imported from German establishments.

JOHANN STAMITZ IN PARIS

Johann Stamitz, already known in Paris through his contacts with French musicians and through his pupils, was a guest of de la Pouplinière from September 1754 to September 1755. His impact on French music was considerable and through him the symphony became the mainstay of the concert programme. On September 8, 1754, the Concert Spirituel put on an all-Stamitz programme—a 'symphonie nouvelle à cors de chasse et haut-bois', a violin concerto, and a sonata for viola d'amore. On March 26, 1755, a symphony 'avec clarinets et cors de chasse' was played. Thereafter Stamitz enjoyed great esteem in Paris, where his works (which included 74 symphonies and numerous concertos) were readily published. At this point in history the cultures of France and Germany were brought together in an *entente cordiale*, of which the German side may now be examined.

FRANCO–GERMAN RECIPROCITY

The principal supports of German music were the Church, the court, the university, the municipality, and the *Collegium Musicum*, with a great deal of interrelated activity. Among the German composers who, so to speak, eliminated class distinction

53

in early baroque music were Dietrich Becker of Hamburg, composer of pieces enticingly labelled *Frülings–Früchte* (*sic*), Sebastian Knüpfer, who introduced variations on folk-tunes into his suites, Buxtehude and Rosenmüller, exponents of *Kirch-* and *Turm-Musik* and *Studenten-Musik* respectively, Beer, of Halle, whose pieces for post-horns and strings represented the zest for variegated instrumentation that distinguished many German composers of the period and anticipated the colourful innovations of Johann Stamitz. Then there were vital influences from the eastern outposts of Europe, Polish, for example, in the case of Kremberg, and Czech in that of Finger. The *Abendmusik* established in Lübeck was supported as a kind of *Concert Spirituel* (which term is applied to it by Blume)[1] by the municipality and by the eighteenth century instrumental as well as vocal works were regularly performed. University music in turn borrowed both from Church and court, or municipality, as particularly in Kiel[2] and in Leipzig.

The German courts, for their part, had, since the end of the Thirty Years' War, settled their general pattern on the model of Versailles, even though the smaller ones maintained a sturdily provincial character. By the end of the seventeenth century German, Austrian, and Hungarian composers, following Gerhard Diessener's lead, were frequently in Paris—on ducal subsistence allowances—in order to study the method of Lully and his colleagues. Erlebach, Mayr, Kusser, Fischer, Muffat, Fux, Telemann, Froberger, were all affected by their visits to France, and on their return composed instrumental music, with pretty titles after the French manner, which pleased their patrons. Johann Sebastian Bach, of course, was influenced by this development, largely through the music of the French school kept in the library at Cöthen. But the composer whose association was closest was Georg Philipp Telemann, perhaps the most successful German composer (excluding Handel) of his generation. He touched the music of his age at every point.

Telemann was born in Magdeburg and went to school in that city until (to take his mind off music) he was sent to Zellerfeld

---

[1] See 'Dietrich Buxtehude', in *Syntagma Musicologicum'*, Kassel, 1963, pp. 307–8.

[2] See 'Augustin Pflegers Kieler Universitäts-Oden', *ibid.* p. 275 *et seq.*

in the Harz Mountains. So far from the parental intention being successful Telemann here found every opportunity to compose; whether for a miners' festival, for the church, or for the town musicians. For the latter he wrote what he flippantly described as *Bratensymphonien* ('Roast-beef symphonies'). In a free-and-easy environment he wrote motets for the Lutherans and persuaded the local Jesuits to allow them, despite their heterodox doctrines, to be performed in the Catholic Church. There followed an undergraduate career in Leipzig, where Telemann helped Kuhnau to establish the *Collegium Musicum*—successor to the *Collegium Gellianum* of 1641.

From Leipzig Telemann went into the service of Count Erdmann von Promnitz in Sorau. 'The brilliance of the Court which the Count had recently established there', wrote Telemann,

> encouraged me to embark on a number of spirited enterprises, especially instrumental pieces such as Overtures with their accompanying movements. These especially pleased the Count, who had lately returned from France with a predilection for this genre. I had mastered the works of Lully, Campra and other good masters, and I wrote some two hundred Overtures in practically the same style in the course of two years.

When this court moved to Upper Silesia for the summer Telemann had an ear for the tavern music, of Polish and Moravian origin, and acknowledged its influence in the concertos which he wrote in an otherwise Italian style.

Telemann next directed the music of the Eisenach court, where he found an orchestra, under Hebenstreit, the dulcimer virtuoso, based on and, he said, as good as that of the French Opera. From this time, about 1712, Telemann had a finger in every pie, adding one court Kapellmeistership (held in *absentia*) to another, and directing church music in Frankfurt—where he composed cantatas for the weekly church concerts, and then in Hamburg. To his activities in Frankfurt and Hamburg reference will be made in the next chapter.

In the autumn of 1717 Telemann went to Paris, where his works were already in demand. He remained in Paris for eight months, and arranged for his quartets and sonatas to be published there. He was as full of praise for the way in which

E   **55**

Blavet (flute), Guignon (violin), Forqueray (gamba), and Edouard ('cello) played his music as they were for the music itself. He composed two Latin psalms expressly for amateur performance, a cantata to a French text, several concerti and trios, and a comic symphony based on a currently popular song—*Père Barnabas*. His largest work during this prolific period was a motet, on Psalm 71, which was twice performed at the Concert Spirituel. Telemann was delighted: the performance, by a hundred picked singers and instrumentalists, was, he said, inspiring.

SYMPHONIC GROWTH

While French influence was great in Germany so also was that which came from Italy. Concert-room music at the German courts was increasingly French in manner, but Corelli and Vivaldi were still in vogue, while every opera-house was dominated by expatriate Italians and their pupils. The point at which the three cultures met was in the new-style, three-movement, *sinfonia*, derived from the overtures of Alessandro Scarlatti, the sinfonia-type works of Vivaldi[1] (who enjoyed esteem in Dresden, for whose royal orchestra he wrote a number of richly scored *concerti*), and defined by Sammartini (1701–1775), Rinaldo di Capua (c. 1715–1771), Porpora (1686–1766), and Jommelli (1714–1774). Among Germans who saw the possibilities inherent in the form and in its amplification through the emotional properties of German melodic style and orchestral resources were Johann Agrell (1701–1765), of Kassel and Nürnberg, Christoph Förster (1693–1748), Kapellmeister to the Prince of Schwetzbourg-Rudolstadt, Johann Fasch (1688–1758), of Anhalt-Zerbst and Leipzig, and Georg Monn (1717–1750), of Vienna. But it was Johann Stamitz (1717–1757), Bohemian by birth, who was the first fully to realise the potential of the symphony and in so doing to lay the foundations of the Classical School and of modern concert music.

Stamitz came into general prominence when he was engaged at Frankfurt in 1741 for the celebration of the coronation of the

[1] See Charles Cudworth, 'Vivaldi and the Symphony', in *Ricordiana*, Vol. 8, No. 1, p. 1 *et seq.*, and 'The Adventurous Vivaldi', in *Ricordiana*, Vol. 9, No. 2, p. 4 *et seq.*

Emperor Charles VII, and was appointed Kapellmeister at the progressive court of Mannheim four years later—at a salary greater than that of any other court musician. Mannheim had been built up as a cultural centre by the Electors Karl Philipp and Karl Theodor. The latter, a friend of Voltaire, was Stamitz's employer. Stamitz, who had perfected his technique as a violin virtuoso and as such had been acclaimed in Frankfurt when he gave a concert in that city in 1742, composed church and theatre music as well as that required for the court concerts. These were given in the summer at Schwetzingen. Stamitz was given considerable freedom to travel by his employer. Hence his long leave in Paris.

Here Stamitz effected his notable advance in the history of music. He combined Italian fluency with the logical attitudes of the Age of Enlightenment that culminated musically in the ground-plan of the sonata, and with the emotional propensities of the Bohemian and German people—their outlet being through a larger, bolder, range of instrumental colouring; and having done so happily coincided with the widening interests of the Paris concert-going public. Out of this intermingling of aristocratic and professional ideals was born the music of the future—the music, that is, of the middle classes.

'The music of the kind that Stamitz provided', wrote Peter Gradenwitz[1],

> was the ideal fulfilment of the demands of the bourgeoisie. Vivid contrasts came right at the beginning of the sonata or symphony. A gentle 'sigh'—a feminine motiv, immediately followed the opening 'heroic signal': this was a sweet, song-like theme to succeed one that was stormy or powerful. The second movement, also song-like, appealed to the lyrical enthusiasm of those who would like to 'return to Nature'.
>
> This music was proper to the bourgeois concert since it was what the public wanted.

[1] *Johann Stamitz*, Prague, 1936, p. 45.

Bourgeois Consolidation in Europe

THE SHAPING OF NATIONAL CHARACTERISTICS

*D*URING THE FIRST HALF of the eighteenth century the concert practices already established were strengthened in Britain and in the German States through a musical alliance of aristocracy and bourgeoisie that helped in some degree to obscure the division between the classes. In due course the results of this alliance became available for a broader section of the public, and for a brief period England could lay some claim to being a thoroughly music-conscious nation. The point is worth some emphasis since any observations in this direction run counter to the general weight of musical-historical convention. This has, in the past, been influenced by those moral issues which will be seen to have bedevilled the whole course of British music since the acceptance of the Handelian oratorio— with its, often somewhat fortuitous, godly references—as a kind of national purgative.

To be truthful the Germans, for different reasons, fell victim to a similar kind of heresy—for Puritanism tended to exert a common influence—and, particularly in Berlin in the last years of the century, oratorio also held considerable sway. But the Germans possessed facilities unknown to the English in the multiple musical establishments maintained, sometimes in conjunction with the civic authorities, in their little courts.

What the courts did was to provide a succession of practising musicians, and composers, from among whom the most skilful might be made available for more public engagement. In this respect the Hanoverian court in London carried on as from its former German base. But, apart from the temporary development of a *Kapelle* by the Duke of Chandos, and the partial maintenance of capital standards in Edinburgh and Dublin, English music became more and more top-heavy, with all major resources centred in London. The pattern then set, both in England and Germany, has maintained itself, with varied inflections, to the present day.

AT VARIOUS GERMAN COURTS

It is often pointed out that Handel's family antecedents, in contrast to those of Bach, were unmusical. In a limited sense this is true, but its significance is diminished when the essential function of music in the Saxony of his day is considered. Halle, enjoying a private but important *Aufklärung* of its own, was full of music of the more solid kind. At Weissenfels[1], where Handel's father was surgeon, and where Georg Frideric visited (surely more than once), was one court musical establishment; at Zeitz, a little further south, another. These, less notable than the more ambitious foundations at Weimar and Köthen, with which Bach was most directly connected, were closely bound up with the lives of the citizens of small communities towards the end of their feudal careers and soon to develop into industrial centres.

The court at Zeitz was, in fact, of interest both to Handel and to Bach, in that they both had family contacts therewith. It was at Zeitz that the only relative of Handel who was a professional musician had been employed. This was Cyriacus Berger double-bass- and timpani-player, and 'week-day' organist, who, earning 50 thalers a year in 1677, was married to a daughter of Handel's uncle Christoph. At this court—which ended in 1718 when it became the victim of a take-over bid by the Elector of Saxony—Anna Magdalena Bach was born and trained as a singer: her father was trumpeter there before transferring to Weissenfels.

[1] For the birthday of the then Duke in 1716 Bach, later to become honorary Kapellmeister, wrote the secular cantata—*Was mir behagt, ist nur die muntre Jagd.* (For an account of this occasion see C. S. Terry, *Bach. A Biography* (1940 ed. p. 108).)

59

Apart from the chapel music, the members of the court ensemble, sometimes augmented by the town's *Stadtpfeiferei*, were employed in a variety of functions which, according to the German taste for classification, were contained in *Morgenständchen*, *Tafelmusiken*, and *Serenaden* and spread over the day. On New Year's Day, and for the principal birthdays of the house, *Morgenständchen* were organised in which the celebratory character of the occasion was lustily outlined by the sonatas of Johann Philipp Krieger, a composer who enjoyed considerable popularity not only in Zeitz, but also Weissenfels, Halle, Eisenberg, and, further afield, in Hamburg. Krieger, a notable composer of stage pieces which moderated Italian style with *Singspiel* elements, invariably included trumpets and drums in his *Morgenständchen* sonatas, and his *Lustige Feld-Musik*, for wind instruments alone, represented that branch of music for the nobility which equated their taste with that of their dependants and pensioners in the countryside, who were often given free access to these familiar musical occasions. In respect of the *Tafelmusik*, sometimes, as the title suggests, performed according to an ancient and royal tradition while the family ate, but sometimes out-of-doors, reciprocity took another turn; for the peasantry would not infrequently be invited to provide their own musical ensembles. An extension of this fraternisation between the extreme wings of Saxon society is, of course, Sebastian Bach's so-called *Peasant Cantata* —*Mer hahn en neue Oberkeet*.

The *Tafelmusik* on the whole gave opportunity for less formal music making, and there was a general preference for small and interesting ensembles, in which lute, theorbo, and harp were conspicuous. *Serenaden* were the evening counterparts to the *Morgenständchen*, and were the most ambitious of the secular musical events. Since they too primarily centred on birthdays, a deferential theme was necessary and was likely to be concentrated in a *Serenata*. That of 1707 (for which there was a programme-book), the text by Christian Naumann, was for five voices, two violins, one viola, two flutes, two oboes, bassoon, two trumpets, two horns, and timpani[1]. It was, perhaps, with memories of such congenialities in mind that Handel produced

[1] See *Städtische und Fürstliche Musikpflege in Zeitz*, Arno Werner, Bückeburg and Leipzig, 1922.

Acis and Galatea (sometimes termed a *Serenata*) for the Duke of Chandos, at Canons, in 1720, and in so doing inadvertently set off a new departure in English music. That the influence of Zeitz was effective in some respects is in fact testified by the fact that one of the few pieces of German music to accompany Handel to England was the *Anmutige Clavierübung* (preludes, fugues, etc., for keyboard) of Johann Krieger, younger brother and pupil of Johann Philipp at Zeitz[1].

It was in the atmosphere of the provincial court that Bach developed; in Eisenach, Arnstadt, and in Celle, where French connections were appreciated by Duke Georg Wilhelm; in Weimar, where a high cultural tone was established by Duke Wilhelm Ernst; and in Köthen. In all these courts secular instrumental music was strong (the ecclesiastical background of Bach has been too long and too much laboured), and at Köthen especially there was a close association with the townspeople. The Kapelle there was called a Collegium Musicum, and its rehearsals were held at one time in the house of a merchant named Lautsch, and at another in Bach's own house: for these rehearsals he was paid twelve thalers a year[2]. It was against this background that Bach wrote secular cantatas, chamber music, orchestral suites and concertos—including the *Brandenburg Concertos*—which formed an invaluable back-list for his later activities in Leipzig.

CONCERTS IN THE MERCANTILE CITIES

Saxony, however, was regarded as a backwater. Fashion and wealth lay to the west and to the north, especially in Frankfurt and in Hamburg. In these cities the music of the mercantile classes was neatly arranged in three categories: *das Hauskonzert* —the domestication of the formerly aristocratic private music-meeting, which was to become one of the main supports of later German supremacy in the more intimate forms of musical expression; *das Unterhaltungskonzert*, concomitant to general sociability; and *das Virtuosenkonzert*, which explains itself, but

---

[1] Handel passed his copy of the *Anmutige Clavierübung* to Bernard Granville, together with his appreciation of the composer. See F. Chrysander, *G. F. Handel*, Leipzig, 1858–67, III, p. 211.

[2] See Terry, *op. cit.*, pp. 121 ff.

which, through the necessary competition to obtain notabilities in the sphere of performance, also developed into a convenient, if collective, status-symbol.

One of the architects of *Hausmusik* in and about Frankfurt in the last quarter of the seventeenth and the first decade of the eighteenth centuries was Wolfgang Briegel, since 1670 Kapell-meister to the Landgraf of Hesse-Darmstadt. Briegel composed a variety of instrumental chamber music of neither more nor less distinction than that of most of his contemporaries. But his chief reputation depended on a counter-revolutionary gesture which in a Germany that was soon to inaugurate a new tradition of amateur choral music represented progress rather than regress. Noticing that the cult of the solo song was on the wane Briegel 'returned to the composition of songs for several voices; he wrote', said Carl Schneider, 'incessantly in all sorts of styles with much fluency but no originality, and with no adequate return for his labours'[1]. It was in 1679 that Briegel published a volume of such music in Frankfurt, of which its claims on the amateur market are well laid out in its title:

Musikalisches Tafel-confect/Bestehend in Lustigen Gesprächen und Concerten von 1. 2. 3. und 4. Singstimmen und Zweyen Violinen Nebst Dem Basso Continuo. Dessen Liebhabern der Musik, zu sonderbahren Ergetzi.~hkeit.

This issue came half-a-dozen or so years after the institution of a Collegium in Frankfurt.

A TOUR BY JOHANN VON UFFENBACH

Among the citizens of Frankfurt at the beginning of the eighteenth century none was more conspicuous for his musical zealousness than Johann von Uffenbach, whose reputation was remembered by Goethe[2]. A lawyer, von Uffenbach had a tenor voice of some quality, sufficient means to be able to travel widely in Western Europe, and the zeal to organise efficiently the musical affairs of his own city in the light of what he had learned elsewhere. In London von Uffenbach attended one of the concerts for the nobility arranged by the expatriate

---

[1] *Das musikalische Lied in geschichtlicher Entwicklung*, Leipzig, *1863–65*. III, p. 155.

[2] *Dichtung und Wahrheit*, I, 2, p. 79 (Insel-Verlag ed. 1958).

Prussian John Christopher Pepusch, who—according to von Uffenbach—used to get up such concerts at the request of various gentlemen. The orchestra was not very strong, consisting of not more than sixteen performers, but it was incomparable. Margherita de l'Épine, to marry Pepusch in 1718, sang, but, compared with her performance at the opera, somewhat carelessly. However, the instrumental part of the entertainment was splendid and von Uffenbach regretted that the performance lasted for no more than two hours. The Frankfurters, as will be seen, spread their pleasures more generously. The name of Pepusch was also familiar in Strasbourg which von Uffenbach duly visited, and praised the comprehensive programmes which he discovered there in 1712. Besides pieces by Pepusch, Vivaldi, and Telemann, there were so-called symphonies by Franz Beck and the Hamburg composer, Tobias.

In Berne, von Uffenbach was impressed with the businesslike organisation of the thirty-year-old Collegium Musicum, which he visited on November 11, 1714[1]. Here was a foundation owing nothing to superior patronage, but entirely self-supporting. And the members had raised the funds to build their own music-room. This was spacious and adequately designed both to provide excellent listening facilities and to safeguard public morals. 'The upper end of the roomy hall is cut off, just as is the choir of a church, by a screen. Here there is a place for the performers. It is remarkable that the dais is protected from the audience by a curtain, so that no-one in the audience can see the performers. They, on the other hand, can see the audience!' The intention was to protect the female singers and gamba players from scrutiny by curious eyes. The main diet of the Bernese at that time was Corelli. The early concerts of the Collegium Musicum took place in a large lecture-room in the Academy, but when a proper concert-room was designed it was established in the Predigerkirche. This was in use for various musical events until 1790, but by now the Hôtel de musique (erected between 1767 and 1770) was also available. Other lively student and middle-class musical organisations of the eighteenth century in Switzerland were the *Musikgesellschaft*

[1] *Die musikalische Reisen des Herrn von Uffenbach, 1712–16*, ed. E. Preussner, Bonn, 1949, p. 50.

beim Kornhaus and the *Musikgesellschaft zur Chorherren* in Zürich and the Collegium Musicum in Thun.

On August 21, 1715, von Uffenbach was a guest at the weekly concert in Lyons. This, following the principle of the *Concert Spirituel*, comprised a motet, a concerto, various opera airs and a miscellany of gamba solos. von Uffenbach did not admire the taste of the French. On the other hand in Venice in the same year he found the concerts of Vivaldi much to his liking, and was enthusiastic to promote the interests of that composer (whose works he was at pains to purchase) in northern Europe.

TELEMANN IN FRANKFURT

The ubiquitous Telemann arrived in Frankfurt in 1712, leaving Eisenach in order to guarantee his independence—'he who wishes to live in all security', he reminded himself according to a healthy proverb, 'should live in a Republic'. Frankfurt was hardly a republic, but in his relations with his patrons there Telemann—whose democratic urges were as powerful as his confidence in his own competence—could dispense with the attitudes expected by court etiquette. He was nominally director of church music in Frankfurt, but also became manager of the Society of the local nobility that met in the Palace of Frauenstein. Herein he learned business methods, since he looked after the finances and superintended the banqueting arrangements. There was also a Collegium Musicum in the Frauenstein Palace, founded by Telemann in 1713, and for its meetings he composed many works. This Collegium, open to visitors, met each Thursday between late September and Easter.

Although the cultivation of oratorio as a sober relaxation is often fathered on to the English, both Hamburg and Frankfurt were earlier in the field of public and popular sacred music, thanks, in the latter case, to Telemann, von Uffenbach, and the Collegium Musicum. On April 2, 1716, Telemann's setting of Barthold Heinrich Brockes's *Passion* was given in the principal Lutheran church for the benefit of the city poorhouse. The word-book, costing 30 Kreutzer, served as a ticket of admission. To ensure that none entered without having paid, a watch was kept on the church doors[1]. According to Goethe, von

[1] See K. Israel, *Frankfurter Konzertchronik*, Frankfurt, 1876.

Uffenbach was the instigator of oratorios as he was of concerts; in respect of both there was a commendable efficiency of organisation. On January 21, 1723, the *Frankfurter Nachrichten* advertised a concert (given in the Grosse Kaufhaus), for which the social élite were invited to contribute according to their means; lesser patrons—'private persons'—subscribed 15 Kreutzer for a performance that lasted from 4 o'clock in the afternoon until 8 o'clock at night. A year later, on September 23, the first 'virtuoso concert' took place, the principal attraction being the new instrument, the *verillon*[1]. In 1727 a diversion was provided by a 'famous horn-player', who could play on two horns simultaneously. Undoubtedly this was Joachim Friedrich Creta, something of an international celebrity, who, it was reported by Burney, visited London in 1729, blowing 'the first and second treble on the French-horns in the same manner as is usually done by two persons'. Another general favourite of those times who helped to maintain good international relations was the double-bass player, Palmerini. He was in Frankfurt in 1726 and again in 1737, by which time he was a member of the Opera band in London. Five years later Frankfurt became aware of Johann Stamitz who was advertised in the *Nachrichten* on July 26, 1742, as about to give a subscription concert, in the Schaffische Saal, at which 'he would produce his new concerto with two choirs, and after that perform on various instruments — violin, viola d'amore, 'cello and double-bass'.

While Frankfurt presented stimulating opportunities both to virtuoso performers and to amateurs, who kept control of the principal non-ecclesiastical and non-operatic occasions and also provided a sufficiency of occupation for music-teachers, Hamburg having secured a metropolitan prestige, continued to maintain it. According to the point of view, this depended on principles that were either conservative or progressive; although in this connection it may be suggested that the greater German composers generally managed to produce revolutionary traits from apparently retrograde characteristics.

---

[1] A set of glasses, containing varying quantities of water, struck by—sometimes muffled—sticks. The virtuoso in Frankfurt was, presumably, C. G. Helmond, of Silesia, mentioned as a *verillon* expert in Walther's *Lexikon* (1732). Helmond played concerti, for verillon and string orchestra.

Inseparable from German musical, and social, development in the century of reconstruction that followed the Thirty Years' War was the trend of nationalism, to reach its first apogee in the life and works of Frederick the Great. Although flirting with Italian and French styles, German composers, sometimes unconciously, sometimes not, worked towards the evolution of a national idiom that could grow from its provincial roots. A conspicuous promoter of this aim was Johann Kuhnau, predecessor of Bach at the Thomasschule, and his views were entertainingly exposed in a characteristically German satirical novel, *Der musicalische Quack-Salber*, published in Dresden in 1700. In this a Swabian adventurer, taking the Italianate name of Caraffa, is able at first to hoodwink the Collegium Musicum of Dresden by his Italian pretensions, but is eventually found out and deflated by the worthy Dresdeners. In Leipzig Caraffa undergoes more thorough humiliation. The moral is clear in this novel. In Hamburg there was more sophistication, but the intention to build on local foundations was equally apparent at an early date.

TELEMANN IN HAMBURG

It was in Hamburg that the young Handel encountered the first German opera, established by Reinken and Theile and made notable through Keiser. German opera in this city ran for a period of sixty years, until 1738, when it was replaced by Italian. But by this time the oratorio and concert had sufficiently engaged the attention of the interested to show directions in which native talents could travel. Regarding the former Johann Mattheson observed in 1739 that 'an oratorio is merely a sacred opera'. As has already been stated, a favourite text for the Hamburg oratorio was Brockes's *Passion*, and—in addition to Keiser—Telemann, Mattheson, and Handel[1], and a score of other composers, were engaged at some time or other in its setting. Telemann came to Hamburg in 1721 as Cantor of the Johanneum and Director of Music in the five principal churches of the city; a plurality of such profit and promise that he could reject a call to Leipzig in 1723—which let in J. S. Bach

[1] Handel's setting of 1716 is an important link between the German and English traditions.

as second-best—and, at the same time, gain fresh guarantees from his employers regarding his freedom to travel and increased emoluments. Telemann remained in Hamburg until his death in 1767, and, in spite of his frequent absences from local duty, he was able to exert a strong influence. He set the pattern of Hamburg oratorio with half-a-dozen works in this genre, and he considerably increased the repertoire of German opera (of operas he wrote as many as Handel, and his *Pimpinone* of 1725 is among the early examples of true *Opera buffa*). With fluency as a composer—he once said that a composer should be able to set a placard to music, and was much admired on this account by Handel—considerable personal charm, and strongly developed managerial capacities, Telemann was the ideal person to direct the Collegium Musicum activities, which had begun in Hamburg in 1660.

A year after his installation in Hamburg Telemann took over the Monday and Thursday concerts which had been held in the barracks of the town guard and transferred them to the 'Zuchthaus' (Penitentiary), at the same time ensuring that the instrumental ensemble employed was professional[1]. This was a significant step forward, for in general concert music at that time was shared between professionals and amateurs. In the interests of general musical education Telemann produced, in 1728, the first musical journal in Germany, *Der Getreue Music-Meister*. The amateur tradition was happily preserved, but its limitations became more obvious during the emancipatory period of the symphony. Dr Burney drew attention to this in respect of a gathering in Hamburg in 1775:

At night I was carried to a concert, at the house of M Westphal, an eminent and worthy music-merchant. There was a great deal of company; and the performers, who consisted chiefly of *dilettanti*,

---

[1] J. Sittard, *Zur Geschichte der Musik und des Concertwesens in Hamburg*, Leipzig, 1890, p. 63.

'Concert' was first separately defined in a modern sense in two publications of this period, Mattheson's *Das forschende Orchestre*, 1717 and 1721, and Walther's *Lexikon*, 1732.

Mattheson: 'Concerte laté genommen, sind Zusammenkunfte und Collegia Musica' (p. 173).

Walther: 'Concerto (ital.), Concert (gal.), bedeutet l. ein Collegium oder ein musikalische Zussammenhaft' (p. 179).

were very numerous. This kind of concert is usually more enter-
taining to the performers than the hearers; however, there were
many young musicians of this party, who had promising hands
upon their several instruments, and who, with pains and experience, would become excellent performers. But in these meetings,
more than others, anarchy is too apt to prevail, unless the whole be
conducted by an able and respectable master[1].

Telemann, a highly professional composer whose merits are
quickly obscured by indifferent interpretation, had the incentive of his own works to insist on adequate standards of public
performance. Nor was he lacking in financial acumen: subscriptions to his concerts were paid to him, at his house.

The Telemann concerts[2] continued and became such a
feature of Hamburg social life that in 1761 a suitable home was
found in the new *Konzertsaal auf dem Kamp*, which was
opened on January 14. At this point management was in the
hands of Friedrich Hartmann Graf, an ex-serviceman who, as
kettle-drummer, had been wounded while campaigning in the
Netherlands. Graf was more particularly a virtuoso flautist and
a composer, and having been well received in Hamburg in 1759,
took over the direction of concerts there. Between 1761 and 1764
he undertook annual series of subscription concerts (eighteen
concerts, on Mondays between 5 o'clock and 8 o'clock), which
began to wean the Hamburgers away from their somewhat
exclusive diet of Telemann. Graf, however, was a bird of
passage. He left Hamburg for Augsburg, and in 1779 went to
Vienna to write an opera for the German theatre. Four years
later he was in London, taking part in the Concerts of Antient
Music (see p. 152), and in 1789 was made a Doctor of Music by
the University of Oxford. Meanwhile, four years after Graf's
defection from Hamburg, concert life in that city came under
the control of Carl Philipp Emanuel Bach.

[1] *The Journal of a Tour*, etc., London, 1775, II, p. 259.

[2] Telemann conducted very little music by composers other than Telemann,
but what he wrote, ranging from the variegated comedy of *Pimpinone*,
the '*Kanarienvogel—Kantate*', and *Der Schulmeister*, through the prototype
Lieder, the pieties of *Der Tag des Gerichts*, the nascent romanticism of *Die
Tageszeiten*, to the suave competences of his instrumental music, was not only
to the taste of his Hamburg friends, but emancipatory for German music in
general. In 1722 Telemann admitted Handel's *Passion* to the repertoire,
where it was followed by instrumental and vocal works of that composer in
1755; and in 1756 Graun's *Der Tod Jesu* went into the programme.

The sons of the great Cantor of Leipzig were impatient of their father's conservatism; but concert life in Leipzig (the foundation of their own experience) was of greater interest and variety than was always admitted in other parts of Germany. In Hamburg and Frankfurt the bourgeoisie sprang quickly to the protection of musical culture. In Leipzig, less prosperous than either of those centres of international trade and finance, the middle classes were slower to move, and progress depended during Johann Sebastian Bach's lifetime on the intelligentsia, the students of the University and Thomasschule, and the ill-paid town musicians.

COLLEGIA MUSICA IN LEIPZIG

Since it is impossible to separate Telemann from most departments of German musical life, it appears as almost inevitable that the principal Collegium Musicum in Leipzig should have been founded by him. After four years of his direction this came under the control successively of Melchior Hoffmann (1705–1715), J. G. Vogler (1715–1719), and Georg Balthasar Schott (1719–1729); the last-named had been a candidate for Bach's cantorship in 1722. By the side of this institution there also flourished a second, which had been inaugurated by Johann Friedrich Fasch. He, a former student of the Thomasschule, was a devoted disciple of Telemann, and taking his overtures and dramatic works as example composed extensively for his society. Fasch, who had been invited to compete against him in 1722, was highly regarded by Sebastian Bach, and also by Carl Philipp Emanuel. In 1723 Fasch was succeeded by Johann Gottlieb Görner, organist of the Nikolaikirche, and one who held an unfavourable opinion of the elder Bach.

When Bach became director of the Collegium Musicum he may not have been blessed with the best of players but he inherited a tradition from which he developed his own. In particular he was indebted to his contemporary, the one-time prodigy, Johann Georg Pisendel, who was a leading violinist. Pisendel had been a pupil of Torelli in Ansbach and as a boy had introduced a solo concerto of Torelli to the Leipzig Collegium in 1709 (in which year Torelli died). In 1716 Pisendel became a pupil of Vivaldi in Venice, and his labours on behalf of that master supplemented those of Johann Joachim Quantz, who was immensely impressed with the first concertos of Vivaldi that he heard in Pirna, near Dresden, in 1714. For Quantz, as for Bach, Vivaldi became a model, and—Quantz so stated on his own behalf—an inspiration. Concertos became the main part of the secular engagements at the Saxon courts and the Collegia Musica, and Bach became a vigorous arranger of other men's works—as were many of his composer colleagues in Saxony: in all some twenty-one such arrangements have survived, of which ten stemmed from Vivaldi. Of Bach's own works in this form there exist eighteen; mostly dating from the Weimar and Köthen periods, they were invaluable in Leipzig[1]. The principle of the concerto was also deeply written into the cantata, a form of music, both in its sacred and secular varieties, in which the members of the Collegium were frequently involved. They were also participant in the Passion settings. It was this integrated music-making, responsive to the local climate of thought, and provincial in the strictest sense, that helped to give to the corpus of Bach's music a particular homogeneity. It may be remarked that in respect of his style the secular element, stemming from the concert tradition, as it was then understood, has been undervalued. By the same token the secular musical institutions with which he was connected have also received inadequate appreciation[2].

Bach's concerts took place at Zimmermann's Coffee House. During the winter season they were given on Fridays between 8 and 10 o'clock, but when the Fair was in progress there were Tuesday performances as well; in the summer the time was adjusted to 4–6 o'clock, and, provided the weather was clement, the music was transferred to the garden. Görner's concerts, also twice weekly during the Fair, were on Thursdays and/or Mondays, and with a rival coffee house as venue. Prospective clients were encouraged by stimulating publicity, which indicated that from among the contributing students there

---

[1] See Hans Engel: 'Johann Sebastian Bachs Violinkonzerte', in *Festschrift zum 175 jährigen bestehen der Gewandhaus 1781–1956*, Leipzig, 1956, pp. 40 ff.

[2] Cf. Friedrich Blume; 'Outlines of a new picture of Bach', in *Music and Letters*, 44, No. 3, 1963, pp. 214 ff. (Trans. of lecture given for the International Bach Society at Mainz, June 1, 1962).

would be those who would in due course achieve fame[1], and which advertised the opportunities available for hearing new instruments such as a freshly acquired *clavicembalo*, or virtuoso players in general[2].

Whatever the results of these occasions so far as posterity is concerned, Bach found the conditions of work in Leipzig often irksome. He was particularly frustrated in respect of the capacity of his players, and if Bach was sometimes held to be conservative in matters of style he could point to the circumstances of his occupation. In fact he did, in a powerfully worded document addressed to the City Council on August 23, 1730:

> . . . Now the present *status Musices* is quite different from what it was, its technique is so much more complex, and the public *gusto* so changed, that old-fashioned music sounds strangely in our ears. Greater care must therefore be taken to obtain *subjecta* capable of satisfying the modern *gustum* in music, and also instructed in its technique, to say nothing of the composer's desire to hear his works performed properly.

> . . . It is astonishing that German musicians should be expected to play *ex tempore* any music put before them, whether it comes from Italy, France, England, or Poland, just as if they were the *virtuosi* for whom it was written, men who therefore have had opportunity to study it, indeed almost to learn it by heart, enjoy large salaries to reward their labour and diligence, and have leisure to study and master their parts. People do not bear this in mind, but leave our players in a position merely to do the best they can, the necessity to earn their daily bread allowing them little leisure to perfect their techniques, still less to become *virtuosi*. A simple *example* may be given: let any one visit Dresden[3] and observe how the royal musicians there are paid. They have no anxiety regarding their livelihood, and consequently are relieved of *chagrin*; each man is able to cultivate his own instrument and to make himself a competent and agreeable performer on it. The lesson is obvious: the withdrawing of the

---

[1] *Mizler's Neu Eröffnete Musikalische Bibliothek* I, 1736: see W. Neumann, *Auf den Lebenswegen Johann Sebastian Bachs*, Berlin, 1957, p. 211.

[2] *Nachricht auch Frag und Anzeiger vom 16 Juni, 1733*; Neumann, *ibid.*

[3] The royal band at Dresden, developed under Jean Baptiste Volumier (1677–1728), Pisendel (1687–1755), and Johann Adolph Hasse (1694–1783), who was chief *Kapellmeister* from 1734, was world-famous, as Quantz testified. The Prussian bombardment and invasion of Dresden in 1760 once again wrought havoc with the cultural life of the city and many of the court musicians emigrated, to take up positions in other establishments.

beneficia formerly provided puts it out of my power to place the musical performances on a more satisfactory footing[1].

Bach was neither the first nor the last to complain of the determination of musical standards through the obtuseness of cheeseparing local authorities.

In 1736 Bach relinquished an honorary *Kapellmeister's* post he had held at Weissenfels since 1729 and received his warrant as Composer to the Saxon Court. A year later he vacated his directorship of his own Collegium in favour of Carl Gotthelf Gerlach, but would appear to have resumed office again in 1739 and continued therein until 1741 or 1744[2]. But on March 11, 1743, there was a new development in Leipzig. On that day the first *Grosses Concert*, under the sponsorship of a committee of sixteen well-known citizens, took place in the house of one of the town councillors. There was a select orchestra of sixteen 'distinguished' players, and the director was Johann Friedrich Doles, whose inclinations were more in the direction of Italian opera than those of Bach. A year later Doles marked the success of the first year's sequence of *Grosse Concerten* in a celebratory motet based on *Ein' feste Burg*. From this institution directly sprang the Gewandhaus Concerts, to be considered in detail between pages 157 and 164.

Meanwhile Carl Philipp Emanuel Bach had moved to Potsdam, which now became a focal point in the history of German music.

[1] Quoted from Terry, *op. cit.*, p. 203.
[2] See W. Neumann in *Bach-Jahrbuch*, Leipzig, 1960.

6

London Institutions in the Age of Handel

ACADEMIES IN LONDON

THE HALF-CENTURY during which the public, or more often semi-public concert, was regularised in German cultural life, and the *Concert Spirituel* in France, and during which the symphony and the concerto were evolved as the consequences and symbols of such activities, English music failed to take advantage of the organisational groundwork of such pioneers as Banister and Britton. It was not that there was not a great deal of musical activity, but that this was impeded by divergent interests: by a too ready submission to Continental influences; by inconsistent patronage on the aristocratic side; by conservative tastes which were not greatly altered by spasmodic curiosity in respect of penny-catching novelty; by a fundamental levity of outlook that relegated music to the casual entertainments of an affluent life; and by the strenuous exercise of private enterprise in all matters of social concern. This was the era which saw the rise and fall of Italian opera; the meteoric and promising incursion into public affairs, and entertainment, of the ballad opera; the emergence of oratorio, as a unique combination of musical, dramatic, and—eventually —moral values; the ratification of the *concerto grosso*, after Corelli, as the focal point of more serious undertakings; but also of the renascence of music in numerous provincial centres. It was, of course, the age of Handel: the answer to every Englishman's prayer, both then and thereafter.

73

London—after taking into account all the discomforts and hazards catalogued in John Gay's *Trivia*—was, however, seen as a city of opportunity, and just as Italian artists rushed speculatively in, in the hope of adorning St. Paul's Cathedral and other monuments of the new-built and expanding city, so also did musicians from France, from Italy, from Germany, and even Scandinavia. From 1705 Italian opera began to provide a talking-point for the *haute monde*, and one after the other virtuoso singers arrived in ever-increasing numbers. Outside of the theatres they took advantage of the opportunities for public relations afforded by the numerous entertainments available to their talents, and in drawing-up contracts singers were careful to have provision made for satisfactory Benefits[1]. As well as singers there was also a new influx of instrumentalists, and of composers.

Two institutions, sponsored by the aristocracy, appeared during this half-century, and these, founded on the best of intentions but both splintered by ultimate dissensions, may be considered at this point as demonstrating the difficulties of effective organisation on a substantial scale. The idea of the *Accademia* was attractive to those experienced in Italian and French ways, and in 1710 an Academy—'for the study and practice of vocal and instrumental harmony'—was set up at the Crown and Anchor, in the Strand. The first controllers of this body were Henry Needler—civil servant, pupil of Banister and Purcell, fiddler and devotee of Corelli, and friend of Handel —Pepusch, and a fellow-German John Ernest Galliard.

Members of the Academy subscribed half a guinea annually, but were not discouraged from making voluntary gifts either of money or of music; a substantial library was acquired; choristers from the Chapel Royal and St. Paul's Cathedral[2], as well as leading instrumentalists, were regularly engaged. This society, the subject of von Uffenbach's commendation[3], continued happily each Friday from 7 p.m. to 9 p.m. until

---

[1] See the documents relating to the engagement of Catherine Tofts, at the Haymarket, quoted in Allardyce Nicoll, *A History of Early Eighteenth Century Drama*, 1700–1750, Cambridge, 1929, pp. 290–291.

[2] See expenses given in 'Papers relating to Academy of Vocal Music 1725/6–31' (B.M. Add. MS. 11732): A Coach for ye Children 2/0, Wine and bread 10/6, for the use of ye room, fire, and candles 5/0, the Drawer 1/0.

[3] See p. 63.

Maurice Greene, organist of St. Paul's, withdrew his support in 1731 consequent on the exposure of a motet by Bononcini (whom he had sponsored as a member of the Academy) as a plagiarism from Lotti. With Greene went his singers, to inaugurate another music-meeting in the Devil Tavern. Three years later Bernard Gates, who in 1732[1] performed Handel's *Esther* at one of the Academy's meetings, also withdrew, taking with him the choristers of the Chapel Royal, whose Master he was. At this juncture the Academy, proud of having supported the interests of Handel against the opposition of a clique led by the Prince of Wales and the Duke of Marlborough, and impressed by the aspirations of the admirable Pepusch—who deserves credit for his pedagogical concern— endeavoured to make up for the loss of its choristers by starting its own school of music. This intention, however, did not proceed far. Of the pupils admitted only one achieved fame, and this devolved from the melancholy fact of his demise at the age of 12. Isaac Peirson, son of the master of a charity school, entered the Academy at the age of seven and within the next year or two, under the tuition of Pepusch, excelled in singing, in organ-playing, and as a prodigy of the violin, with which he executed the new and difficult sonatas of Geminiani to perfection. Young Peirson shared his studies with Pepusch's own son: both, alas, died in their early youth.

In 1719 another Academy of Music, with an initial flotation of £50,000 was founded under royal patronage—for what that was worth—and with a powerful committee of management. The purpose of this Royal Academy, however, was to develop Italian opera, and to this end Handel was coaxed from Canons, Bononcini from Rome, and Ariosti from Berlin. While Handel initially undertook his commitments to this body with zest, ranging Europe for the best performing material, internal dissensions soon broke out, and after an uncertain career of nine years this ambitious venture also folded up.

While certain members of the aristocracy used such undertakings to further their own reputation, or to work off private enmities, to form agreeable liaisons with female singers, or

[1] On April 20, 1732, *Esther* was publicly performed by Gates in the 'great room' in Villiers Street, and from this occasion the Handelian oratorio as a public entertainment may be said to have stemmed.

simply to appear to be in the swim, others took a lively, if limited, interest in music for its own sake. The Duke of Bedford, as has been seen, supported Haym and James Sherard; Lord Burlington, sometime host to Handel, brought Castrucci, the subject of Hogarth's *Enraged Musician,* to England; the Duke of Rutland, himself an amateur violinist of some quality, returned from Italy on one occasion with Carbonelli under his wing; and the Duke of Newcastle is said to have given employment to 'the Swedish virtuoso', Johan Helmich Roman. Under such protection private concerts, in which the noble patrons participated, flourished, to the satisfaction of Handel, who conducted

> concerts at the Duke of Rutland's, the Earl of Buckingham's, and the houses of others of the nobility who were patrons of music. There were also very frequently concerts for the royal family, at the Queen's Library in the Green Park, in which the Princess Royal, the Duke of Rutland, Lord Cowper, and other persons of distinction performed[1].

TAVERN MUSIC

As has been seen the English tavern sometimes took its responsibilities seriously, and even if this was with one eye on an increase in trade, the democratisation of music in this way was a steady factor in the popular dissemination of musical experience. After the break-up of Britton's establishment other informal associations were formed. One such was at the Angel and Crown in Whitechapel, where the principals were a writing-master, a mathematical instrument-maker, and a carpenter—all keen Purcellians. William Caslon, the type-founder, held monthly concerts at his house (at full moon for the greater safety of his visitors).

> The performances consisted mostly of Corelli's music, intermixed with the Overtures of the old English and Italian operas . . . and the more modern ones of Mr Handel. In the intervals of the performance the guests repasted themselves at a sideboard, which was amply furnished; and, when it was over, sitting down to a bottle of wine, and a decanter of excellent ale, of Mr Caslon's

[1] A. Burgh, *op. cit.,* II, p. 233.

own brewing, they concluded the evening's entertainment with a song or two of Purcell sung to the harpsichord, or a few catches, and about twelve retired[1].

Woolaston, the portrait painter, who had formerly deputised for Banister and Corbett (who gave their services freely) at Britton's, held Wednesday evening meetings at his house in Warwick Court, off Newgate Street, at which the guests were men of substance, mostly Dissenters. Woolaston had an interest in various similar activities in the City and from his connection with John and Talbot Young, instrument-makers, Maurice Greene, and other professionals, a more ambitious series of performances were undertaken in the Castle Tavern, in Paternoster Row.

On the first of these concerts the *Daily Post* of October 17, 1724, reported as follows:

We hear that near one hundred gentlemen and merchants of the City, have lately form'd themselves into a musical society, the one part Performers the other Auditors in St. Paul's Churchyard. They opened the Consort last week with a very good Performance, to the entire satisfaction and Pleasure of the Members. Mr [John] Young of St. Paul's Churchyard, a noted Master of Science, and one of his Majesty's Chapel is President of the Same. As musick must be allow'd to be the most innocent and agreeable Amusement, and a charming Relaxation to the Mind, when fatigued with the Bustle of Business, or after it has been long bent on serious Studies, this bids fair for encouraging the Science, and seems to be a very ingenious and laudable Undertaking.

The tired businessman, who in later times has found other entertainment of, perhaps, less innocent character, was no doubt most fascinated by the singers from the Italian Opera who were the main attraction at these affairs for many years.

Similar concerts took place at the Swan Tavern for twelve years from 1728, and among the instrumental players there engaged were Obadiah Shuttleworth, John Clegg, Abraham Brown, and Michael Festing. The musical director at both, for some time, was the blind organist John Stanley, whose talents as performer, and skill as a composer, though restricted by the Handelian influence, were accompanied by attractive personal

[1] Hawkins, *op. cit.*, V, p. 128.

qualities conducive to the satisfactory development of these musical-social meetings. The Castle concerts were at first supported by subscriptions of two guineas from each member, but when they expanded to include oratorio in 1744, at aldermanic insistence, the subscription went up to five guineas. In due course the concerts were moved, first to the Haberdashers' Hall and then to the King's Arms, in Cornhill, where they continued into the last quarter of the century[1].

INCIDENTAL MUSICAL PERFORMANCE IN THE THEATRE

The theatres, which were regarded rather as establishments for general amusement than intended solely for the purpose of drama or opera, gave frequent concerts during this period. Singers often arranged their Benefits therein, and dramatic entertainments were consistently varied by musical interludes which at various times helped to circumvent censorship of purely dramatic entertainments[2]. The bands at Drury Lane and Covent Garden were splendid in executive skill, but restricted as to repertoire. 'Handel, Corelli, and Geminiani, with some introductory *Musicks* of Purcell, furnished both the bands with all the pieces they ever attempted[3].'

As in the Restoration period music was introduced interstitially into theatrical representations. Indeed as the playhouses increasingly competed against each other the entr'actes became more important—and more extravagant.

At the Lincoln's Inn Fields Theatre (one which had difficulty in surviving) *The Cautious Coxcomb* was interspersed on three occasions in April 1704, with

> three several New Entertainments of Musick perform'd in Consort by seven Young Men (upon Hautboys, Flutes, and German Horns), lately brought over by their Master the famous Godfrede Pepusch, Musician in Ordinary to His Majesty the King of Prussia. The Composition being made entirely new for that purpose by his Brother, the Eminent Master, Mr John Christopher Pepusch[4].

(At that time Pepusch was in the orchestra at Drury Lane: after his appointment with the Duke of Chandos be became

---

[1] T. Busby, *Concert Room and Orchestra Anecdotes*, London, 1825, I, p. 66.
[2] See p. 81 and, in respect of America, p. 104.
[3] Burney, *History*, IV, p. 663.
[4] *The Daily Courant*, April 3, 1705.

more closely associated with Lincoln's Inn Fields and composed there for many years. Such intimacy with theatrical hackwork made him an ideal collaborator with Gay in *The Beggar's Opera*, in 1728.)

On December 12, 1705, Dryden's *All for Love*, at the Haymarket, was diversified with a sequence of dances, while a week later the Drury Lane management advertised not only dances but also songs by 'Mr [Lewis] Ramondon[1] and "the Boy",' and violin sonatas by Gasparini[2] and Paisible[3] during the performance of John Crowne's *Sir Courtly Nice*. Sir Richard Steele's *Love's Last Shift* was always a popular draw, and when it was played at Drury Lane on April 30, 1705, Purcell's 'Frost Music' from *King Arthur*—'with the proper Scenes belonging to the Musick'—made an *intermezzo*. Two years later, at the same theatre, the musicians capped Richard Brome's *The Northern Lass* satirically, with 'an Equi-Vocal Epilogue after the old English manner, Compiled and Spoken by the famous Singer Signior Pinkethmano, upon an Ass that never appear'd but twice on either Stage'. This could not be allowed to pass by the Haymarket management, so to John Banks's *The Unhappy Favourite* was added 'the last new vocal Epilogue, Compos'd and Perform'd by the famous Signior Cibberini, after the newest English, French, Dutch, and Italian Manner'[4].

In the theatres the musicians were highly favoured and, being much sought after, were able to command substantial fees. The actors complained, and their objection to the misplaced enthusiasms of their audiences and their own relative inferiority were indicated in the following quatrain which appeared in *The Diverting Post* on May 16, 1705:

> Thin Pit, and Cheating Turnkeys, for five-days
> Secure us little Pay; and Saturdays,

[1] English (French?) bass singer in the 'English Opera', and composer. In 1716 Ramondon composed songs in ' "The Merry Musician, or a Cure for the Spleen"; among which there is a favourite hymn upon the execution of two criminals, beginning, "All you that must take a leap in the dark". This is one of the tunes in the "Beggar's Opera", adapted to the words, "Would I might be hanged" '. *Musical Biography* [W. Slingsby], London, 1814.

[2] Gasparo Visconti, known as Gasparini (Violin Sonatas, Op. 1, 1703).

[3] James Paisible, or Peasable, of French extraction, was a flautist, and his compositions for the flute were popular. He was a member of the royal band.

[4] See Allardyce Nicoll, *op. cit.*, p. 48.

Italian Singing Tacking to our Scenes,
L'Epine, and Tofts sneak off with all our Gains[1].

In Cibber's *The Rival Fools*, Drury Lane, January, 1709, an extract from a dialogue between Young Outwit and Sir Oliver Outwit, the latter having complained at the size of the musicians' bill, bears on the same topic:

Y.O.   Death! Sir, they are all *Italians*.

Sir O.   Why, what then, Sir, mayn't an *Italian*
be a Scoundrel, as well as an *Englishman?*

Y.O.   Lord! Sir, I wou'd not have this heard for
the Universe. Does not the whole nation adore 'em,
Sir? Is any man allowed common sense,
Among the better sort, that is not ravish'd
With their musick? And is any thing
a more fashionable mark of a gentleman,
than to pay an extravagant price for't?

The taste of the theatre-going public was responsible for certain concessions by Handel. In 1734 he rearranged *Il pastor Fido* in order to accommodate the *danseuse*, Sallé, who also took part in *Alcina*, and in the intervals between the acts of his oratorios he introduced his *concerti grossi* and organ *concerti*. In fact with a varying amount of purely instrumental music in the oratorios themselves, with favourite (or less-than-favourite) singers performing their recitatives and arias non-dramatically, and with the intermittent extra *concerti* the eighteenth-century English oratorio was much nearer a concert than some would like to think: an advertisement from Birmingham, quoted on page 102, indeed, shows that the two terms could be accepted as coterminous. If oratorio, backed by moral prejudices, represented one triumph of music over drama, other instances can be seen. For instance: 'Oct. 15 [1740]: At the late Theatre in Ay[c]liffe Street—a concert of vocal and instrumental Musick in 2 parts—between the parts of the Concert will be presented *gratis* a Comedy, called the Stratagem—by persons for their diversion[2].' Or, again: 'Sept. 19 [1741]: Concert at the Theatre

[1] See Michael Tilmouth, *A Calendar of References to Music, etc.* (R.M.A. Research Chronicle No. 1, 1961), p. 61.

[2] J. Genest: *Some Account of the English Stage*, London, 1832, III, p. 636. See also *Remains . . . of the Chetham Society*, Manchester, 1857, Vol. LXX, II, p. 56. The theatre in Aycliffe Street was that known as Goodman's Fields.

in Goodman's Fields in 2 parts: interlude—Life and Death of King Richard III, with *Entertainments of Dancing* and a 1 act Ballad Opera . . . *The Virgin Unmask'd*: 6 p.m. 3/-, 2/-, 1/-.'[1] In the interlude David Garrick made his first appearance on a London stage.

That drama should apparently run second in importance to music was, however, due not to any sudden reversal of taste but to the Licensing Act of 1737. A concert, with dramatic interludes, was easier to get past the censorship, and the arrangement spread to the provinces. Nevertheless it was from this circumstance that musicians began to realise that some sort of order in the arrangement of concert items was desirable. Thus Carbonelli's Benefit Concert at Drury Lane ('at Playhouse prices') was advertised in this manner in the *Daily Courant*:

ACT I   A new Concerto for two trumpets, composed and performed by *Grano*[2] and others;
A new concerto by *Albinoni*, just brought over;
Song by Mrs *Barbier*[3];
Concerto composed by Signor *Carbonelli*.

ACT II   A concerto with two hautbois and two flutes, Composed by *Dieupart*[4];
A Concerto on the bass-violin by *Pippo*[5];
Song by Mrs *Barbier*;
By desire, the eighth concerto of *Arcangello Corelli*.

[1] Genest, *op. cit.*, III, p. 636.

[2] Or Granom, a trumpeter and flautist, who incurred Burney's displeasure as 'a kind of *mongrel* dilettante', i.e. 'semi-professional'.

[3] Mrs Barbier first appeared in the Opera *Almahide* in 1711, when her shyness on the stage called forth a sympathetic piece by Addison, in *The Spectator* (No. 231): six years later her elopement provoked an amusing poem by John Hughes.

[4] Charles Dieupart, a Frenchman, violinist and harpsichordist, was associated with Haym and Thomas Clayton in the production of *Arsinoe* at Drury Lane in 1707. In 1711 he took part in concerts in Clayton's house. 'In the latter part of his life he grew negligent, and frequented concerts performed at ale-houses, in obscure parts of the town, and distinguished himself not more there, than he would have done in an assembly of the best judges, by his neat and elegant manner of playing the solos of Corelli'. Hawkins, *op. cit.*, V, pp. 169–70.

[5] Filippo Mattei, or Amadei.

ACT III   Concerto by *Carbonelli*;
Solo on the arch-lute by Signor *Vebor*;
Song by Mrs *Barbier*;
A new Concerto on the little flute, composed by
Woodcock[1] and performed by *Baston*;
Solo, Signor *Carbonelli*;
and for *finale*, a concerto on two trumpets by
Grano, etc.

SUBSCRIPTION CONCERTS AND
HICKFORD'S 'GREAT ROOM'

Amid the informalities and prodigalities of London music the
more extensive Subscription Concerts canalised a good many
disparate interests. These, taking up where the Villiers Street
Music Room left off, firmly established the public character of
concert-room music. A number of such concerts took place in
the Halls of the City Companies[2]. But the most significant
centre was further west, in the development area of Georgian
London, in Hickford's Room where concerts were given before
the end of the seventeenth century and continued until the days
of Mozart (who gave a concert there in 1765), John Christian
Bach and Abel, and Edward Jones, the pioneer of Welsh music,
who engaged Hickford's Room in 1775.

Thomas Hickford was a dancing master, and the concerts that
had been given irregularly since 1697 in his 'Great Room' off

[1] Robert Woodcock, flautist and composer of flute concertos. His brother'
Thomas, kept a coffee-house in Hereford, where he gave performances on the
violin of country-dances. That he also played the sonatas of Corelli with some
skill was apparently not known in Hereford.

[2] See, for example, the advertisements in *The Spectator*, No. 224, of
November 16, 1711, and *The Daily Courant* of December 29, 1712, and
February 27, 1717. The first concerned a concert 'For the Benefit of Mr
Anthony Young, Organist of St. Clement Danes, at Stationers Hall on
Thursday the 22nd instant being St. Cecilia's Day, [there] will be performed a
Consort of Vocal and Instrumental Musick, most of which will be entirely new;
and Mr Leveridge sings that celebrated song, beginning "Genius of England".'
The second also referred to a concert in Stationers' Hall 'by a Band of Thirty
Performants, compos'd all after the Italian Manner . . . [and] "the most
Celebrated Voices in Town": the third to one in Leathersellers' Hall, where
"No Footmen are to be let in; but there is without the Hall, a Cover'd Walk,
where they may wait".'

the Haymarket became more frequent from 1713, at which time the room was re-designed the better to fit it for the purpose. Hickford's Room rapidly became the establishment at which the best musicians of the day, from home or abroad, could be heard. On March 25, 1713, at the first event in the refurbished auditorium, William Corbett was a beneficiary—together with Claudio Roieri. Corbett, leader of the Opera band from 1705 to 1711, was a particular link with Italy, for in 1711 he went to Rome for two years. When he returned he was glad to take advantage of Hickford's establishment to build up a connection. Being as ambitious as a composer as he was excellent as a violinist, he made good use of this opportunity until he went back to Italy for a further period of foreign study in 1716. After eight years he was once more in England, with so much new music, and so many new and expensive instruments, that it was commonly rumoured that his own modest resources had been increased from Government funds, in return for which he had engaged in espionage in respect of the refugee Stuarts.

When he published his Opus VIII concertos, or, as he called them, *Le Bizarie Universali*, Corbett was reported to have endeavoured to show the several styles of Milan, Rome, Naples, Florence, Bologna, Brescia, the Tyrol, England, Ireland, Scotland, Flanders, Hungary, Denmark, and 'Muscovy': an exercise in international relations that drew the comment from Hawkins that 'in music . . . there can be no such discrimination of style as will enable the hearer to distinguish the music of one country . . . from another[1]'. In his gazetteering intentions Corbett was somewhat ahead of his times—or so it might appear; but his reading of public expectation, for the exotic, was accurate. A good deal of impetus to this cult came from Scotland. In 1725 William Thomson published his *Orpheus Caledonius* in London, where he taught and sang, and Scottish airs became so

---

[1] *Op. cit.*, V, p. 172. Corbett's score was advertised for 2 violins and tenor, with thorough bass for harpsichord or organ, alternatively for two hautboys and flutes (recorders) or German flutes, 'on all the new Gusto's in his Travel thro Italy'. The separate concertos were designated *alla* (1) Genouse, (2) Turinese, (3) Parmegiana, (4) Olandese, (5) Gremonese, (6) Ventiana, (7) Todesca, (8) Modonese, (9) Pollonese, (10) Spagniola, (11) Paduana, (12) Francese. Of these only the last—Overture, Fugue, Aria, Minuet—is recognisably characteristic.

popular[1] that even composers of Italian operas for the English needed to be aware of them. The more public musical exposition became the more it also entertained the colourful, the spectacular, the sensational. Instrumental music in the concert-room had to compete with the opera and with theatrical performance in general, with which, in any case, it had its direct connections.

In 1714 Hickford's Room promoted six concerts, all of them promising on the publicity side. On February 1, there was a 'consort' for the Benefit of one Mr Rogier by the 'Masters of the Opera'. On March 17 Haym's former pupil, the German soprano expert in the Italian style known as 'the Baroness' [Johanna Maria Lindelheim?] took a Benefit: but this concert was made notable by the appearance of 'the famous Signor Veracini'. Veracini remained in England for three years, during which time he led the Opera orchestra and gave numerous recitals: in 1717 he went to Dresden as solo violinist in the Electoral *Kapelle*. After his first appearance at Hickford's Room Veracini did not delay his second, and took a Benefit on April 22, the programme consisting entirely of his own compositions. Five days later Signora Stradiotti sang for the first time in England, and at the end of the songs played a harpsichord solo. The next foreign guest was a Signor Pardini, on May 20. If, so far, the stranger had dominated the proceedings— in contrast to the more local performers favoured in the City Club-concerts—the last artiste of that year was the native Matthew Dubourg. He, who at a tender age had stood on a stool to play at Britton's, was eleven years of age when he gave his performance at Hickford's on May 27, 1714. A protégé of Handel, and pupil of Geminiani (who arrived in London only that year) he made frequent attendances at Hickford's, until, in 1728, he was promoted to be leader of the royal band in Dublin, where, in due course, he again crossed the path of Handel, on the occasion of the first performance of *Messiah*.

[1] See also John Walsh's *A Collection of Original Songs* (c. 1720) with settings by Henry and Daniel Purcell, Jeremiah Clarke, and William Croft; songs popularised by John Abell ('at his concert in Stationers' Hall), Mrs Barbier, and Mrs Robinson; and some genuine folk songs, among which was *The Yellow-hair'd Laddie* (see also p. 92).

Concerts at Hickford's Room continued after this manner for more than twenty years. Among the more important performers—in addition to those like the Baroness and Dubourg and Geminiani, who were consistent in appearance—were Castrucci, Corbett's successor as leader of the Opera orchestra, Francesco Scarlatti, brother of Alessandro, Jack Kytch, the flautist and oboist in the Opera orchestra, Giovanni Battista Sammartini, who came to England as oboist in 1723 and was later appointed director of chamber music to the Prince of Wales, John Clegg, the Irish virtuoso violinist, Adolph Kuntzen, a seven-year-old harpsichord prodigy from Wittenberg who remained in London for some time and there published his Opus 1—a pair of sonatas dedicated to the Prince of Wales.

In general the virtuosi played their own compositions, it being given out to the more gullible that none else had the technique to do so. Castrucci, who kept one hand firmly on the apostolic tradition by playing works by 'his master, Corelli', was not averse from showmanship—with concertos full of echoes, or punctuated by double-stopping which was thought to be a splendid representation of the effect of two trumpets. Versatility was applauded generously, and the multiple talents of Sarah Ottey enabled her to perform with equal skill on harpsichord, bass viol, and violin. Mrs Ottey struck a blow for female emancipation by becoming the first of her sex to practise as a professional violinist.

By 1731 the concert at Hickford's was a social obligation, and for his twenty Thursday Subscription Concerts which began on December 9, Geminiani charged four guineas and issued non-transferable silver tickets similar to those needed at the Opera. For these concerts Geminiani designed his *concerti grossi*, which were published in 1732, 'and which', said Burney, 'placed him at the head of all the masters then living, in this species of composition[1]'. Geminiani, in spite of his inconsistencies as an orchestral leader, detailed both by Burney and Hawkins, his apparent waywardness in taste (encouraged by the climate of concert music), his individuality, his pose as an art dealer, and occasional smart practice, exerted a strong influence over instrumental music, the more so since he had little or no

---

[1] *Op. cit.*, IV, p. 642.

inclination to the dramatic, and was a brilliantly successful teacher. He supervised concert arrangements for many years and in 1748 introduced a concert of unknown Italian music to Drury Lane under the heading of *Concerto Spirituale*, one of the rare occasions when this term was used in England[1]. Some years later Geminiani went to Paris, and then, at the end of his life, to Dublin, where Dubourg was pleased to welcome him.

In 1729 Hickford's Room off the Haymarket was closed, and new premises were taken in Soho—in Brewer Street, near Golden Square—and the concerts became more ambitious. If, however, they became more ambitious they also became more parochial, in that, picking up the stray threads of the by now established oratorio tradition, they featured the contributions to this genre of John Christopher Smith, John Ernest Galliard, and Johann Adolph Hasse—who was in London in 1740 in opposition to Handel. Among the performers during this period were Festing, Caporale and Cervetto, the violoncellists, Millar, the bassoonist, Weidemann, the flautist, Mrs Arne, and John Beard, and most of the other singers associated with Handelian oratorio.

ROYAL SOCIETY OF MUSICIANS

Almost from the beginning, concerts at Hickford's Room had sometimes served charitable ends. In 1738 the fraternity of orchestral players, their solidarity enhanced by frequent playing together, took a step which, in fact, served as the starting-point for any further collective activity on the side of professional welfare.

The improvidence of an oboe player, named Kytch, reduced his family to extreme distress at his death. Some members of the musical profession having witnessed the forlorn condition of the young family, determined to raise the children from their abject state; and, whilst in so doing, they extended the benefit of their charity, and formed a general fund to alleviate the miseries of the indigent members of the profession, their widows and orphans[2].

[1] But see p. 154 in respect of the use of the term in Sheffield.
[2] *Musical Directory*, London, 1853, p. 63.

The originator of this fund was Michael Festing, who 'by good sense, probity, prudent conduct, and a gentleman-like behaviour, acquired a weight and influence in his profession, at which hardly any musician of his class ever arrived[1].' The leaders of English music—Handel, Boyce, Thomas Arne, Greene, Pepusch, and Anthony and John Young (junior) among them—readily supported Festing's conception, Handel giving the proceeds of performances during his lifetime and a handsome legacy in his will, and royal patronage was also forthcoming. Fifty years after its inception[2] the 'fund' received a charter and became the Royal Society of Musicians.

[1] Burney, *op. cit.*, IV, p. 669
[2] The Declaration of Trust was signed on August 28, 1739.

The Breaking of New Ground in the Eighteenth Century

MUSIC IN SCOTLAND

*E*VEN BY COMPARISON with the modest living standards of the majority of the English during the era of Handel the prevailing conditions for the Scots and the Irish, subject to additional political hazards, were deplorable: yet both Edinburgh and Dublin, the one formerly, the other currently, seats of government, were worthy culturally to be judged in an international rather than a British-national context. The former city, after the Act of Union in 1707, took the rational step of providing for the future of the country of which it was the true capital by strengthening its system of education; the latter, increasingly peopled by English aristocrats and officials who were learning the arts of imperialism in a congenial setting, erected in its new facade the handsomest skyline in the British Isles. In these two satellite metropolises music flourished, before its final subjugation by alien forces.

In the last years of the seventeenth century Edinburgh could provide an orchestra of twelve violins, five 'cellos and viols da gamba, six flutes, two oboes, and harpsichord. Of the players led by a German 'professor', Henry Crumbden, eleven were professional and the rest amateur—of the 'first rank and fashion'. In 1695 the Festival of St. Cecilia was duly celebrated, and thereafter effort was mostly concentrated on the works of Bassani and Corelli. The chief patron of this society was Lord Robert Colville of Ochiltree, harpsichordist and organist, and an avid collector of music books, many of which he had brought back from Italy. It is said that the German flute was introduced into Scotland by Sir Gilbert Elliot of Minto—who had helped to organise the Earl of Argyll's Rising, been sentenced to death but pardoned, was appointed a judge of session, and had opposed the Union. On the professional side there was Daniel Thomson, one of the royal trumpeters, and the father of William Thomson[1].

In 1716 and 1721 Allan Ramsay alluded to the principal musical functions of Edinburgh, Corelli's works being admixed with Scottish folk-song in the programmes[2], and Hugo Arnot's account[3] supplies the information that the music club then met in the Cross Keys tavern, whose landlord, Steil, was himself an excellent exponent of his country's songs. In 1728 the undertaking became more formal; seventy members comprised a Society, presided over by a governor, deputy-governor, treasurer, and five directors, which met weekly, on Friday, in St. Mary's Chapel in the Niddry Wynd. In 1741 another concert agency was established by Thomas Este in the Taylors' Hall. This, however, was a familiar subterfuge, disguising a theatre. On February 12, 1745, the *Caledonian Mercury* reported Este's death, noting that he was 'one of the managers in the Taylors' Hall, who has for these four years past, most agreeably entertained the town with his excellent performances on the stage'.

The Society in the Niddry Wynd pursued its more earnest course across the remainder of the first half of the century, to be commended by Smollett in *Humphrey Clinker*, in 1756[4], until

[1] William Tyler, 'On the fashionable amusements and entertainments in Edinburgh . . . with a plan of a grand concert of music on St. Cecilia's Day, 1695', in *Transactions of the Society of Antiquaries of Scotland*, Edinburgh, 1792, I, p. 506 and R. Chambers, *Domestic Annals of Scotland*, Edinburgh and London, 1858, III, pp. 139–40.

[2] *The City of Edinburgh's Address to the Country* (1716); *To the Music Club* (1721); see also *An Epistle to James Oswald on his leaving Edinburgh* (1741); *Poems* of *Allan Ramsay*, Paisley, 1877, 2 vol.

[3] Hugo Arnot, *History of Edinburgh*, Edinburgh, 1779.

[4] Jeremy Melford to Sir Watkin Phillips: 'Edinburgh, August 8th . . . Here is a well-conducted *Concert*, in which several gentlemen perform on different instruments. The Scots are all musicians. Every man you meet plays on the flute, the violin, or the violoncello, and there is one nobleman whose compositions are universally admired.' For Smollett's comments on musical life in Britain in general, see Percy M. Young, 'Observations on Music by Tobias Smollett', in *Music and Letters*, XXVII, 1946, p. 18, *et seq.*

in 1762 a concert hall, the funds coming from voluntary sources, was built to the design of Sir Robert Mylne, and 'after the model of the great opera-theatre at Parma, but on a smaller scale'. This was St. Cecilia's Hall, in the Niddry Wynd—perhaps the most romantic title ever bestowed on a concert hall. During the first period of the Society the programmes were heavily weighted by Corelli, Handel, and Geminiani, and guest artists— one was Gordon the Handel singer[1]—sometimes diversified the arrangements. Foreign notabilities were also suitably entertained, and when the Prince of Hesse was in Scotland in 1745–1746 he was greatly impressed by the Scottish and English songs, hitherto unknown to him, to which he was introduced. The then Governor was Lord Dunmore, on the occasion of whose death in 1755 the Society provided a Funeral Concert, 'in the manner of a *concerto spirituale*'. Oratorio came within the ambit of the Society and two or three were performed annually: it was said that Handel permitted manuscript copies to be made for the use of the Society[2].

From this devoted activity arose one composer whose fame was more than local. This was Thomas Erskine, grandson of Dr Archibald Pitcairn, who succeeded as sixth Earl of Kelly in 1756. Erskine went to Mannheim and became a pupil of Stamitz, the robustness of whose music was attractive to a nobleman whose aesthetic proclivities were toughened by a natural, and notorious, coarseness. Erskine was among the first British symphonists, but his *avant-gardisme* was hardly approved by his more sedate countrymen. Thus Dr John Gregory, Professor of Medicine first at Aberdeen and then at Edinburgh University, wrote:

> The present mode is to admire a new noisy stile of composition, lately cultivated in Germany, and to despise Corelli as wanting in spirit and variety. The truth is, Corelli's stile and this will not bear a comparison. Corelli's excellence consists in the chastity of his composition, and in the richness and sweetness of his harmonies. The other sometimes pleases by its spirit and wild luxuriancy, which makes it agreeable variety in a concert, but possesses too little of the elegance and pathetic expression of music to remain

---

[1] Who also gave a concert in Glasgow in 1722.
[2] Arnot, *op. cit.*, quoted in D. Fraser Harris's: *Saint Cecilia's Hall . . .*, Edinburgh, 1911, p. 205.

long in the public taste. The great merit of the Earl of Kelly's composition, who first introduced this species of music into this country, and his own spirited performance of them, first seduced the public ear. They are certainly much superior to any of the kind that we have yet heard; though by the delicacy of the airs in his slow movements, he displays a genius capable of shining in a much superior stile of music[1].

Gregory was the leading light of the Musical Society in Aberdeen that was founded on January 29, 1748. This Society, similar in intention to that in Edinburgh, was primarily stimulated from within the University and, bearing in mind the earlier essays in concert given by John Abell, combined with the old song-school tradition of the city by enlisting the aid of Andrew Tait, organist of the Sang Schule of St. Nicholas, and Francis Peacock, a dancing master, with the newer traditions of the south. The sixth Resolution of the new Society thus defined the nature of the meetings:

That a Plan be laid down every Night of the Musick to be per-form'd at next Meeting, which is to be kept to, and no Member to propose any other Musick till at least that is finished. That the Plan be so contrived as to be divided into three Acts, in each of which some of Corelli's Musick shall be performed: each Act also, if a Voice can be had, to end with a song; and the whole so contrived as to end at Eight O'Clock at Night, and not to exceed two Hours in Continuance. That such Members or Others as are Hearers only shall take their seats, and not mix with the Performers, in time of Musick, and strict silence to be kept, except in the Intervals between the Acts[2].

The records of the Aberdeen Musical Society having survived in the Minute Books preserved in the City Library there is a wealth of detailed information available concerning its activities. The inventories show that by purchase and bequest the Society maintained a supply of orchestral instruments and also a well stocked library. In 1749 the latter contained the overtures of Arne, Handel, and Barsanti, the concertos of Avison, Corelli, Geminiani, Hasse, John Hebden—a London gamba and bassoon player—Jomelli, Rameau, Sammartini, John Humphreys,

---

[1] J. Gregory, *The State and Faculties of Man*, Edinburgh 1765, p. 180.

[2] Quoted by H. G. Farmer, in *Music Making in the Olden Days*, London, 1945, p. 15.

Scarlatti, and John Stanley. Native music was enthusiastically cultivated, and an effort to furnish a new market is represented by Geminiani's *Scots Tunes in Score*—from which kind of example there later devolved John Christian Bach's symphonisation of Scottish modality and pentatony[1]. In the eighteenth century Scotland stood on the threshold of a genuine musical independence; but any ambitions in that direction were eliminated by the more insidious forms of southern politeness and by the end of the century the societies in both Edinburgh and Aberdeen had declined.

MUSIC IN DUBLIN

The pattern of musical advancement in Dublin was similar to that in Edinburgh and Aberdeen; but one great climactic occasion—the première of *Messiah* on April 13, 1742—gave to the city a unique place in the annals of music. It is, perhaps, fitting that the origins of the tradition that culminated in the production of this oratorio should be in choral music and in an early association of Church and tavern. Before the end of the seventeenth century[2] the singing-men of Christ Church Cathedral were in the habit of meeting regularly for the laudable purpose of singing catches and drinking. At the beginning of the eighteenth century the Dean and Chapter of Christ Church obligingly converted a property in Fishamble Street, formerly a private house, into the Bull's Head Tavern. Here the singing-men met each Friday between Michaelmas and May and, with the surplus from the weekly half-crown subscription and the profits on the annual Dinner in December, supported certain charities. An especial interest was that in aid of imprisoned debtors, many of whom owed their eventual liberty to these harmonious evenings. In or about 1710 an instrumental-music society was established in the Cross Keys, the initiative for which came from Patrick Beaghan, the first President, and Gregory Byrne, a shopkeeper. Other citizens who took part in the early administration were Alderman James Malone, a printer, Laurence Whyte, a mathematics teacher and poet,

---

[1] See Variations on 'The Yellow-hair'd Laddie' in Op. XIII, No. 4, and arrangements of 'Lochaber' and 'The Broom of Cowdenknowes'.

[2] 1679–80, Grove (5th ed.), II, p. 786.

John Neal, a music publisher, and his son William. Neal assumed the Presidency of the Society in 1723, when the Bear Tavern became its headquarters, and under his aegis the association, also conspicuous for its generous donations to charity, accumulated a solid backing both from the aristocracy and the bourgeoisie. The title then became the 'Charitable and Musical Society', and because the Bear proved inadequate to house the enlarged membership the meetings were transferred to the Bull's Head, also the meeting-place for Irish Freemasons.

A realistic picture of the Society was limned by an anonymous poet quoted in Gilbert's *History of Dublin* (1861)[1]. Despite benefactions to the Charitable Infirmary (f. 1724), the Mercer's Hospital (f. 1734), and the Fund for the Releasement of Prisoners, the behaviour of some of the members was sometimes a cause of scandal. Thus in 1741 Dean Swift instructed his Sub-dean and Chapter at St. Patrick's to punish those of the singing-men of the cathedral who should appear at 'the Club of Fiddlers in Fishamble Street, as songsters, fiddlers, pipers, trumpeters, drummers, drum-majors, or in any other sonal quality, according to the flagitious aggravation of their respective disobedience, rebellion, perfidy, and ingratitude'. Messrs Taberner, Phipps, and Church came under special interdict since, says the Dean, 'they have in violation of my sub-dean's and Chapter's order in December last, at the instance of some obscure persons unknown, presumed to sing and fiddle at the club above-mentioned'. Nevertheless, these recalcitrant singers were sufficiently restored to favour by the spring of 1742 to be able to take their place in the chorus for *Messiah*, for which performance the Dean and Chapter were, indeed, duly enthusiastic[2].

[1] For reference to eighteenth century music see pp. 67–89 and p. 94.

[2] Minutes of the Governors of Mercer's Hospital for January 23, 1742: '. . . The Dean and Chapter of St. Patrick's are ready to concur with the Dean and Chapter of Christ Church in permitting the Choir to assist at the Musical Performance of the Philharmonic Society, if the Dean and Chapter of Christ Church will concur with them in permitting the Choir to assist at Mr Handels. They think that every argument in favour of the one may be urged with equal strength at least in favour of the other, particularly by that which with them is of greatest weight, the advantage of Mercer's Hospital. Mr Handel having offer'd and being still ready in return for such a favour to give the Governors some of his Choicest Musick and to direct and assist at the performance of it for the benefit of the Hospital.'

Although in general the social disadvantages of having a court at Dublin Castle far outweighed the advantages, it was this that gave an incentive to the cultivation of instrumental music in Ireland; for the Lord Lieutenant maintained a Kapellmeister. From about 1706 this was Johann Kusser, a Hungarian composer of wide experience, who had been a pupil of Lully in Paris, sometime director of the opera in Hamburg, and member of various court ensembles in other parts of Germany. Kusser wrote *Serenatas* for royal celebrations in Dublin, and was concerned in one way or other with music in Trinity College and also Christ Church Cathedral[1]. He died in 1727 and was succeeded by Matthew Dubourg, who remained in Dublin until 1765.

It was in 1736 that Dubourg was first publicly engaged in a performance that engaged the name of Handel with the Dublin charities, and with the cream of the city's musicians, both professional and amateur. On April 10 Dean Madden preached a sermon at St. Andrew's Church for the Mercer's Hospital, and 'at the same time was performed a grand Te Deum, Jubilate, and an anthem composed by the famous Mr Handel. Mr Dubourg played the first violin, Signor Pasqualini the first bass ... The performers were upwards of seventy in number, among whom were several noblemen and gentlemen of distinction'[2].

When Handel came to Dublin at the end of 1741 he found a new concert room—Neal's Music Hall—which, under the superintendence of Richard Cassels, had been erected in Fishamble Street. It was opened on Friday, October 2, 1741, and impressed by its splendid acoustics, to which Handel alluded in a letter to Charles Jennens, of April 19, 1742. Before undertaking *Messiah* Handel gave two series of subscription concerts in Neal's Hall[3] and the future of the establishment seemed assured.

In 1743 Arne organised concerts in the Music Hall and a steady stream of virtuosi came over from London, and the

---

[1] Probably during the periods of suspension suffered by Daniel Roseingrave, organist from 1698–1727, notorious for his foul language and aggressive behaviour.

[2] *Pue's Occurrences*, April 10, 1736.

[3] See Percy M. Young, *The Oratorios of Handel*, London, 1950, pp. 104 ff.

Continent, to supplement local talent. In 1749, however, the concerts were rudely disturbed:

> Whereas several Evil minded Persons have of late frequented the Galleries, and have thrown Stones and other Things at the Band of Musick during the Time of Performance, to the great Disturbance of the Audiences, & Peril of the Musicians, I do hereby offer a Reward of ten Guineas for the Discovery of any Persons who shall throw any Thing at the said Band of Musick, to be paid by me immediately upon the Conviction of such offenders.
>
> B. Victor, Treasurer[1].

If such interventions were caused by dissatisfaction at the quality of the music the directors of the concerts could claim that they had been, and were, trying to maintain this by persuading Arne's German brother-in-law, John Frederick Lampe, for long a familiar figure in the popular music of London, and Niccolò Pasquali, the violinist, to live in Dublin. Both, however, were there but briefly, preferring the attractiveness of Edinburgh and the St. Cecilia's Hall in the Niddry Wynd[2].

The last phase of Dublin's musical *grand siècle* was ushered in in 1757 when Garrett Wellesley, graduate of Trinity College, and to become the Earl of Mornington in 1760 and Professor of Music at Trinity in 1764, established a Musical Academy— for 'persons moving in the highest sphere of society', and excluding 'professors and teachers'. This late offshoot of the Italian Renaissance graded its members into Academics, Probationers, and Associates, with only the 'male academics' enjoying the 'right of suffrage in the Academy[3]'. The orchestra, led by another John Neal, a surgeon, and 'one of the best amateur violinists in Europe', comprised seven violinists, one viola, four 'cellos, four flutes, two bassoons, and there were five available harpsichordists. Among these was Quin, also a surgeon, who had been friendly with Handel when he visited

---

[1] *Dublin Courant*, October 3–7, 1749.

[2] Lampe died in Edinburgh in 1751, after a year of concert life there during which he initiated open-air concerts (with the necessary qualification, 'in case the weather is not unfavourable'—*Edinburgh Evening Courant*, June 3, 1751).

Pasquali, engaged as 'professional musician' for the Gentlemen's Concerts in 1752, also died in Edinburgh, in 1757. Both musicians were buried in the Canongate Church yard.

[3] Gilbert, *op. cit.*, p. 76.

Dublin. Passing through oratorial respectabilities the Academy laudably promoted the interests of amateur composers, such as Dr Murphy who produced a setting of Pope's St. Cecilia's Ode in 1769, but came down in the end to catches and glees (a particular province of Mornington), and at this point the music of Dublin slumped into the commonplace. A review of the political situation gives sufficient cause for this conclusion to an era of high noonday promise.

OXFORD AND A NEW MUSIC ROOM

The University of Oxford, whether in the intimate atmosphere of college life or on a bigger, corporate, scale, had encouraged public performance of music certainly since the days of the Commonwealth—and before that time in various, honorific, musico-dramatical displays. Benjamin Rogers, Henry Aldrich, and Matthew Locke were among the earliest holders of commissions to compose odes for performance in the Sheldonian Theatre[1], while more recreative vocal and instrumental musical meetings took place from 1671[2]. In 1713 Pepusch, required to perform his Doctor's Exercise, not only affronted the dignities of academic life by enlisting the aid of London professionals for this purpose, but sensibly aimed to recover some of his expenses by giving a series of Subscription Concerts. Twenty years later —in 1733—the five Subscription Concerts given by Handel in the Sheldonian proved a greater incentive, and in 1742 a scheme for erecting a public Music Room was launched. Like most musical ambitions in Handelian and post-Handelian England, this was set astride the vogue for oratorio, soon to become a national disease. After personal canvassing had resulted in a basic sum of nearly £500 (of which one-fifth was dedicated to the purchase of land), two oratorio performances in the Hall of Christ Church contributed another £120. It was, however, not until 1748 that the new Music Room in Holywell was ready for use; until that time monthly concerts of choral music were given in the King's Head. The Music Room was described by William Hayes as

[1] In 1669, 1672, and 1673.
[2] Anthony à Wood, *Survey ... of the City of Oxford*, ed. A. Clark, 1889, II, p. 802.

An elegant stone edifice appropriated to Music, and therefore called the Music Room; the dimensions are 65 by 32 and 30 feet high. The north end, being a Segment of a Circle, is occupied by the Performers. The orchestre rises gradually from the Front, where the Singers stand, partly screened by a Balustrade. On the uppermost Stage, in the Center stands an excellent Organ . . .[1]

The organ, built by Byfield, was a bequest from William Freeman, of Hamels (Hemels) in Hertfordshire, a graduate of Magdalen College, and one with which Handel himself was acquainted[2]. The Oxford Concerts prospered under the direction of Hayes, who was Professor in the University, and whose earlier experiences in respect of extramural music-making in another place will shortly be noticed, and for many years the cream of professional talent—including Thomas Pinto[3], Peter Hellendaal[4], Edward Jones[5], Miss Barsanti[6], the Linley family of Bath, Mrs Bathélemon[7], John Crosdill[8], Johann Fischer[9], Johann Cramer[10], Salomon Ignazio Raimondi[11], Andreas Lidl, the baryton-player from Esterház—was available.

The Oxford Concerts, of which the climax was the visit to the city by Haydn in 1791, were quite as attractive as any in London. More important, perhaps, their inauguration had set a seal on music as a social accomplishment. In 1750 it was

---

[1] Wood, *op. cit.*, I, pp. 390–2.

[2] The libretto of *Alexander Balus* was inscribed to Freeman, and there is reference to his organ in a letter from Handel to Jennens of September 30, 1749.

[3] ? 1714–?, violinist, who played in London, at the Three Choirs Festival (see page 98), and, after failure as impresario, in Edinburgh and Dublin.

[4] 1721–1799, Dutch violinist and pupil of Tartini, who migrated to England because of lack of opportunity in Holland and took up organ appointments and also arranged concerts, particularly in East Anglia.

[5] 1752–1824, famous Welsh harpist.

[6] Singer, and daughter of Francesco Barsanti (d. 1776), oboist in London and Edinburgh.

[7] c. 1749–1799, née Mary Young, opera singer and wife of François Barthélemon, violinist.

[8] 1751–1825, the best English 'cellist of his time.

[9] 1733–1800, oboist at Dresden and Berlin before settling in England, where he married the daughter of Gainsborough.

[10] 1745–1799, violinist, born in Mannheim and after 1772 leader of the royal band in London.

[11] c. 1773–1813, Italian violinist, who settled in London in 1762, after having previously directed concerts in Amsterdam.

written that 'a Taste for Musick, modern Languages; and other polite Entertainments of the Gentlemen have succeeded the Clubs and Bacchanalian Routs'[1].

CONCERTS IN OTHER PROVINCIAL TOWNS

The generally held notion that during the Hanoverian era English music subsided into a state of near-atrophy is somewhat wide of the exact truth. That was the age, in fact, in which its cultivation and particularly its appreciation became generously diffused. At the same time the virtues of its main channels of expression being exposed before their time prevented adequate expression on the side of composition, and when in the nineteenth century a new generation of composers appeared to meet the challenge of industrial England they were insufficiently equipped to fulfil their obligations satisfactorily. The lack of patronage on any scale comparable to that obtaining in Europe was a disadvantage in this particular, but it was, on the other hand, a reflection of a state of comparative political maturity and comparative social balance. The association of aristocracy and bourgeoisie accomplished notable deeds in what were the principal cities of Britain, but others also played their part in promoting musical entertainment.

Among these cities were those which had cathedral musical establishments and traditions. In Worcester, probably in 1717, the Three Choirs Festival—the progenitor of all such Festivals—was born out of a sound local musical tradition (such as supported a gala performance of Purcell's *Te Deum* to celebrate the Peace of Utrecht in 1713, and a Musical Society in 1720) and the necessity for raising money for charitable performances[2]. Between 1731 and 1734 William Hayes was organist in Worcester, and the usefulness of concerts in enlarging his emoluments is indicated in notices in the *Worcester Journal* of July 7/14, 1732, and July 20, 1733. They read respectively as follows:

> On Tuesday, August 1, 1732, in the evening, at the Town Hall, will be performed a Concert of Vocal and Instrumental Musick, for the benefit of Mr William Hayes, Organist of the Cathedral. N.B.—There will be a Ball for the ladies when the Musick is ended.

[1] A. D. Godley, *Oxford in the Eighteenth Century*, London, 1908, p. 136.

[2] See Watkins Shaw, *The Three Choirs Festival*, c. 1713–1953, Worcester, 1954.

On Monday, July 30, 1733, will be perform'd a Concert of Vocal and Instrumental Musick, for the benefit of William Hayes, Organist at the Cathedral. N.B.—The place of performance will be mention'd in the next paper.

In Salisbury, too, a combination of Cathedral and town provided exhilarating performances for the people of Wiltshire. On October 25, 1744, the *Salisbury Journal* announced that the Festival of St. Cecilia would be celebrated as usual in the Cathedral 'for the Benefit of the Town Music [i.e. town musicians], assisted by several bands from Bath'[1]. Among the works performed was Handel's *Dettingen Te Deum*. At the Assembly Rooms there was an additional concert, with a ball, for which the tickets cost 2/6. Behind these activities in Salisbury, and for many years to come, stood James Harris (1709–1780), an independent gentleman related to the House of Shaftesbury, who was a fervent Handelian. Although he had wide musical interests[2], which inspired a variety of music in intimate musical meetings at his house, the power of Handel was such that before long the Salisbury Festival ran its programmes almost exclusively from the works of that master.

Some light on the condition of music in another of the southern cathedral cities comes from the record of the early career of Charles Dibdin. He may not rank among the major English composers, but there were few who could outdo him in the more sociable genres. His talents might have been buried in the Church of England, for which he was intended and therefore sent to school in Winchester in 1754. But a capacity for music, increased by the expert tuition of the Cathedral organist, was at first developed towards its conclusion thus:

He learned enough . . . to enable him to take a part in the anthems at the Cathedral, and to sing at concerts given during the races and assizes. There was a weekly amateur concert, of which several

[1] Benson Hatcher, *The History of Modern Wiltshire*, etc., Salisbury, 1843, p. 585.

[2] See Introduction to *The Works of James Harris* . . . , Oxford, 1841: at the Musical Festivals in Salisbury there were selections from the best Italian and German composers . . . adapted . . . to words from the Scriptures or from Milton's *Paradise Lost*, sometimes to compositions of his own'.

of the principal clergymen and gentry of the town and neighbour-hood were members, and at which he was the chief vocal performer. His musical propensities being thus nourished by the popularity which his attainments, slight as they must have been, gained for him, he abandoned his ecclesiastical studies, and devoted himself wholly to his favourite pursuit, resolving to depend on it as his means of subsistence[1].

In Bath, Bristol, and Devizes, as in Salisbury, the Handel influence was profound, as from 1749, and *Boddeley's Bath Journal* from that year faithfully records an impressive row of oratorio performances, interspersed however, especially in Bath, by Subscription Concerts. A strong choral tradition was developed under Francis Fleming, author and amateur musi-cian, Thomas Chilcot, organist of the Abbey, and Thomas Linley, singing-master and father of a talented family. Concerts took place in the Old Theatre Royal and the town Assembly Rooms, and the quality of Bath heard such original Handel singers (he himself took a cure in Bath in 1751) as Galli, Frasi, Cuzzoni, Passierini, and Guadagni, and oratorio choruses brought together the combined choirs of Wells, Bristol and Salisbury. Bristol had its new Musick Room[2] by January 14, 1756, on which day it was opened with a performance of *Messiah*, between the Acts of which Broderip, organist of St. Mary Redcliffe, in the authentic manner, interspersed organ concerti. At this time the organist was a figure of importance in provincial England and from him stemmed a great deal of professional initiative. It was, for example, the organist of St. Nicholas's Church in Newcastle upon Tyne, Charles Avison, who first arranged Subscription Concerts, in 1736, in that city.

Avison, a native of Newcastle, was unusual among his organist colleagues in the wealth of his interests. It is said that he studied in Italy (his reported inheritance of a violin of Corelli is recorded on page 26), and that later he was a pupil of Geminiani[3]. In addition to playing the violin, as well as organ and harpsichord, he advertised himself as a teacher of the

---

[1] *The Songs of Charles Dibdin*, Memoir by George Hogarth, London, 1842, p. xii.

[2] Concerts had previously taken place in Wiltshire's Rooms on the Walks.

[3] Geminiani, who tried to persuade Avison to Edinburgh, visited him in Newcastle in 1760.

German flute. He was also a philosophical, and critical, student of music. His *An Essay on Musical Expression* (1752) in which he extolled Marcello and Geminiani and which provoked a reply by William Hayes, attained some celebrity, went into a second edition (in which he offered some mitigation of his previous criticisms of Handel); Avison instituted his concerts 'at the Assembly Rooms in the Great Market and at Mr Parker's Long-Room in the Bigg Market' soon after his appointment to St. Nicholas, and continued them until his death in 1770. Avison, whose concertos formed a welcome addition to the resources of contemporary musical societies—as, for instance, the inventory at Aberdeen shows—was strongly supported by three prominent citizens of Newcastle, the Rev. Mr Alut, traveller and collector of music, Sir Lionel Pilkington, and Dr Brown[1]. As had become customary Avison made his contribution to charity:

'Mr Charles Avison is to give an annual Concert and Mr Joseph Baker, of York, an annual Play, gratis, for the Benefit of the Infirmary[2].' The concert took place in September, at the Assembly Rooms, 'to a numerous and polite audience; which we hear produced £36 15s 0d the Performers giving their Assistance gratis, & Mr Avison being at the Expense of Lights etc.'

In Manchester, too, there was, by the middle of the century, a 'numerous & polite audience' to be found at the Subscription Concerts of which there is a record from November 2, 1744. Among the first subscribers[3], one hundred and sixty-five in number and each contributing 5/–, were some prominent in subversion and to be among the supporters of the Jacobite rebellion in the next year. As a result of this and its calamitous conclusion the membership of the Subscription Concerts was considerably reduced, as also, necessarily, the fees disbursed.

The records of these concerts, which flourished between November 2, 1744, and August 20, 1745, are informative in general. Thus supernumerary professionals' fees ranged between half a guinea and a guinea and a half; hire of harpsichord

---

[1] See *The Gentleman's Magazine*, 1808, p. 581 ff.

[2] *Newcastle General Magazine*, April, 1751.

[3] A *Mr Anonymous*, who stands thus in the records, has, not unreasonably, been suggested as Charles Edward Stuart, the 'Young Pretender': see 'Manchester Concerts in 1744' in *Remains Historical and Literary ... published by the Chetham Society*, Manchester, 1867, pp. 66–76.

stood at one guinea, and its tuning cost 15/–; hire of a room required 5/–, while ancillary payments included 5/4 for candles, 3/6 for door-keeper, and 6d for 'drink to porter'; and advertising and tickets accounted for 5/6. Regarding the purchase of music the members paid out £2 2s 0d for 48 overtures by Handel, 15/– for concertos by Corelli (binding 15/– extra), and £2 17s 0d for Geminiani's concertos, including the binding. Of the first concert the programme was:

ACT I	Overture to *Otho*	Handel
	Song	
	Concerto for the German flute	
	First [Concerto?]	Tessarini[1]
	Sonata No. 3	Corelli
ACT II	Concerto No. 2	Corelli
	Lesson for harpsichord	
	Song	
	Sonata No. 2, Second Set	Corelli
	Flute Solo	
	Third [Concerto?]	Tessarini

Other composers represented in subsequent concerts were Vivaldi, Hasse, John Humphreys, Arne, and William Felton, the latter, a clergyman, having some local reputation[2]. After this promising start concert life in Manchester disappeared from notice, to be resuscitated—so far as the records are concerned—in the Gentlemen's Concerts which began in 1770 and continued, unbroken, until 1920.

Of the other cities to play a significant part in the later stages of English music, Birmingham maintained concerts of a different order. Thus:

> At the New Theatre, Moor St., Birmingham.
> On Tuesday, November 13, 1744
> An ORATORIO, or
> Concert of Vocal and Instrumental Musick.

[1] Carlo Tessarini, b. 1690, was a pupil of Corelli and in 1762 was still active as violinist in Amsterdam.

[2] He was educated at Manchester Grammar School, and the *Andante & Variations* ('Felton's Gavotte') from his Concerto Op. 1, No. 3 (published 1745) was said to have been played when the forces of the Young Pretender left Manchester in December 1745, and in the next year at the execution of the Manchester Jacobite, Jemmy Dawson.

In which will be introduced the celebrated comic opera of the *Dragon of Wantley*. With select pieces of music between every act.
To which will be added:
A Modern Matrimonial Dialogue between a Drinking Husband and a Scolding Wife. The whole by H. Hallam and set to music by Mr Gunn.

The composer of this curiosity was Barnabas Gunn, organist in Birmingham before going to Gloucester: his principal claim on posterity lies in the List of Subscribers to his *Two Cantatas and Six Songs*, for among them was Handel. The musical life of Birmingham was marked at this time by an inclination to the bizarre, as indicated by this notice:

On Thursday, July 16, 1747, at Mr Sawyer's Great Room, will be a Grand Concert of Vocal and Instrumental Music, wherein will be performed several full Pieces and a Concerto Obligato on the Harpsichord: with a handkerchief over the keys which no other Master ever performed. Also several songs by Signor Pescatore[1], Italian Master of Music, and several Pieces of musick on the Cymbal by Israel Nowell. After the Concert a Ball. Tickets 2/– each[2].

Standards were raised when, in 1779, the Hospital was opened and its sustentation depended on oratorio performances.

THE RELATIONSHIP BETWEEN AMATEUR
AND PROFESSIONAL

The period under review is, to all intents and purposes, the last in which the amateur and the professional could come together on more or less equal terms. The conservative style of the *concerto grosso* which prevailed in Britain was ideal material for this purpose (as, indeed, it still is, and it is on this style largely that the amateur orchestra of the twentieth century has been built), which is one reason for its long perpetuation there. The fact that professionals and amateurs could thus meet on an agreeable footing, which for the former was made more palatable by the prospect of steady engagements in

---

[1] Who also appeared in the Edinburgh Concerts.
[2] See J. Sutcliffe Smith, *The Story of Music in Birmingham*, Birmingham, 1945, p. 15.

performance and teaching[1], ensured the committee principle on which concert organisation was bound, and, in the long run, the ultimate dominance of the amateur, especially in programme selection. The institution of the public concert therefore appealed to the bourgeois citizen of cultural aptitudes, since it guaranteed his social standing and, in due course, led him towards positions of greater power. He was, in fact, emulating the progress of the aristocrat, though in a smaller circle and to a lesser extent. During the eighteenth century the arrangement worked well in the provincial towns of Britain; later, when the technical ability of the amateur diminished or disappeared entirely and he retained only a shadow of knowledge and a profusion of prejudice, it worked a good deal less well. Paradoxically, it was from the authoritarian systems of continental Europe that the real musical independence of the artist really stemmed.

However, the establishment of the public concert in the social order of the era of Handel was a notable achievement. And it carried to the New World.

EARLY CONCERT LIFE IN AMERICA

In the seventeenth century American music consisted largely of psalmody, and the standards of piety, therein enshrined, that supported the burgeoning democracy of New England and underwrote its economic and social viability, had a powerful influence on cultural advancement. The theatre was held in disfavour, and in Boston several instances of suppression occurred in the late seventeenth and early eighteenth century. On the other hand concerts, after the London manner, were free from moral opprobrium and were introduced into Boston in 1731, by one Peter Pelham, an artist and teacher who had emigrated from London in 1726. On December 16/23 the *Boston News-Letter* advertised as follows:

[1] The relationship between the professional musician attached to a 'Gentleman's Concert' organisation is paralleled by that obtaining in modern times in golf clubs. On the aristocratic side life for the player was more hazardous. The 'nobleman would send his butler or steward to haggle with the musicians for their price'. They were often not free agents even so, but represented by a 'fixer', such as, *c.* 1750, Giardini, who 'regulated the terms . . . according to the different grades of talent'. W. T. Parke, *Musical Memoirs*, London, 1830, I, p. 234.

On Thursday, the 30th of this instant December, there will be performed a 'concert of Music' on Sundry instruments At Mr Pelham's great Room, being the house of the late Doctor Noyes near Sun Tavern. Tickets to be delivered to the place of Performance at 'Five Shillings' each. The Concert to begin exactly at Six o'clock, and no Tickets will be delivered after Five the day of Performance. N.B.—There will be no admittance after Six.

From this beginning sprang a series of Gentleman's Concerts —to use the English term—for which the authorities of the town allowed the use of the Faneuil Hall, and by 1754 Boston was able to boast its own Concert Hall. Meanwhile the same pattern was being inaugurated in New York.

On Wednesday the 21 of January Instant there will be a Consort of Musick, Vocal and Instrumental, for the Benefit of *Mr Pachelbel*, the Harpsicord Part performed by himself. The Songs, Violins and German Flutes by private Hands. The Consort will begin percisely [*sic*] at 6 'a-Clock. In the House of *Robert Todd*, Vintner.

Tickets to be had at the Coffee-House, and at *Mr Todd's* at 4 Shillings[1].

Karl Theodor Pachelbel (1690-1750) was a son of Johann Pachelbel and the first notable link between the music of Germany and that of America. Pachelbel was in Boston in 1732 or 1733, and when he left, for Newport, New York, and Charlestown, he took with him Peter Pelham's son as pupil. In 1743 the younger Pelham returned to Boston as organist.

After Pachelbel's visit to New York benefit and charity concerts took place there, mostly under the direction of William Hulett and Alexander Dienval, members of a theatrical company, and in 1760 this partnership organised the first Subscription Concerts of New York.

In 1741 Bethlehem, in Pennsylvania, became the centre for the Moravians, and their transposition of traditions native to Saxony—their previous refuge—brought to America the familiar institution of the *Collegium Musicum*, from which grew the Bethlehem Philharmonic Society in 1820.

If the period under consideration is epochal in its acceptance of the potential of the dilettante, it is also notable as one in which musical standards were preserved by due consideration

---

[1] *The New York Gazette*, January 6, 1736.

of international affairs, and also by a general insistence on the superiority of contemporary music. (In the latter respect the British were increasingly throwing backward glances, but the real idealisation of the excellences of the past did not set in for another generation.) No one better illustrates the interdependence of musical thought and practice at this time than the Swede, Johan Roman.

JOHAN ROMAN, AND SWEDISH MUSIC

Roman lived at a peculiarly propitious time. Imperial Sweden, after the romantic misadventures of Charles XII, was in decline, and in place of military and diplomatic power the ruling classes looked to culture to restore prestige. The interests of Queen Christina, who was among the admirers of Corelli when she lived in Italy, were later adopted by Princess Ulrika Eleonora, sister of Charles XII, who became Queen in 1718. It was she who recognising the talent of Roman sent him to study in London. In 1720 he returned to Stockholm to become deputy director of the royal orchestra—with which he had played as a boy. In 1729 Roman took complete control of the court music and, with the experience of London behind him, began the concert life of Sweden in performances in the House of the Nobility (still used as a concert room). These, with amateurs and professionals co-operating, were after the manner of *Concert Spirituel* but with programmes dependent on music brought from London. The dominant influence was that of Handel, which is also strongly represented in Roman's own compositions. In 1735 Roman took two sabbatical years and visited England again, as well as France, Italy, and Germany. Roman, whose concerti, sonatas, symphonies, and motets reflect his travels, was the principal figure in Swedish music for many years, even after his retirement from the post of Royal Kapellmeister in 1745; so much so that he is termed the 'father of Swedish music'. Even though he did not, as a composer, depart from the international conventions he did by his executive skill and vision lay the foundations of a national respect for music, which was greatly assisted when, in 1771, the Royal Academy of Music was founded as a teaching institution.

Swedish music prospered when Roman had a free hand and when royal patronage was enlightened. Ulrika Eleonora and Frederik I set an example that was followed by Adolf Frederik and Louisa Ulrika. The latter, who became Queen in 1751, was a sister of Frederick II of Prussia, and like him she was passionately interested in the theatre and in music. With mention of Frederick the Great we enter the last great period of royal patronage.

Patronage on the Grand Scale

THE SYMPHONY

$\mathcal{A}$S HAS BEEN SUGGESTED, in a quotation from Gradenwitz on page 57, the achievement of the form of the symphony and its allies represented a dividing-line in the social development of instrumental music. For the first time an abstract musical form became a vehicle for the aspirations of the many rather than of the few. The reasons for this were various. On the technical side there was the attraction of a highly developed and particular skill: the instrumental virtuoso whether alone or in company with others was a public spectacle, and the factor of display was in itself compelling. On the psychological side the power now inherent in a trained instrumental ensemble to provoke and to satisfy the emotions was considerable, and collateral with a new recognition of the emotional life of the individual: to this the up-grading of wind instruments was notably contributory. Structurally, the comprehension within the symphony of all the basic elements of music—song, dance, harmony, counterpoint, and so on—not only gave scope to the instruments involved, with an intensification and rationalisation of timbres, but also realised a new ideal of musical unity. There was too a general shift in emphasis which in itself caused a greater relative appreciation of music.

The first age of the symphony was also the age of Kant (1724–1806) and some connection between the philosophic evaluation of pure ideas (in the *Critique of Pure Reason*, 1781) and the increasingly exploratory quality of instrumental music was not altogether to be wondered at in view of the German interest in both; it was also an age in which the critical scepticism of

Voltaire (1694–1778) and the optative attitudes of Rousseau (1712–1778) undermined older responses to art—especially in the field of theological alignment—and underwrote the condition of dissatisfaction that is the essence of all new forms of artistic expression. The term Classical, as applied to music of the symphonic era, is misleading, as also it is in respect of the literature of Goethe, Schiller, Klopstock, and Kant himself, if it indicates mere excellence in detachment. In fact the reverse is the case. Symphonic music may now be seen, as formerly it was felt, to be emancipatory, just as was the *Lied*, of which the full fluorescence was somewhat later. Within symphony there was the possibility of synthesis, of naturalism—the capacity of instrumental music to mirror nature was a tenet even of Baroque musical philosophy and of popular belief—and of Idealism, and a satisfaction for the wish for some stylistic uniformity.

FREDERICK 'THE GREAT', OF PRUSSIA

New situations emerge only gradually, despite revolutions, and by frequent coincidences of paradox. Among these paradoxes lies the liberation of music, and its full emergence into wider fields, under the protection of authoritarianism. Berlin and Potsdam, Mannheim and Schwetzingen, Dresden and Pilnitz, Paris and Versailles, Esterház and Eisenstadt, Vienna and Schönbrunn—in each case palace and 'summer residence': these were the real fulcral points of musical advancement during the second part of the eighteenth century. That they were so was due to such accidents as the discord between Frederick William I, King of Prussia, and his eldest son, the infiltration of Bohemian impulses into the court of the Palatinate, the independent and hopefully expansionist aims of the Saxon royal house, French esteem for the *style moderne* which preceded the Revolution, the personal aptitudes of the Habsburgs, and the reinforcements of all such casual circumstances by various, indigenous traditions.

Frederick the Great ascended the throne of Prussia in 1740 and carried with him the interests in music, literature, philosophy, that he had been happily able to indulge in his rustication at Rheinsberg. A visit to Dresden in 1728 had greatly impressed him, and something of the Dresden method was carried to Berlin by Quantz—who was a member of the Saxon royal orchestra from 1728 till 1741—and others who were appointed to the Prussian *Kapelle*. Intent on making Berlin worthy of the State it was his ambition to build, he employed Georg Wenzeslaus von Knobelsdorff (1699–1753) to start on a metropolitan building campaign, of which the Opera House was ready for occupation by 1742. But von Knobelsdorff was also given his commission at Potsdam where, one year later, Frederick removed his court. To the existing palace at Potsdam Knobelsdorff had added by 1747 the charming fancy of Sanssouci, in which Baroque and Rococo phrases are spoken with a strong German accent. Sanssouci being no more than a summer residence and the needs of State and of dependants calling for further architectural expansion, Knobelsdorff's successor, Karl von Gontard, was called on to design the *Neues Palais*, which was in being by 1769. In each of these palaces Frederick had his Music Room. His pattern of life being regular these were in constant use.

Between 5 and 7 in the evening the King was read to,

and his Reading is succeeded by a Concert, which lasts till Nine. He takes great Delight in, and understands Musick extremely well, and few can equal him upon the Flute[1]. His daily Concert consists chiefly of wind instruments [*sic*], which are the best in Europe; namely, three Eunuchs, a Counter Tenor Voice, and Mademoiselle *Astra*, an *Italian*[2]. These singers cannot be equalled, for he will admit of none that are not superlatively excellent. There is seldom any singing, except in the Company of Favourites, tho' sometimes on particular occasions, Young Lords making Interest with the King's Favourites gain Admittance[3].

[1] In some respects the so-called German Flute was mightier than the sword. This instrument conquered whole armies of European dilettanti, so that, for instance, when, in 1760, the Gentlemen's Concerts were constituted in Manchester all the founding members were flautists.

[2] Besides Astr(u)a the Opera singers of this period included Carestini and Concialini (male soprani), Porporino (male contralto), and Benedetta Agricola, Italian-born soprano and wife of J. F. Agricola.

[3] *A Succinct Account of the Person, the Way of Living, and of the Court of the King of Prussia, translated from a curious transcript in the French Found in the Cabinet of the late Field Marshall Keith*, London, J. Reason, 1759.

After the evening concert the King collected half-a-dozen or so 'wits', took supper, and thereafter engaged in intellectual discussion until midnight. On Mondays and Fridays concerts did not take place, as on those evenings the court attended the Opera.

THE MUSICIANS OF POTSDAM AND BERLIN

Frederick was an indefatigable flautist, dexterous but irregular in tempo. In regard to this defect he found himself at odds with Carl Philipp Emanuel Bach, who became cembalist to the court in 1740, remaining there for twenty-seven years before going to Hamburg, where he took over the Monday Concerts from October 27, 1768[1]. Carl Philipp Emanuel was also irritated by his employer's conservatism of taste, finding sympathy from the King's sister-in-law, the Princess Amalia, and on numerous occasions made efforts to move. But Frederick both disliked changes in his musical establishment and was not unimpressed by the reputations that his employees made for themselves. Principal among the court musicians at Potsdam in addition to Emanuel Bach were Johann Joachim Quantz, Johann Gottlieb, and Karl Heinrich Graun, Franz (František) Benda, Johann Friedrich Agricola, Johann Philipp Kirnberger, Carl Friedrich Fasch, and Johann Friedrich Reichardt, who, with their colleagues, assistants, and pupils made a closely knit community, strengthened from time to time by intermarriage. Compared with the musicians of Mannheim, this group, excepting Bach, were conservative in outlook and accomplishment, yet progressive in their general intellectual interests and in their vigorous promotion of bourgeois music in the city of Berlin. Most of these musicians, according to German practice and the example of the monarch, were philosophical and literary in outlook and accomplishment, and in their various writings laid the foundations of scientific method whether in the practice or the appreciation of music. Quantz wrote a classic on flute playing, Bach on clavier playing, Agricola on singing; Kirnberger provided ballast on the theoretical side, to which

[1] See J. A. Hiller, *Wöchentliche Nachrichten und Anmerkungen die Musik betreffend*, Leipzig, 1766–1770.

Friedrich Wilhelm Marpurg, an acquaintance of Voltaire and director of the government lottery in Berlin from 1763, also made valuable contributions; Johann Georg Sulzer, a member of the Academy of Sciences in Berlin, wrote a work esteemed by Burney, of some aesthetic significance; while Reichardt, whose literary style was supported by copious reading in the works of Jacopi, Kant, Moses Mendelssohn, Rousseau, Klopstock, and Edward Young, explored the interdependence of the arts and social and political affairs in a flood of works that served as a point of departure for all German musical journalism in the nineteenth century, though not all his successors possessed Reichardt's lively capacity for clear and racy exposition. By his sponsorship in writing of unfamiliar works Reichardt may also be accepted as the pioneer of the programme note.

Quantz (1697–1773), was chamber musician at Potsdam from 1741 until his death. He taught Frederick the flute, composed more than three hundred concertos for him in an old-fashioned idiom attractive to the King, and assisted the cause of German letters by settings of moralising poems by Christian Gellert. The concertos, symphonies, and chamber music of Emanuel Bach, on the other hand, revealed all kinds of new possibilities, and his talents were recognised as beyond those of the other royal musicians. So Reichardt could pay tribute to

> . . . unserem Bach—mit seeleerhebendem Stolze nenn ich ihn unser—wer kann ihm wohl je an Originalität, an Reichtum der edelsten und schönsten Gedanken, und an überraschender Neuheit im Gefange und in der Harmonie gleich?
> Seine Seele ist ein unerschöpfliches Meer von Gedanken; und so wie das grosse Weltmeer den ganzen Erdball umfasset, und tausend Ströme ihn durchdringen, so umfasst und durchströmt Bach den ganzen Umfang und das Innerste der Kunst . . .[1].

The two Grauns, Johann Gottlieb (1703–1771) and Karl Heinrich (1704–1759), had been with Frederick at Rheinsberg and on his accession both moved to Berlin and Potsdam, the

---

[1] *Schreiben über die Berlinische Musik*, Hamburg, 1773. 'Who can compare with our Bach—I call him our Bach with tremendous pride—in originality, in profusion of noble and beautiful ideas, in the surprising novelty of conception and harmony. His mind (soul) is an inexhaustible sea of ideas. Just as the great ocean surrounds the earth and sends thousands of streams through it, so Bach contains the whole of art and permeates its innermost parts . . . '

latter being appointed musical director. Both, formerly choristers in the Kreuzchor, were from Dresden, and Johann Gottlieb, trained instrumentally under Pisendel and a violinist, was largely responsible for the excellence of Prussian orchestral playing[1]. Karl Heinrich, a tenor singer, was expert in opera and was reponsible for the direction and the composition of operas in Berlin. His interest in Church music, however, was strong and his *Der Tod Jesu*, which was first performed in the Cathedral in Berlin in 1755, was a landmark in German oratorio. Both Grauns were also composers of concerti. Benda, a Czech, had caught the fancy of Frederick when he was Crown Prince and introduced to his suite in 1732 remained in the royal service (like so many of his colleagues) until his death. Benda provided his quota of concerti, chamber music, and technical studies for violin, and his daughter Juliane married Reichardt.

Agricola and Kirnberger were pupils of Sebastian Bach and as guardians of his reputation maintained an interest in his works that intensified, through the choral tradition to which they both adhered, in sacred music of somewhat academic character, and developed into the so-called Bach revival. This in turn derived in some part from the nationalism extruded from Frederick the Great's statecraft, but also from deeply-rooted affiliations of musical and literary thought and practice, dating from the time of Luther. Karl Friedrich Fasch also had his Leipzig connections, being the son of Johann Friedrich, founder of the second of the *Collegia Musica* there, and like Agricola and Kirnberger was conservative and scholarly in respect of composition. His musical place at court was that of harpsichordist—it was his talent for accompaniment that first recommended him to Benda, who was responsible for his coming to Potsdam—but he also gave lessons in composition. These increased when, as the result of the Seven Years' War

---

[1] In 1774: 'The orchestra is very large, and arranged after that at Dresden. The band consists of about 50 performers, among whom are,

Two composers	One harp
The concert-master	Four tenors [violas]
Eleven violins	Four flutes
Five violoncellos	Four hautboys
Two double bases [*sic*]	Four bassoons, and
Two harpsichord players	Two French horns.

Burney, *The Present State of Music*, etc., II, pp. 96–97.

from 1756 to 1763, his salary decreased[1]; as examples for his pupils he wrote innumerable pieces of intricate counterpoint and ingenious canons. Again this kind of academicism represented a constant factor in German music and was apparent throughout the nineteenth century, from Mendelssohn to Brahms, and into the twentieth, with Reger and Hindemith.

Concerts at court, at Potsdam, flourished as has been seen and, as Burney testifies[2], became less exclusive, but by 1754 Berlin was rich in parallel performances. These designated at various times as *Musik(aus)übende Gesellschäfte, Academies, Assemblées, Concerts,* the term *Collegium Musicum* now being limited to pedagogic usage, were at least half public and a great attraction to the professional and mercantile classes. On Mondays Kammermusikus Schale[3] superintended one series; on Fridays Johann Janitsch, court official and double-bassist, held an academy; on Saturdays it was the turn of Agricola. After the war (during which retrenchment hit subsidies for music, but most of all those for the opera, which was the least of the King's interests), in 1770, a celebrated *Liebhaberkonzert* was instituted by Friedrich Benda (son of Franz, and also a violinist) in conjunction with his colleague Karl Bachmann, a viola player. The *Liebhaberkonzerte* took place each Friday during the winter, and once a month during the summer, and lasted until 1797, Bachmann sustaining them after the death of Benda.

Meanwhile Reichardt, whose impetuosity as director of the renewed opera since 1776 was one aspect of an abundance of vitality, had brought Berlin into line with Paris by introducing a Lenten *Concert Spirituel.* This was held on Thursdays, between five and eight, and the admission charge for a lady and gentleman was two ducats. From his various travels Reichardt brought back different ideas, and the *Concert Spirituel* of his

---

[1] During this period the State revenues ran very low and Prussia was reduced to a state of misery similar to that suffered during the Thirty Years' War.

[2] In the long section on music in Berlin and Potsdam, *op. cit.,* II, pp. 87–235.

[3] Christian Friedrich Schale (1713–1800), violoncellist and organist of Berlin Cathedral (St. Hedwig's) from 1764: his *Musikausübende Gesellschaft,* founded in 1749, and held in the house of Johann Philipp Sack (1722–1763) the then Cathedral organist, was the first of many amateur orchestras in the city.

initiation also owed something to the Antient Concerts (see page 152) he had attended in London. Thus the score of Leonardo Leo's *Kain und Abel*, acquired in Italy, was a natural choice for an early performance. In the relevant programme book Reichardt wrote an appreciation of Leo as a composer, and this may be regarded as the starting-point of the programme note[1]. As a pioneer Reichardt was inevitably going against the tide (not least in political matters in which he declared himself a supporter of the Revolution). His antiquarian interests were those of a minority, the general public preferring virtuoso performance, and, since his ambitions were accompanied by a frequent lack of tact and his many absences were detrimental to finished performances, he eventually met with considerable hostility, not least from a by now effective and critical press[2].

CHORAL MUSIC IN BERLIN

While Reichardt was prodigal of enthusiasm his colleague Fasch was, as his diaries reveal, methodical, industrious, and amiable. He had the capacity for canalising the potentialities of others and also a well-developed social sense that ensured a genuine personal respect in different quarters in Berlin and Potsdam. Fasch was enthusiastic for choral music, and when Reichardt showed him another of his Italian souvenirs, a Mass in sixteen parts by Grazio Benvoli (1605–1672)[3], he realised that adequate presentation of such music was only possible by a well-trained choir of mixed voices. He had many singing pupils[4] among the army and the civil service and their wives and girl friends, and instead of persuading them all that they were

[1] See H. M. Schletterer, *J. Fr. Reichardt*, Augsburg, 1865, 1 vol. only published.

[2] *Allgemeine Musikalische Zeitung*, 1803, pp. 248 ff. This journal, edited by Johann Friedrich Rochlitz, was founded in 1798.

[3] Benvoli, of French parentage, was a church musician in Vienna and Rome. His contrapuntal technique was notable and he wrote Masses in 12, 16, and 24 parts, and a motet—for the consecration of Salzburg Cathedral in 1628—in 48 parts disposed among 12 choirs.

[4] Whose enthusiam was privately catered for by examples of the *Lied*, now a serious part of a German composer's activity. Regarding the work of the Berlin composers, especially Johann Schulz (1747–1800) sometime Kapellmeister in Berlin), Reichardt, and Zelter, and their settings of Goethe, Schiller, Burger, Voss, Claudius, Klopstock, and Hölty, see Georg Knepler, *Musikgeschichte des XIX Jahrhunderts*, Berlin 1961, II, pp. 736 ff.

brilliant soloists he urged on them the merits of co-operation. This also meant that with a choral ensemble to hand he could conveniently rehearse his own works. To aid the amateurs Fasch brought in members of the Berlin Singchöre and personnel from the Opera, and was grateful by 1787 to be able to meet in Councillor Milow's house near the Spittelmarkt, or in the Councillor's 'garden-house'. By 1791 Fasch had a steady body of twenty-seven choralists (seven sopranos, five contraltos, seven tenors, eight basses), who practised weekly (on Monday evening) in different houses, and in the next year presented a public performance of his own eight-part setting of Psalm LI in the Marienkirche.

On November 5, 1792, Fasch's organisation became constituted as the Sing-Akademie, under the patronage of two Ministers—von Herzberg and von Heinitz, and was given a room in the Academy of Arts. Fasch appointed an assistant director, this being his former pupil Carl Friedrich Zelter[1] (1758–1832), who was approved by Goethe for settings of his poems. Public performances given in 1794 included motets by Sebastian Bach, Durante and Prince Louis Ferdinand, himself a composer, gave the Singakademie his blessing and encouraged others from the court to patronise it. By now Fasch's choir had expanded[2], and in 1795 began the popular rehabilitation of Handel as a German composer by a performance of *Judas Maccabaeus*. In 1796 Graun's *Passion* was undertaken, and on June 21 the society received a visit from Beethoven, who delighted the members by extemporising on a theme by Fasch. Two years later Prince Radziwill, brother-in-law of Louis Ferdinand, was also a visitor, and the influential Abbé Vogler was an honorary member.

In 1800 Fasch died and, according to his wishes, the Singakademie, Zelter now being Director, gave the first performance in Berlin of Mozart's *Requiem*. This performance was of exceptional interest and the unprecedented receipts from the public of 1200 Thaler presented a problem which was solved by the endowment of a worthy but impecunious family. The

---

[1] Zelter wrote a biography of Fasch, published in Berlin in 1801.

[2] 29 sopranos, 22 contraltos, 14 tenors, 19 basses. It continued to increase so that the respective figures for 1799 were, 53, 22, 18, 21; for 1812, 89, 38, 42, 36; and for 1813, 111, 67, 62, 61.

membership of the Singakademie in the early years of the nineteenth century was representative, embracing students, actors, artists, schoolmasters, clergymen, doctors, city councillors, soldiers, merchants (among whom the booksellers were prominent), and professional musicians.

Performances were given in church or in a room in the Opera House, and from 1806[1] Handel had become as essential to the Singakademie as to the English Festival Choirs, though the former body was somewhat less restricted in its choice of oratorio. The success of the society was such that in 1823 Ottmer was commissioned to build a permanent headquarters, with concert-room. This Singakademie building, across from the Opera, is now used as the Maxim Gorky Theatre. In the formative days of the society the Mendelssohn family were firm supporters of its activities, and so it was that in 1829 Felix, abetted by a fellow-member, the actor, Eduard Devrient, was able to produce his historic revival of the *St. Matthew Passion*. In spite of the difficulties created by the fact of Mendelssohn's youth and Zelter's age and experience it is clear that Zelter— for whom, through Fasch, Bach was an heroic figure in German music—was glad of this initiative. In 1830 the *Passion* was repeated, as also in 1831, 1832, and 1833; while in 1834 the first half of the *Mass in B Minor* was given, the second half coming in the year following.

DEVELOPMENT OF NATIONAL PRIDE

Frederick the Great commenced his long reign with a contempt for German values in art, philosophy, and literature. If at its conclusion, in 1786, his esteem for his subjects was little higher, theirs for him was enormous. He had converted a backward State, devoid of natural advantages, into an efficient and potentially prosperous society, the most capably administered, perhaps, in Europe; he had secured it against the ambitions of France, Austria, and Russia; he had invested nationalism with a new significance and imbued the Germans

---

[1] 1806, *Alexander's Feast*; 1813, after the interruption caused by the Napoleonic Wars, *Judas Maccabaeus*, as being particularly suitable to the times; 1827, *Joshua*; 1828, *Judas Maccabaeus, Alexander's Feast, Samson*; 1829, *Messiah, Jephtha*; 1830, *Dixit Dominus*; 1831, *Israel in Egypt*; 1832, *Messiah, Solomon*; 1833, *Saul*; 1836, *Joseph*.

with a pride in their collective quality; the German 'soul' existed, a complex of metaphysical introspection—the result of so many disasters from the time of the Thirty Years' to the Seven Years' War, and Protestant theology—native industry, and a growing faith in the potency of these characteristics under the protection of adequate military strength. There was also the matter of history. Frederick himself made no appeal to this to guarantee his philosophy, but the philosophers increasingly did so. Music was something of a centripetal force. It was the one department of life in which Frederick was conservative and parochial, his personal inclinations being permitted their maximum freedom in this field, and his musicians, both by temperament and the necessity in the system of patronage to consider the patron, were content to develop along lines laid down by tradition and circumstance. Indeed, they were altogether content. Their provision at Potsdam was not ungenerous, their standing was recognised, and they had additional and ample opportunity to expand their interests in Berlin. The end of this was the Singakademie; a consequence of royal patronage, but also a fundamental of bourgeois musical experience. Through the Singakademie, and the many societies which stemmed from it in all parts of Germany, the amateur was once again involved in music. But now the milieu from which interest was drawn was far wider than in former times. A revolution of this kind had not been foreseen, but it took place: the only silent (in one sense) revolution in German history.

THE ELECTOR OF THE PALATINATE AT MANNHEIM

Frederick the Great was Francophile, but his tastes were subordinated to his duties as he conceived them, and himself to the State. Karl Theodor of Mannheim (1742–1799) was at first equally Francophile, but his capacity for ruling was inhibited by indolence. Karl Theodor prided himself on his cheerful accessibility and his excellence in cultural judgment. The prosperity of the Electorate had been assured by the acumen of his predecessors, particularly by the energetic Karl Ludwig who had made Mannheim a profitable trading-centre, especially between the other German States and Holland. Karl Theodor held his court in Mannheim from 1743 to 1778, when it was

5.   Collegium Musicum, Thun, Switzerland.

(a) Quantz, Handel, Bach, Tartini, Gluck, and Jommelli, by an anonymous eighteenth-century German artist.

(b) Cambridge performance, c.1770.

6. Concerts in Caricature

transferred to Munich, and during this period it became, as Jacopi described it, 'das Paradies der Tonkünstler'.

Karl Theodor initially made Mannheim a home from home for French artists, particularly actors, and so many were there resident that Christian Schubart observed in 1773 that it could at one time have easily been taken for a French colony rather than a German provincial community. Like the King of Prussia, the Elector of the Palatinate determined to illuminate the German mind through the principles of enlightened France, for he too was on sociable terms with Voltaire. Karl Theodor's first contributions to the *Aufklärung* were a National Theatre, an Academy of Art, a Library, an Observatory, and a variety of Museums. Since the Elector took some delight in his understanding of human nature there was also a brothel ancillary and convenient to the other institutes of culture. In 1770, recognising the strength of the wind of political change, he sent the French actors home and substituted a German troupe who played German pieces or, since that repertoire was limited, classical plays in translation. In 1775 a further turn towards a national culture came with the inauguration of the *Kurpfälzische Deutsche Gesellschaft zur Pflege der nationalen Sprache und Literatur*, under the auspices of which Heribert von Dalberg, Otto von Gemmingen, and the painter Friedrich Müller worked out the idea for the German National Theatre. This was ready for occupation in 1777. It was in this year that Mozart visited Mannheim[1] where he commented on the excellence of the orchestra, but the relative indifference of the singers, and the substitution of German operas by Schweitzer and Holzbauer for Italian, did not seem to him promising so far as his own prospects were concerned. It was, however, the orchestra and its performances that were the magnetic feature of the Mannheim court. Best of all were the summer days when everything took place at Schwetzingen.

The scene was described by J. J. Heinse:

When the Elector was in residence in his summer palace at Schwetzingen his superb orchestra was also there. There was music all the time. Mermaids, gnomes, salamanders all chased one another; and so did melodies—over the water, in the air, on

[1] See *Letters of Mozart and his Family*, ed. Emily Anderson, London, 1938, II, pp. 511–756, 936–949.

the ground, and through the fireworks—from which the most wonderful symphonies were shaped. One believed oneself to be on an enchanted island. Everyone played and sang. From the pavilion near the bathing-place in the 'Garden of the Hesperides' there came the most voluptuous music in the evening. . . [1].

Mannheim was a splendid attraction for the tourist who saw only what he wanted to see. Beneath the surface of its splendours, however, reposed many of the factors that destroyed the way of life it represented. 'The expense and magnificence of the court of this little city', reported Burney, 'are prodigious; the palace and offices extend over almost half the town; and one half of the inhabitants, who are in office, prey on the other, who seem to be in the utmost indigence.' Moral standards were low, and the Elector, as has been suggested, did little to raise them. There was, as Mozart discovered, a spate of intrigue, jealousy, and back-scratching. The autobiography of Karl von Dittersdorf is a cogent demolition of the aristocratic principle obtaining at this time, the more so because he was urbane, amusing, and—having been himself elevated thereby—without prejudice. Arthur Coleridge summarised Dittersdorf's story:

> A strange world is depicted in this book. The modern baby appears to be, in some respects, less childish than the potentates who then controlled Europe. Life was a perpetual and rather a prosaic fairy-tale. Emperors were amused with islands that floated about of themselves, and bagpipe-players who capered and frisked like goats. Princes went out hunting, seated in an armchair, and took their pet sopranos with them. Sopranos . . . married theatrical wig-makers in order to escape the importunities of Dukes . . . As for Bishops, they seem to have occupied themselves principally in match-making, in the construction of operatic librettos, in the design of Turkish masquerades, and in hiding so many ducats in the snuff-boxes or under the table-napkins of their favourite servants . . . [2].

Music could flourish; at Mannheim it did. The Elector was a flautist and 'cellist and, like Frederick the Great, he provided a concert every evening when there was no opera. The musicians, something like a hundred being on the payroll, were well treated and, at the end of their service, eligible for pensions.

[1] Quoted by B. Paumgartner, *Mozart*, Zürich, 1945, p. 196.
[2] *Autobiography of Dittersdorf*, London, 1896, Preface, pp. xix-xx.

So many of them were there that 'Schwetzingen . . . must seem to be inhabited only by a colony of musicians[1].' In the midst of social reaction this colony of musicians, not discontented with their own circumstances, and insulated from the main rigours of life, made of their activities a focal point for the rest of Europe. Their influence spread north to Aberdeen, south to Vienna, east to Hungary, and west to, and beyond, Paris.

THE STAMITZ SCHOOL

Given the favourable circumstances obtaining at Mannheim there was every reason why music should develop. This happened at other similar centres. But the direction it took was another matter. The character of the court ensured, perhaps, that practice would prevail over theory, and the extrinsic over the intrinsic. Thus the colour of music, as shown in a contrariety of keys and timbres, and its possibilities of graciousness, as limned in melodic patterns and rhythmic formulas, were considered more particularly than, say, in Berlin, where the emphasis was on its serious, character-building aspects. In Berlin the tendency was inward-looking, at Mannheim outward-looking, and the *Kapelle* at the latter court international in constitution. Johann Stamitz (christened Jan Václav Stamic) was a Bohemian, a member of one of many families compelled to emigrate in the seventeenth century, and the element thus introduced into the main stream of European music was, at this time, vital.

'We will not grieve because we must present this laurel to a Bohemian and not to a German. It required such a primitive element to off-set the dry formalism that the Berlin school especially began to adopt.' In writing in this manner Riemann[2] anticipated aesthetic doctrines enunciated through the same terms, but at greater length, in some parts of Europe during the middle years of the twentieth century.

Stamitz inculcated efficiency into the orchestra he directed, and especially into the string ensemble. But he also infected his colleagues with something of his own imaginative vision, so

---

[1] Burney, *Present State of Music*, etc., I, p. 98.
[2] In *Denkmäler Deutscher Tonkunst*, Leipzig, 1902, vol. 3, 1, p. 24.

that the players who appeared as an 'army of generals' were hardly inferior in their creative capacity. Among the first generation of Mannheim composers, in addition to Stamitz, were Toeschi and Danzi, who were Italians, Richter and Holzbauer, both Austrians, and Filitz, of Bohemian stock. Alessandro Toeschi joined the Mannheim court at about the same time as Stamitz, after having been chamber musician at Stuttgart. He composed flute pieces, concerti, and ballet music, and his talent for the latter was inherited by his son Carlo Giuseppe (c. 1722–1788), who, after being tutored by Stamitz also became a prolific symphonist. Innocenz Danzi (c. 1730–1798) was a 'cellist, and was succeeded in his office by his son Franz (his mother was a daughter of the elder Toeschi), who, in turn, became one of the pioneers of German opera in Munich. Franz Xaver Richter (1709–1789), singer and violinist, covered a wide field as a composer and was much esteemed in Mannheim on account of the excellence of his symphonies, of which he wrote sixty-four.

Ignaz Holzbauer (1711–1783) travelled widely (spending some time in Italy), before being appointed director of Count Franz Anton Rottech's orchestra at Holleschau (Holešov) in Moravia, where he had ample opportunity for experiment[1]. In 1753 he went to Mannheim, where he was in charge of the opera and conductor of the orchestra. He also wrote more than two hundred symphonic works, as well as masses, motets, and miscellaneous works for trumpet, horn, and clarinet, behind which stood his long experience as a composer of opera. It is significant that Mozart found in Holzbauer's *Günther von Schwarzburg* the qualities of 'spirit and fire'. This opera was, in fact, a response to the new mood of the time, being based on a German subject and with German recitative to replace the spoken dialogue of the *Singspiel*; and the overture, in its semantic underwriting of a conventional musical form, showed the direction in which the later Mozart and Beethoven symphony should develop. Anton Filitz (c. 1730–1760) was leader of the Mannheim 'cellos, and in addition to much chamber music, composed thirty-nine symphonies, some of which were printed in Paris, Amsterdam, and London. These were the

---

[1] K. M. Klob, *Drei musikalische Biedermänner*, Ulm, 1911, p. 7.

composers who 'stimulated by the productions of Jomelli, first surpassed the bounds of common opera overtures, which had hitherto only served in the theatre as a kind of court cryer, with an "O Yes!" in order to awaken attention, and bespeak silence at the entrance of the singers[1].'

Of Stamitz's pupils the most important was Christian Cannabich (1731–1798), son of Martin Cannabich who taught the flute to the Elector. The younger Cannabich joined the orchestra as an apprentice at the age of thirteen and was put on the regular strength three years later. He was favoured by the Elector to the extent of having a travelling scholarship to Italy, where he worked with Jommelli, and in 1757 he succeeded to Stamitz's post as leader of the orchestra. In 1760 he became director of all the instrumental music, in which capacity he ultimately transferred with the court to Munich. Cannabich was regarded by Mozart as the best conductor he had ever encountered, and responsible for an exemplary team-work. It was under Cannabich that the orchestra reached its peak of excellence and in Schubart's testimonial may be discovered the *ons et origo* of modern orchestral style:

'Its *forte* is thunder, its *crescendo* a cataract, its *diminuendo* the splashing of a distant brook, its *piano* a rustle of spring'[2].

For his orchestra Cannabich wrote ninety-one symphonies. In addition to the younger Toeschi the pupils of Stamitz included J. Ritschel, Franz Beck (1723?–1809), who was obliged to defect from Mannheim after a duel, first to Venice to study with Galuppi, then to Paris where a symphony of his was played at a *Concert Spirituel* in 1757, and finally to Bordeaux, Ernst Eichner (1740–1777), a bassoonist who settled in Potsdam and composed thirty-one symphonies, and Anton I, Carl and Anton II, sons of Johann Stamitz. Carl went to Paris in 1770, and eight years later visited London, while Anton also migrated to Paris. All were symphonists.

The theory of inheritance of musical ability was given as much validity at Mannheim as anywhere. Some dynasties have already appeared. Other musical families produced Caspar Bohrer (1744–1809), trumpeter, and virtuoso double-bass

---

[1] Burney, *op. cit.*, I, pp. 95–6.
[2] *Ideen zu einer Aesthetik der Tonkunst*, Vienna, 1805, p. 84.

player; Wilhelm (1745–1799) and Johann Cramer (1771–1858), who as pianist, violinist, and conductors, exerted a powerful influence on English orchestral music after their settlement in London; and Johann Friedrich Eck (1766–1809), pupil of Danner, who was declared by Reichardt to be, except for Salomon, the best violinist he had ever heard. Johann Baptist Wendling (1730–1797), the flautist, Friedrich Ramm (1744–1811) and Ludwig August Lebrun (1746–1790)[1] oboists, Franz Anton Dimmler (1753–c. 1819) and Franz Lang (b. 1751) horn-players, and Jacob Tausch and his son, Franz Wilhelm (1762–1817)[2] clarinettists—with most of whom Mozart was acquainted during his stay in Mannheim in 1777–1778—were all members of families with numerous representatives in many fields of music and across several generations.

In 1775 Georg Joseph Vogler (1749–1814), who had lately returned from four years of foreign study at the Elector's expense, was—since he was in Holy Orders—given the sinecure of Court Chaplain at Mannheim. One of the most intelligent musicians of his age, Vogler realised that musical excellence should depend on prevision and coordinated preparation rather than on the haphazard system of casual apprenticeship and occasional good luck in patronage that had hitherto been the rule, and he inaugurated the *Mannheimer Tonschule*, the first *Musikhochschule* in Germany. At this Burney cast envious eyes, and that he was unable to found a similar institution in London was a source of grief to him[3]. Among the pupils of Vogler's school were Peter von Winter (1754–1825), Joseph Martin Kraus (1756–1792), Bernhard Anselm Weber (1766–1821), Peter Ritter (1763–1846), and Franz Danzi (1763–1826), son of Innocenz—all of whom were conspicuous, if secondary figures, in the transition of music from classicism to romanticism, from the private to the public zone.

---

[1] Lebrun married Innocenz Danzi's daughter, Franziska, a soprano. In 1779–1781 both Lebruns were busy in London, where Franziska had also sung in 1777.

[2] The younger Tausch is said to have popularised the clarinet in Berlin, where he settled as court musician in 1789. He was a great teacher and among his pupils was Heinrich Joseph Bärmann.

[3] See *Memoirs*, London 1832, I, p. 234.

THE MUSIC LIBRARY OF MANNHEIM

Karl Theodor became Elector of Bavaria in 1778. The court, apart from a few old retainers who refused to move, went to Munich, where the musical establishment was much smaller and where, in due course, interest was concentrated in opera. The glory of Mannheim faded. But in the library were kept the most famous symphonies of the pre-Beethoven era[1]. These included works by:

Johann Andreas Amon (1763–1825), Johann Anton André (1775–1842), Georg Benda, Fr Blyma, Cannabich, Dittersdorf, Anton Eberl (1766–1807), Ernst Eichner (1740–1777), Friedrich Fleischmann (1766–1798), Gossec, Gyrowetz, Josef Haydn (fourteen symphonies), Michael Haydn (1737–1806), Holzbauer, Jommelli (the Overture for *Fetonte*), Ed. Kunz, Ludwig Lachnith (1746–1820), Leduc (the Overture to *Julius Caesar*), Mozart (K.297 and K.425) Neubauer, Ignaz Pleyel (1753–1831), J. Reitha, Heinrich Riegel (1741–1799), Andreas Romberg (1767–1821), A. Roselti, J. Rösler, Anton and Karl Stamitz, Stertzel, Jan Tomaschek (1774–1850), Tommaso Traetta (1727–1779), Peter von Winter and Paul Wranitzky (1776–1808). These composers mostly had direct connection with Mannheim and they were of different nationalities, amid which the Bohemian strain was strong.

Among the works in the Mannheim Library were some that directly reflected the growing popularisation of music and a new attempt to come to terms with realism. Romberg's *Symphonie alla Turca* caught an impulse brought across the plains of Hungary at the end of the Turkish occupation of that country, while Haydn's *Jagd-* and *Abschiedsymphonie*, and idealisation of the *verbunkos* idiom, showed a new awareness of popular undercurrents of humour and feeling. Neubauer produced a 'Battle' symphony (adagio—Le matin; *Allegro*—allarme au camp; *Andante*—harangue aux guerriers; *Allegretto*—les deux armées se rangent en ordre de bataille; *Allegro*—la bataille; *Andante*—retour au camp; *Allegro*—célébration de la victoire), and Wranitzky an even more programmatic work

---

[1] Fr Walter (ed)—*Archiv und Bibliothek des Grossh. Hof- und Nationaltheaters in Mannheim 1779–1839*, 2 vol., Leipzig, 1899.

in his *Symphonie* (Op. 31), *caractéristique pour la paix avec la république française*. Of this the movements ran: (1) *Andante maestoso and Allegro molto*—Revolution, English March; *Tempo di marcia piu maestoso*; *piu Allegro*—Austrian and Prussian March. (2) *Adagio affetuoso*—Destiny and the death of Louis—Funeral March. (3) *Tempo di marcia*; *Allegro*—English March, March of the Allies, Getümmel eines Schlacht. (4) *Andante grazioso*—Peace Treaty negotiations; *Allegro vivace*— Rejoicing over the ratification of the Peace Treaty.

ENCOURAGEMENT FOR SYMPHONIC MUSIC IN PARIS

In spite of Berlin, Mannheim, Stuttgart—where the Duke of Würtemburg's orchestra which had been under Jommelli's control from 1753 to 1757 also qualified for the title of 'one of the best in the world'[1]—Bayreuth, where the Margraf Friedrich founded an *Akademie der Musik* in 1760, Salzburg, Esterház, and many other courts, and the public concerts of Hamburg, Frankfurt, Quedlinburg (1757), Zittau (1768), Dresden, Kassel, Munich (1784), Stettin[2], Leipzig (to which we shall return), Amsterdam, and London, the *Concert Spirituel* in Paris still took pride of place in European instrumental music. To appear at, or to be performed at, one of these functions was the ambition of every virtuoso and every composer. For the latter there was the additional incentive of possible publication, for Paris was a principal centre for the issue of symphonic works.

Jean Mondonville took charge of the *Concert Spirituel* after Royer and in 1762 was succeeded by Antoine d'Auvernge. From 1773 to 1777 Pierre Gaviniès, his pupil Simon Leduc, and Gossec were the managers, and from 1777 to 1789 Joseph Legros and Isidore Bertheaume. Gossec, much influenced by Mannheim through Johann Stamitz, was the most notable of the directors of the *Concert Spirituel*[3], stabilising horns and clarinets in the orchestra, and laying the foundations of symphonic appreciation both by his selection of the works in this form of others and the compositions of his own. A piquant composer, Gossec, the first French symphonist, is one of the few in the second rank whose works have distinctive character. In 1789 the King returned

[1] Schubart, *op. cit.*, p. 94.

[2] See Karl F. Kramer, *Magazin der Musik*, . . . 1783–9, *passim*.

[3] J. B. de La Borde, *Essais*, III, p. 428.

to the Tuileries and there was no place for the concerts. Legros, however, maintained a tenuous hold of his official position until, in 1791, the institution of the *Concert Spirituel* collapsed under the pressure of events. Thereafter its affairs were administered by the Théâtre Feydeau, and finally it was embodied in the Conservatoire Impérial.

The quality of the playing in the latter years of the *Concert Spirituel* aroused no marked enthusiasm on the part of such peripatetics as Burney, while Mozart was thoroughly discontented with the standard there encountered[1]. But it could justly be said that ' . . . the great benefit arising from the institution was the opportunity which it afforded the students of music, and the public in general, of hearing, judging, and comparing the compositions of the great masters of foreign schools, and the spirit of emulation which it naturally inspired . . .[2]'.

The inspiration afforded by the progressive programmes of the *Concert Spirituel* is epitomised by Charles Henri de Blainville, all of whose academic reserves were broken down by the sensibilities of the new music:

> But a new kind [of music] announces itself. The voice no longer tries to stand out by its brilliance or by repetitive warbling in the throat. A precise, marked rhythm replaces a soft, ineffectual prosody. We have, in short, a kind of music that pleases, is seductive, and paints Nature in new forms . . . The obedient instruments give new beauties to melody and to harmony. Nothing resists them, and everything is delicate and exquisite; there is—in the music—full explanation, to which one must listen[3].

As for the notable composers of the era we read: 'Meanwhile if I examine the works of our great men, such as Jommelli, Galuppi, J. C. Bach, Holzbauer, Pergolesi, etc, I find therein great and beautiful things. When I look again I discover this beautiful character inseparable from an art of which the effects are so sensitive, subtle, and short-lived[4].'

[1] See letter to Leopold Mozart of July 3, 1778: ' . . . never in my life have I heard a worse performance. You have no idea how they twice scraped and scrambled through it ['Paris' symphony, K. 297]'.
[2] *Harmonicon*, 1824, p. 57.
[3] *Histoire générale critique et philologique de la Musique*, Paris, 1767, 'Discours Préliminaire', p. xi.
[4] *Ibid.*, p 176.

CONCERTS DES AMATEURS

This attitude was in large measure conditioned by Gossec, whose influence lay not only behind the *Concert Spirituel* but also the derivative *Concerts des Amateurs*, which, founded by M Delahaye and the Comte d'Origny in 1773(?), were conducted by Gossec and the Chevalier de Saint Georges. The relationship with the French style of concert on the one hand and the Mannheim school on the other is indicated by the first programme, of March 25, 1773:

Symphony	Toeschi
Motet for solo voice	sung by Olivini
Flute concerto	played by Rault
Motet for 2 voices	J. C. Bach
sung by Richa and Mme Billini	
Symphonie Concertante	C. Stamitz
soloists Leduc and Besozzi	
Motet for solo voice	sung by Mme Larrivée
Violin solo	Jarnowick [*sic*]
Motet for chorus, *Qui confident*	Matthieu

At the *Concerts des Amateurs, concertante* symphonies were immensely popular, and favourite composers were Cambini, Boccherini, J. C. Bach, Toeschi, C. Stamitz, and Karl Ditters [Dittersdorf]. Dittersdorf, a cosmopolitan figure with a finger in every pie, from Esterház to Paris by way of Vienna, the confidant of crowned heads and the friend of Haydn, was a *succès d'estime* wherever he went. Ten of his symphonies were published in Paris by Cousineau[1], among them one which, while obeying the general dictates of fancy as shown by Romberg and Wranitzky, may be taken as the putative foundation for a European Common Market—in terms of music. This was the *Sinfonia nel gusto di cinque Nazioni* of 1768. The movements of this work were, *Andantino—Tedesco*; *Allegro assai—Italiano*; *Allegretto—Inglese*; *Menuetto—Francese*, with a trio marked *Turco*; and a final *Allegro* rondo of a 'general' nature of which the sections are marked in succession—*Tedesco, Italiano,*

[1] Among Dittersdorf's, other publishers were Venier in Paris; Bremner, Longman and Broderip, Preston, T. Skillern, and Thomas Tilley, in London; S. Markordt in Amsterdam; J. M. Goetz in Munich; Breitkopf in Leipzig; and B. Schott in Mainz.

Inglese, Tedesco, Francese, Tedesco, Turco, Tedesco. As a parody symphony this work is unusual, and the presumed national characteristics are defined with wit. It should be heartening to find that in 1768 the English were accorded a place in the symphonic scheme. Comparison between Dittersdorf's Symphony and Corbett's similarly intentioned *Bizarerie* (see page 83) shows to what extent the definitive properties of instrumental music had developed under the influence of expanding audiences.

HAYDN AND MOZART; THE COMPOSER'S GROWING REPUTATION

In 1779 the *Concerts des Amateurs* were re-named as *La Société de la Loge Olympique*, which, under the patronage of Marie Antoinette, Lahaye, the 'fermier-général', and numerous other persons of high standing in the army and society in general, also functioned in the Tuileries, in the *Salle des Maréchaux*. For this Society Viotti composed his second *Symphonie Concertante*, which was played by his pupils Guérillot and Grasset, and Haydn six symphonies (Nos. 82–87), which were conducted by the Comte d'Origny in the season 1785–1786. In the following year Haydn was able to write to William Forster, of London, in respect of these: '. . . the following works may be had of me, *viz*: 6 elegant Symphonies . . .'[1].

If the argument that musical forms are not self-generated, but the effect of conditions in general, has any force it may reasonably be argued that the symphonies and concertos of Haydn and Mozart resulted in large measure from the proliferation and particular character of concert activities during that part of the eighteenth century that preceded their major output.

The prospects for an infant prodigy when Mozart and his sister arrived on the scene were alluring. (What happened before their time to the many such who are noted is too often obscure.) Skilful management, a willingness to swallow insult[2], to disregard

---

[1] H. C. Robbins Landon, *The Collected Correspondence and London Notebooks of Joseph Haydn*, London, 1959, p. 59.

[2] Leopold Mozart to Lorenz Hagenauer, July 11, 1763, from Ludwigsburg: '. . . the Duke [of Würtemburg] has the charming habit of making people wait interminably before hearing them and then making them wait as long again before giving them a present'.

matters of taste[1], and to sleep in strange beds, was necessary; but the ambitious Leopold was prepared for all contingencies and in organising the European tours of his progeny showed more than enough initiative. He played up the aristocracy, submitted to the catechism of the curious, and in so doing unlocked the gates of genius by making Wolfgang a rebel. The symphonies and concertos of Mozart, at first conditioned by Johann Christian Bach and Carl Friedrich Abel, and later by the examples available for study in Mannheim and Paris, were initially in conformity with patronal requirements; but the last half-dozen or so of each was ahead of expectation. The composer himself became the arbiter of taste. This, in a sense, was what the French Revolution was about—or should have been about: the integrity of the individual. Haydn played his hand differently. The conditions of the system he could accept— which Mozart could not: his reward was a superior living from the Esterházys, and a dinner-place among the guests and the family rather than the retainers. In late life Haydn, his symphonies having preceded him, had some opportunity to travel, and his London visits were the climax of his career as a composer in that there he found the ideal audience (if not always quite ideal players), willing to meet the composer more than half-way, and to treat him without the reservations implicit in the European patronage system.

By this time the peripatetic composer had established himself, if he was good enough, and the international pre-eminence of Dittersdorf, Mozart, and Haydn gradually began to send the local composer into decline—sometimes unjustly. The ideal medium for the virtuoso composer was the symphony, or, if like Mozart he was also a performer, the concerto, and the proportions of such works enabled far more commissions to be fulfilled in many more places than did those of opera. Haydn served his apprenticeship to symphonic music in the modest musical establishment of Count Ferdinand Morzin, and when the orchestra was disbanded after the Count's marriage, he passed to Esterházy. Fortunate in that this prince both wielded considerable influence and approved progressive music, Haydn

[1] At Frankfurt Wolfgang had to play an item on the clavier with the keyboard hidden by a cloth (see also page 103). Newspaper announcement of August 30, 1763, quoted in Willi Reich, *Bekenntnis zu Mozart*, Lucerne, 1945, p. 24.

came into contact with the best people in Vienna. The Empress, Maria Theresa, was among them, and the honorific symphony (No. 48 in C major) composed in respect of her stay in Esterház in 1772 may be taken to symbolise Viennese acceptance of the new mode of instrumental music.

ROYAL MUSIC IN VIENNA

The dynasty of the Habsburgs was full of musical talent[1]. Ferdinand III, Leopold I, and Karl VI, were composers; Maria Theresa, the pupil of Hasse, was a competent singer; so too was her daughter; while the Crown Prince, the future Joseph II, was a 'cellist and a harpsichordist, a competent hand at realising a figured bass. The Court set the general tone, and in 1783 Reichardt, visiting Vienna, noted how the nobility practised music 'with passion' and how it was impossible to conceive of a more musical society. The first influential musician at court, at the beginning of the eighteenth century, was Georg Christoph Wagenseil (1715–1777). He was the royal music master, a conservative composer but an early symphonist, and one from whom Leopold Mozart expected more in the way of support for Wolfgang than, in fact, he got. There was also Johann Adam Reutter (1708–1772), Kapellmeister of St. Stephen's Cathedral —to which he brought Haydn as a boy chorister—and of the court, who, although preferring to write masses, oratorios, and operas, also helped to lay the foundations of a Viennese symphonic style. Reutter, however, was less notable for his musical efficiency—he reduced the Court *Kapelle* to an undistinguished condition—than for his smooth tongue. For being able to say the right thing at the right time he was ennobled. Under Wagenseil and Reutter concerts in Vienna were organised by the 'Academies'[2] which, from 1750, met in the theatre. Dittersdorf used to play accompaniments[3] at these until a row with

---

[1] See H. V. F. Somerset, 'The Hapsburg Emperors as Musicians', in *Music and Letters*, XXX, 1949, p. 204 *et seq.*

[2] As in other cases such concerts at first took the place of dramatic entertainments during Lent. *Wiener Diarium*, No. 14, 1750, quoted in K. Kobald, *Klassische Musikstätten*, p. 109.

[3] 'Ich musste bei den alle Freitage gehaltenenen Theater-Akademien accompagnieren, wo sie auch alle 14 Tage Concerte spielen.' *Lebensbeschreibung*, Vienna, 1804, p. 101.

Count Wenzel Sporck, in 1764, discouraged him from staying in Vienna and brought him into Michael Haydn's (now in Salzburg) old job with the Bishop of Grosswardein at Pozsony (Pressburg) in Hungary.

In 1764 Florian Gassmann (1729–1774) was appointed to the Viennese court as ballet composer in succession to Gluck. Like Gluck Gassmann was a Bohemian—indeed he was educated at the same Jesuit school at Komotar as Gluck—and he was approved, not only by the Viennese, as an extremely good representative composer of his period. On Reutter's death Gassmann was also appointed to his place as court conductor, a position he enjoyed for only two years, for he died, in 1774, as the result of a road accident: he fell out of a coach. Gassmann got on with Count Sporck rather better than had Dittersdorf, and the two were responsible for the foundation, in Vienna, of an independent concert organisation, the *Tonkünstler-Societät*.

This, the oldest concert society in Vienna, was founded, under royal patronage and with a royal nominee (this being Sporck at the time of foundation) as 'Protector', or President, in 1771. The intention, however, was not to supplant the private academies, which continued to flourish, but to provide a means of sustentation for the widows and orphans of Austrian professional musicians. In this case it resembled the society set up in London in 1738, and it similarly met with the whole-hearted support of the professional fraternity. Thus the performances could be relied upon to reach a high standard of competence. With side-glances at the *Concert Spirituel* and in consideration of a local tradition of some strength the meetings of the *Tonkünstler-Societät*—of which there were four annually, two in Advent and two in Lent[1]—were primarily centred on oratorio. Thus on March 29, 30, and 31, 1772, the main work of the first meeting was Gassmann's *La Betulia Liberata*. This, however, was preceded by a symphony by Josef Starzer[2] succeeded by another by Franz Asplmayr[3], and with a violin concerto played

---

[1] Each meeting was twice repeated, so in all three evenings were involved.

[2] 1726–1787, Viennese violinist and composer, who interrupted his Austrian career to lead the orchestra in St. Petersburg from 1760–1768.

[3] 1721–1796 Viennese court composer, now chiefly interesting on account of his settings for stage pieces based on *Macbeth* (1777) and *The Tempest* (1781).

by Lamotte[1] during the interval[2]. On December of that year the oratorio was Hasse's *Santa Elena al Calvario*, and a viola concerto was played by a travelling virtuoso, 'Herr Stramitz' [Carl Philipp Stamitz?]. Mixed concerts, in which oratorio was moderated and excerpts only were included, were more popular after Gassmann's death, as a specimen programme from 1778 shows: symphony by Johann Sperger[3], aria by Dittersdorf, chorus by Handel, violin concerto composed and played by Sperger, aria by Anton Teyber[4], chorus by Antonio Sacchini, aria by Giardini, a new symphony by an unnamed composer, a second chorus by Handel, a violin concerto played by Joseph Zistler[5], a terzetto by Sarti, and a final chorus by Handel[6]. In 1778 Haydn proposed joining the society, and indeed, paid his subscription; but he withdrew his application when the society tried to pull a fast one by asking him to sign an agreement to provide compositions when required. It was not until 1797 that this *gaffe* was corrected. In that year, sponsored by the Counts Johann Esterházy and Johann von Kufstein and the more highly esteemed after his triumphs in London, Haydn was elected a 'Senior Assessor' for life, in token of which he presented to the society the scores of *The Creation* and *The Seasons*.

Behind the concerts of the *Tonkünstler-Societät* lay the influence of Gottfried van Swieten, who was Ambassador to the Prussian Court from 1771 to 1778. Having established himself as a patron by commissioning six symphonies from Carl Philipp Emanuel Bach (1774) and having discovered the glories of the elder Bach and of Handel, van Swieten returned to Vienna full

---

[1] Franz Lamotte (1753–1781), Flemish violinist educated in London under Giardini, who gave a concert at the Burg Theatre in Vienna at the age of 13. Appeared in London in 1776 and 1778–1789.

[2] On the second night there was a flute concerto played by A. Schulz.

[3] d. 1812; double-bass player in Haydn's orchestra at Esterház, in 1780.

[4] 1754–1822; he served in the courts of Vienna and Dresden. His oratorio *Gioa* was performed at the Tonkünstler-Societät, in December 1786.

[5] Orchestra leader at Poszony 1782, see Mozart to Michael Puchberg, December 29, 1789.

[6] An excellent account of a 'mixed' concert compounded exclusively out of Mozart's works is given in Wolfgang's letter to his father of March 29, 1783. This, however, was a private 'academy'.

of good intentions, and with the means to carry them out[1]. Hence the strong Handelian influence in the Viennese programmes. Haydn, Mozart, and Beethoven were all among van Swieten's protégés; and that high standards should be established by the principals of society led van Swieten (who was made President of the Education Commission in 1781) to found the *Musikalische Gesellschaft* (limited to twenty-five aristocrats), which preceded the more widely based *Gesellschaft der Musikfreunde* of 1808.

THE AUGARTEN CONCERTS

In addition to Mozart and Haydn the mainstays of instrumental music in Vienna were Leopold Kozeluch[2], Huber[3], Dittersdorf, Johann Vanhall[4], and Leopold Hoffmann[5]. Opportunity came through the Societät through countless dilettante- and Liebhaberkonzerte, but also after 1782 in the more public ones organised by Philipp Martin, of Regensburg, in the Gartengebäude in the Augarten, a public garden in the suburb of Leopoldstadt. These concerts began on April 30, 1775, as a sequel to a successful set of winter concerts which had been given in the Mehlgrube in the Neuer Markt.

> You know that there are a great many amateurs in Vienna, and some very good ones too, both men and women. But so far these concerts have not been properly arranged. Well, this Martin has now got permission from the Emperor under charter . . . to give twelve concerts in the Augarten and four grand serenades in the finest opera places of the City. The subscription for the whole summer is two ducats . . . The orchestra consists entirely of amateurs, with the exception of the bassoon-players, the trumpeters and drummers[6].

[1] See Mozart to his father, March 12, 1783, and elsewhere.

[2] 1752–1818; Bohemian composer who became the fashionable music teacher in Vienna. He refused to succeed Mozart at Salzburg on account of the way the Archbishop had treated Mozart. Kozeluch arranged Scottish songs for Thomson of Edinburgh.

[3] 'a poor man, who plays the tenor at the playhouse', Burney, *Present State of Music*, I, p. 285.

[4] 1739–1813; of Dutch extraction, Wanhal or Vanhall was a pupil of Dittersdorf. Having no official appointment he depended entirely on private patronage. A voluminous composer, his works, of no more than moderate difficulty, were popular in England.

[5] c. 1730–1793; Kapellmeister of St. Stephen's Cathedral from 1772.

[6] Mozart to his father, May, 1782.

7. Music in Vauxhall Gardens, c.1770.

8.   Jubilee ticket for Vauxhall Gardens.

The Augarten concerts reflected something of the character of the popular concerts of London, and the virtuosi engaged to vary the productions of the amateurs were of a more or less sensational order, being experts in the harp (Mme Josepha Müllner), the guitar (Abbate Costa), the mandoline, for which Kozeluch wrote a concerto, the baryton, the 'Lyra tedesca', and the glass harmonica. If there was one place where a concertante work for piano, mandoline, trumpet, and double bass could be heard it was the Augarten.

Of the music of this era the modern listener is, by glossy performances, made aware of elegance, of *galanterie*, of a sweet reasonableness. While such agreeable ends were, no doubt, envisaged by some the picture of the composer at work is more sober; behind the music lie the dissonances, as well as the concords, of society, and ranges of taste that could meet in the pleasaunces of the public park. In this respect the Gardens of London were remarkable.

9

A Variety of Tastes

A GERMAN VIEW OF ENGLAND

AMONG THE FOREIGN OBSERVERS of the English people at the end of the eighteenth century none was more analytical and more outspoken than the conscientious Friedrich Augustus Wendeborn, whose *A View of England* appeared in German in about 1785 and in English some five years later. On the subject of the place of the arts in England he was critical, but, at the same time, aware of underlying philosophical and political problems that others, less thoughtful, would overlook: 'Liberty,' he wrote,

is most favourable to trade and commerce. Of this the English nation affords the strongest evidence. The spirit of gambling and commerce are nearly related; to gain riches by means of genius and enthusiasm for the arts, is exceedingly precarious. It is far more easy to obtain a fortune as a tradesman or merchant, assisted with the good luck of a gambler, and his not always very honest maxims. No wonder, therefore, if the greatest part of the English, whose *summum bonum* is money, are tasteless in the arts, and treat them with neglect, or even look upon them with a kind of disdain; no wonder if a tradesman or merchant, favoured by liberty, regards the accumulation of money above all, and considers a man of talents and learning, or an artist endowed with excellent genius, as beings far below him[1].

Elsewhere Wendeborn, conscious of his own frugal, Prussian, heritage, animadverts on the condition of an affluent society, on the 'prevalent inclination to get rich as soon as possible, and to lead an indolent life'[2], and in so doing outlines problems

[1] *A View of England*, II, p. 183.
[2] *Ibid.*, I, p. 412.

which are of twentieth-century significance, and no less intractable. In dealing with English institutions Wendeborn notices one in particular that both stated his case but also afforded some kind of solution.

> The famous gardens of Vauxhall, so celebrated on the continent, and of which there are so many feeble imitations, are within the parish of Lambeth. Various classes of people resort thither in the evening during the summer, for different kinds of amusements; but, even a philosopher may spend there agreeable hours at a small expense. He may hear good music and singing; he may refresh himself in the cool of the evening; he may make observations on men and manners, retire in good time, and rise the next morning without in the least repenting the pleasures of the last evening. This, indeed, may not be the case with a great number of those who frequent those gardens, and derive from thence causes for a long repentance[1].

VAUXHALL GARDENS

Institutions founded on good intentions and high ideals seldom lead directly to noble ends, while those of more indifferent origin may, in a more or less cohesive community, arrive at satisfying conclusions. The musical life of the pleasure gardens, of which those at Vauxhall were the most celebrated in eighteenth-century London, represented a higher point in popular musical culture than is generally conceded. Music, ranging from the concerti of Handel to the symphonies of J. C. Bach, from the songs of Arne to the ballads of Hook and Dibdin, became classless—that is, there were no divisions between 'serious' and 'light'; and available, performed by the best hands, at minimal cost. The consequences of this institution were the formation of an English school of symphonists— who suffered later neglect through an unfortunate prejudice on the part of musical institutions in favour of respectability and oratorios on the one hand, and foreign eminences on the other, and of a fundamental, and plebeian, regard for music that was irreparably damaged by the ravages of Victorian philistinism. The cult of the concert at Vauxhall and at Ranelagh (the

[1] *Ibid.*, I, pp. 352–3.

foundation for latter-day South Bank adventures in the provision of art for the many) stemmed from 'private enterprise' and was killed by it. Wendeborn was right, and was wrong.

The enterprise at Vauxhall belonged to Jonathan Tyers, a speculator in a speculative age. In 1730 Tyers took a lease for the Gardens, that had formerly been a favourite walking-out ground both for the quality and the commonalty, as Evelyn, Pepys, and Addison all noted. Since their inauguration in 1661, first as the New Spring Gardens, Vauxhall had provided some kind of musical entertainment[1]. Tyers, investing £250 a year in his lease, signified his intention of making something special out of his undertaking by a well-calculated publicity drive, symbolised in the *Ridotto al fresco* of the opening night[2] to which the Prince of Wales lent his patronage. The success of this occasion encouraged others of a similar nature.

Tyers organised his Gardens into a quadrangle, crossed like a Roman city by main thoroughfares interlinked by subsidiary paths, relieved by arbours named as imaginatively as the sectors of a Butlin's Holiday Camp and nicely sheltered for the more seductive purposes the Gardens served, ennobled by classical colonnades, theatres, temples, and pavilions for musical performance, and adorned by trees amid whose branches hung a myriad of fairy lanterns. On the material side clients in the cheaper confines, having paid a shilling for admission, could enjoy a spacious menu on which were such palate-titillating fancies as frothed syllabub, fragrant tea, sliced ham, scraped beef, and burnt champagne. Sitting in boxes decorated with murals designed by Francis Hayman, the wealthier patrons were soon able to enjoy the best of music, of food and drink, and of company: a sybaritic existence.

In 1737 Tyers installed an organ in the Gardens and, having appointed James Worgan (1715–1753) as organist—he also held appointments in city churches—entertained the multitude with organ concertos by Martini, Arne, Felton, Handel and others. On his retirement in 1751 James Worgan was succeeded by his brother, John (1724–1790), who served both as organist and

[1] Samuel Pepys, *Diary*, May 28, 1667: 'But to hear the nightingale and other birds, and hear fiddles, and there a harp, and here a Jew's trump (i.e. Jew's harp) . . . is mighty diverting.'

[2] June 7, 1732.

official composer to the Gardens, on and off, until 1774. The opening of the summer season of 1738 saw another captivating gesture by Tyers, when the statue of Handel by Roubiliac, for which he had paid £300, was unveiled. This statue presided over the scene until 1818.

In the summer of 1745 Tyers . . ., extending the performance of his orchestra to vocal music, presented at that evening retreat, then so simple, natural, and perfectly rural in its scenery and decorations, the combined powers of Lowe, Rheinhold, and Mrs Arne[1]. From this bower, where they were first heard, issued the strains of the most charming of our ballad composers, to be rapidly circulated all over the kingdom. The band was led by the strength and agility, if not the taste and elegance, of Richard Collett[2], whose tone was full, clear, and smooth. Sometimes the principal violoncello, and sometimes the first bassoon, was ably managed by the abilities of Hebden[3]. The silver tones of the trumpet of Valentine Snow[4] spread around their full and softened force; and Vincent's[5] interesting hautboy mingled with them its delicate tones[6].

Vauxhall Gardens were in their heyday during the last half of the eighteenth century, although they continued to function until the middle of the nineteenth, by which time their musical significance had been submerged by the more spectacular

[1] Thomas Lowe (d. 1783), tenor, appeared first at Drury Lane in 1760, when he was especially associated with Arne's Shakespeare songs. He was also engaged for Handel's oratorios, as were Thomas Rheinhold, a German bass, reputed to be a bastard son of the Archbishop of Dresden, who arrived in London in 1731, and Cecilia Arne.

[2] Burney added that 'having neither task nor knowledge of Music, he always remained an inelegant player.'

[3] John Hebden, also viol da gambist and bassoonist, whose portrait was painted by Philip Mercier.

[4] d. 1770: the trumpeter for whom Handel wrote his obbligato parts; Sergeant-trumpeter to the King, in succession to John Shore in 1753.

[5] There was a large family of Vincents, the most celebrated being Richard (1701–1782) and Thomas II (1720–1783). Both were oboists and the latter a pupil of Sammartini. Through Vincent's cultivation of 'delicate tones' the oboe became accepted as a solo instrument. Cf. Fanny Burney, in her vivid description of Vauxhall Gardens in *Evelina*: ' . . . there was a concert, in the course of which, a hautbois concerto was so charmingly played, that I could have thought myself upon enchanted ground, had I spirits more gentle to associate with. The hautbois in the open air is heavenly.'

[6] T. Busby, *Concert Room and Orchestra Anecdotes*, London, 1825, III, p. 3: the passage is lifted direct from Burney, *General History*, IV, pp. 667–8.

entertainments that the proprietors then put on in the hope of saving a declining property. Few foreign visitors missed Vauxhall, and the place was also a convenient venue for fictional intrigues. Among other writers, another German, the Pastor Moritz, found himself, as it were, at home:

> ... as I walked along ... I seemed to transport myself, in imagination, once more to Berlin; and forgot for a moment that immense seas and mountains and kingdoms now lie between us. I was the more tempted to indulge in this reverie, as I actually met with several gentlemen, inhabitants of Berlin in particular ... with whom I spent the evening in the most agreeable manner. Here and there (particularly in one of the charming woods which art has formed in this garden) you are pleasingly surprised by the sudden appearance of the statues of the most renowned English poets and philosophers; such as Milton, Thomson, and others. But, what gave me most pleasure, was the statue of the German composer, Handel, which, on entering the garden, is not far distant from the orchestra.

> This orchestra is among a number of trees situated as in a little wood, and is an exceedingly handsome one. As you enter the gardens you immediately hear the sound of vocal and instrumental music. There are several female singers constantly hired here to sing in public. On each side of the orchestra are small boxes, with tables and benches in which you sup. The walks before them, as well as in every other part of the gardens, are crowded with people of all ranks. I supped here with Mr S . . . r and the Secretary of the Prussian ambassador; besides a few other gentlemen from Berlin; but what astonished me was the boldness of the women of the town, who, along with their pimps, often rushed in upon us by half-dozens, and in the most shameless manner importuned us for wine, for themselves and their followers[1].

A culture which embraced prostitutes and pickpockets (of whom Moritz was also made aware that evening) could at least be said to be broadly based, and it is herein that the English symphony found its first home.

RANELAGH AND OTHER GARDENS

In addition to Vauxhall there were other Gardens in London. Those at Ranelagh, in which the Rotunda—amphitheatrically anticipating the Albert Hall—was the musical centre, were

[1] Moritz, from *Pinkerton's Travels*, London, 1771, I, p. 502.

somewhat more socially select, and the admission price was half-a-crown. Ranelagh was also a speculative venture, undertaken by Lacey, a patentee of Drury-lane Theatre in partnership with David Garrick, and it was opened in 1742. Michael Festing led the orchestra at first and after the installation of an organ by Byfield a few years later John Keeble (1711–1786) became organist. In the early days excerpts from oratorios were presented at morning sessions—which were altered to the evening when Sir John Barnard, Member of Parliament for the City of London and an authority on finance and questions relating to apprenticeship, persuaded the magistracy to insist on the change owing to the loss of trade caused by absenteeism among young workers who found the allurements of Frasi and Beard, and Handel and Arne, irresistible. There were moral disadvantages to evening meetings, as Pehr Kalm pointed out in 1748, for 'married ladies and mistresses of establishments and the young girls become in many ways altered and ruined . . . and all lose all pleasure in household duties'[1], and two decades later Moritz found himself accosted by a too friendly lady before entering the Gardens. The authorities, however, did their best to reduce the hazards, by the improvement of street lighting and the provision of patrols against highway robbery. Fielding's Mrs Ellison, in *Amelia*, thought of Ranelagh that 'Paradise itself can hardly be equal to it'. In 1764 Mozart performed there[2], and six years later Charles Burney became organist. In 1805, however, Ranelagh, also in decline, was sold. In due course the site was occupied by the buildings of Chelsea Hospital.

Vauxhall, Ranelagh, and Mary[le]bone (which operated from 1660 to 1778) Gardens, and Sadlers Wells, varied in their clientèles, were constant in their support of music. Their influence—the result of finding the lowest common denominator

---

[1] *Kalm's Account of his visit to England on his way to America in 1768*, translated by Joseph Lucas, London, 1892.

[2] Leopold Mozart, June 28, 1764: 'On Friday, June 29 . . . there will be a concert or benefit at Ranelagh in aid of a newly established Hôpital de femmes en couche, and whoever wishes to attend it must pay five shillings entrance. I am letting Wolfgang play a concerto on the organ in order to perform thereby the art of an English patriot who, as far as in him lies, endeavours to further the usefulness of this hospital which has been established pro bono publico. That is, you see, one way of winning the affections of this quite exceptional nation.'

among an infinite series of social grades—broadly speaking was beneficial. Musicians could guarantee full engagement-books, and composers found no great difficulty in selling their compositions—even though their returns were usually slender. And what went on in London also went on in the provinces. For instance, Holte Bridgman, a Birmingham impresario, instituted open-air concerts in the Apollo Gardens at Aston. Later in the century another Vauxhall Gardens was opened in Manchester, while in Liverpool John Sadler, of Harrington Street, was engraving the best songs from the tradition—which were also sung during theatrical performances in Liverpool— in such collections as his *Apollo's Cabinet* (1757).

POPULAR MUSIC

With the elegances of polite Europe on the one hand and the rough edge of their own vulgar public on the other most composers compromised somewhat, but since compromise led to succinctness and direct statement this was not always a bad thing. Certainly there were qualities astir in English music not ashamed to own Continental affiliations that led towards something that could be called a national style; in the songs and ballads of Dibdin, Arne, Hook, and Shield, the overtures, symphonies, and concertos of John Collett, John Marsh, Thomas Morris, William Smethergell, and many others, and the works of the anglicised Johann Christian Bach.

So far as song was concerned the Pleasure Garden acted as an emulsifier. The repertoire included items from oratorio, Italian opera, ballad opera, folk song (especially Scottish, for reasons which have already been stated), and adaptations of favourite instrumental tunes[1]. These were scored for chamber orchestra— strings, often with violas omitted, flute (well favoured for its demonstrative provocation to prima donnas to emulate its runs and roulades), and harpsichord, with oboes and clarinets[2]

[1] Burney's observation on Arne's style was generally applicable: 'The general melody of our countrymen, if analized, would perhaps appear to be neither Italian nor English, but an agreeable mixture of Italian, English and Scots. Many of his ballads, indeed, were professed imitations of the Scots style; but in his other songs he frequently dropped into it, perhaps, without design.' *A General History, etc.*, IV, p. 673.

[2] Bach first introduced the clarinets into England in the score of *Orione* (February 19, 1763).

establishing themselves in the popular numbers of Christian Bach. The words furnished a prelude to later developments in sentimental and commercial association. In "The Amazon" Samuel Howard[1] fulminates against foppery in a sturdy, 'English', four-square melody; in 'When Sappho tun'd the raptur'd strain', the words attributed to Smollett, James Oswald plaintively indicates the erotic stimulant provided by the popular female singer; in 'The Highland Laddie' 'Master' Arne proposes that love-making behind Scottish bushes has more delightful possibilities than West End luxury can afford; for a commercial in favour of red wine the anonymous 'The Praise of Burgundy', 'sung by Mr Lowe', was available, while 'The Jolly Toper', 'sung at the public Gardens', gives a more broadly directed recommendation of alcohol. Developing patriotism burgeoned in such direct propaganda as is contained in songs like 'Old England'. Undercurrents of urban vice are contained in those like 'A Cant Song', 'the words by Mr George [?] Stevens', which abbreviated the most squalid aspects as from *The Beggar's Opera*, while half-way from this to the degeneracies of Victorian sentimentality is Arne's setting of 'My Grandmother's Cot'. In such songs of the eighteenth century is the true index of popular taste, and from them stemmed the ideas that declined in one sense but flourished in another in the ballad concerts later founded by William Boosey, and their commercial exploitation was hardly less than of their twentieth-century successors. It may be added that however unseemly or trivial the texts the melodies were invariably recognisable as such.

THE ENTERPRISE OF J. C. BACH AND K. F. ABEL

Of all the composers associated with the Pleasure Gardens none is more important than J. C. Bach[2], who, after arriving in England in 1763, summed up the situation with the opportunist eye of the Saxon eminence he replaced and foresaw profit in it.

---

[1] 1710–1782: . . . 'this honest Englishman, thought of in the Chapel Royal, preferred the style of his own country to that of any other so much, that he never staggered his belief of its being the best in the world, by listening to foreign artists or their productions'. Burney, *ibid*, p. 672.

[2] See Percy M. Young, *Johann Christian Bach, Der 'Englische Bach'*, in *Musa, Mens, Musici*, Leipzig, 1965.

He wrote operas, contributed to ballad operas, arranged folk-songs—making agreement between Scottish pentatony and Mannheim instrumentation, invented songs in rondo and minuet style, and anglicised the symphony. A favourite at Court, affable with the aristocracy and the intelligentsia, and easy in lower circles, Bach also took in hand concert promotion. Here he was assisted by another immigrant, Karl Friedrich Abel, a former pupil of J. S. Bach and friend of Johann Adam Hiller in Dresden, where Abel was gambist from 1743 to 1758. Abel had given his first concert at the Music Room in Dean Street, Soho, in 1759, where he displayed his remarkable powers as a virtuoso performer. On Bach's going into partnership with him Abel turned from Spring Gardens, where they gave their first concert, to the establishment of the notorious Theresa Cornelys, and in 1764 superimposed a symphonic concert pattern on the indecorous background of balls and masquerades that had hitherto brought notoriety to Carlisle House. Abel and Bach gave concerts there and also in Almack's, and in 1775 moved to the newly built Rooms in Hanover Square (which were regularly used from 1775 until 1874).

These concerts became famous and fashionable. In addition to the symphonic works of Bach and Abel the best of European music was made available[1]. Bremner, Freeman, Longman, Straight, Vogler and Welcker and other publishers issued the works of Stamitz, Dittersdorf, Filitz, Holzbauer, Haydn, Mysliveček, and the Earl of Kelly, and the newest Mannheim devices were exploited. The third movement of Holzbauer's 'Periodical Overture', No. 29 in R. Bremner's series, subtitled *La Tempesta del mare*, contained the lot, while No. 25 of the same set, by Kelly, is a complex of dynamic markings. English symphonists, particularly Smethergell, took the hint, and if aiming at a more modest target, produced works of some charm and even distinction. The concerts were approved by the

[1] Less familiar composers—showing the force of the symphonic impulse—included the Dutchman C. E. Graaf, Kapellmeister to the Prince of Orange (six symphonies, Longman, Lukey) and J. D. Meder ('Periodical Symphony' for the entry of the Prince and Princess of Orange into the Town Hall of Amsterdam on May 30, 1768), Michel Esser, the German composer whose Op. 1, symphonies dedicated to the King of Denmark were imported into England from Holland, and the Princess Royal of Saxony (who contributed a set of six overtures collected by Antonio Kammell and published by Welcker).

majority, and von Archenholtz could later write that 'The concerts in London are allowed to be very grand, and the English in general prefer them to the music of the opera-house[1]'. Gentlemen like the Rev Thomas Twining came up to London specially to attend these performances, and W. J. Parke recorded his tribute to the Bach style: 'He seems', he wrote, 'to have been the first composer who maintained the law of contrast as a principle . . . His symphony for a double orchestra in the key of C (composed for his own concerts) is perhaps one of the most original, noble, and effective compositions I have ever heard[2].'

But there were also censorious voices:

> The performer in music is now anxious to produce sounds that strike the ear; but is little ambitious of moving the heart. Where, however, there is nothing in music but mere harmony, it wastes its most essential quality, it becomes a mechanical art, it dazzles, but cannot affect the mind. This is a reflection which the greatest part of modern performers never make. Charmed with the trick they have of writing sounds that seem not to be made for each other, they seek for nothing more[3].

REGULAR PROFESSIONAL CONCERTS

The Bach–Abel concerts were highly professionalised. In addition to the regular players at the Gardens and the theatres Bach, as 'Musick-Master' to Queen Charlotte, had access to the royal band (at the beginning of the reign only eight wind players, but increased to twenty to maintain the twice-weekly concerts at court), and with the competition thus involved it was possible to keep the standard of performance reasonably high. After Bach's death in 1782 and the temporary departure of Abel for Germany the quality declined somewhat, but in 1785 the concerts took on a new lease of life and were re-named the Professional Concerts. These were especially associated with William Cramer (1745–1799) who, coming to London from Mannheim in 1772 to join the royal band, showed himself to be

---

[1] Johann Wilhelm von Archenholtz, *A Picture of England*, London, 1791, p. 244.

[2] *Musical Memoirs*, I, p. 350.

[3] *Annual Register*, 1772, pp. 183–4.

a remarkable orchestral leader. In this capacity he exerted influence throughout the country—for in addition to certain royal duties he played at the Professional, the so-called 'Anacreontic'[1], and the Musical Fund Concerts in Hanover Square, had led the mammoth orchestra for the Handel Commemoration of 1784, was leader of the Three Choirs Festival Band, and appeared in Manchester and other provincial centres, and in fact, 'led all the festivals of that day[2]'. John Baptist Cramer (1771–1858), pupil of Abel and Clementi and also of his father, also appeared at the Hanover Square Concerts.

SALOMON AND HAYDN

It was the elder Cramer who first interested Haydn in coming to England; this was in 1787 when it was hoped that the master might appear in person at the Hanover Square Rooms, where his symphonies were already known. It was, however, not until 1791 that Haydn was able to visit England. The agent for his visit was Johann Peter Salomon (1745–1815), whose private enthusiasm for Haydn dated back to his office of *Konzertmeister* at Rheinsberg, where he had been in the service of Prince Henry of Prussia. Salomon arrived in London in 1781, after his Prussian master had served redundancy notices on his musicians, and made his name first as a violinist. Seceding from the Professional Concerts Salomon aligned himself with Gertrude Mara, the German soprano who ran concerts at the Pantheon[3] and elsewhere. Mara was distinguished as a Handel singer, a fact which commended her to Richard Edgcumbe, and caused him to wonder whether the Parisian *Concert Spirituel* was all it was reputed to be:

[1] 1766–1794: a Society of noblemen and wealthy amateurs dedicated to songs, catches, glees, etc. The Society collapsed when the Duchess of Devonshire took offence at the nature of the words of the songs presented to her at one concert.

[2] See *Remains . . . of the Chetham Society*, Manchester, 1867, LXXII, p. 84.

[3] The Pantheon, in Oxford Street, was built in 1770–1771 to a design by James Wyatt, to serve as a 'winter Ranelagh', with concerts, balls, and masquerades: '. . . in its original state the largest and most beautiful room in London, and a very model of fine architecture . . .', Edgcumbe, *Reminiscences*, 1773–1823, pp. 71–72. See also Burney in *An Account etc . . . .in Commemoration of Handel*, Dublin 1785, pp. 49–50.

During my stay in Paris (1785), one *Concert Spirituel* took place in the old theatre of the Tuilleries, at which for the first time I heard Madame Mara, just then returned from England, where she had performed at the Commemoration of Handel in Westminster Abbey. Amongst other things, she sung 'I know that my Redeemer liveth', which was announced in the bills as being, musique de Handel, paroles de Milton. The French had not the taste to like it . . .[1].

In 1786 Salomon undertook his own Subscription Concerts at Hanover Square, where he promoted the cause of both Haydn and Mozart. Thus it was that when Haydn arrived in London his music was by no means unfamiliar, and there was a solid body of support ready for him, including the Anacreontic Society and the subscribers to the Ladies' Concerts, as well as Dr Burney and his coterie. Salomon put Haydn under contract to compose six symphonies. He himself led the orchestra (of thirty-five to forty players), and the first of the concert series got off to a brilliant start on March 11, 1791.

Of his London visits Haydn left his own record[2] and those comments which are immediately pertinent are quoted therefrom. On January 1, 1792, Haydn took part in Mara's Benefit Concert—that lady just then rejoicing at having got rid of her tiresome husband—and the audience was entertained by a German soprano, partnered by an Austro-Hungarian accompanist, performing a 'very difficult English air'—Purcell's 'From rosy bowers'. During the performance of two of his symphonies Haydn conducted, as was his practice, from the keyboard. In respect of orchestral behaviour during performance Haydn noted this carefree episode: 'Just as the director of a grand concert was about to begin the first number, the kettle-drummer called loudly to him and said he should wait a moment, since his two kettle-drums were not yet tuned. The leader could and would not wait any longer, and said he should transpose in the meantime.'

On March 26, 1792, Haydn took part in Barthélemon's Benefit (in fact Sophia Corri's) and reported that 'an English

---

[1] *Reminiscences*, p. 45.
[2] See *The Collected Correspondence and London Notebooks of Joseph Haydn*, H. C. Robbins Landon, London, 1959.

147

clergyman was present who fell into the most profound melancholy on hearing the Andante [of Symphony No. 75 in D major second movement] because he had dreamt the previous night this piece was a premonition of his death. He left the company at once and took to his bed. Today, the 25th of April, I heard from Herr Barthélemon that this protestant clergyman had died.' The idea that a symphony should be listened to in unbroken silence has no warrant in the authentic tradition. Thus on February 17, 1792, when the Symphony No. 93 in D major was given, Haydn was surprised that 'only the Adagio of the new symphony was repeated', whereas on February 24 the first Allegro was encored as well as the Adagio. On March 2, 'the new Symphony in B flat [No. 98] was given, and the first and last Allegros encort [sic]'.

Haydn's first visit to England was enormously successful and a tremendous incentive to the new kind of concert based on the symphony. His character endeared him to players and public alike[1]. And even when, as in 1792, the Professional Concerts, piqued at Salomon's success, engaged Ignaz Pleyel as a counter-attraction, the move only enabled Haydn to renew a friendship with a former pupil. In 1794–1795 Haydn returned to England and wrote a further set of symphonies for Salomon. On one occasion during this visit he took an unkindly view of the slap-dash methods that sometimes prevailed. 'On 30th March, 1795', he wrote in his *3rd London Notebook*, 'I was invited by Dr [Samuel] Arnold and his associates to a grand concert in Free Maisons [sic] Hall: one of my big symphonies was to have been given under my direction, but since they wouldn't have any rehearsal, I refused to co-operate and did not appear.'

Of the old school Haydn came across Giardini, whose *Ruth* was once again performed at Ranelagh at that time, and who was the only musician in London to dislike Haydn. 'I don't want to see the German dog,' he said. Which was capped by Haydn's terse diary description: 'Giardini played like a pig.'

---

[1] 'The papers say he has been bowed to by whole orchestras when he has appeared at the play-house.' Rev Thomas Twining to Dr Charles Burney, February 15, 1791.

Among the younger musicians Haydn encountered Viotti[1], Yaniewicz[2], Clement[3], Bridgetower[4], Dragonetti[5], and George Smart, whose enthusiasm was instrumental on the one hand in carrying the Haydn cult behind the Handel cult in the British provinces, and in leading to the foundation of the Philharmonic Society on the other.

CLAGGET'S CONCERTS

The ardent music-lover who lived in London during the reign of George III had no reason to complain of lack of opportunity to hear music; indeed he might well have felt the danger of superabundance. In addition to the main entertainments as so far outlined there was a multiplicity of concerts put on more speculatively. Charles Clagget (1740–1795) was an Irish musician of fortune, who, after playing in theatre bands in Dublin and directing musical performances in Liverpool and Manchester, moved to London, where he became well-known as an inventor. He applied his inventive skill to all kinds of musical instruments—which formed an impressive museum collection in his home in Greek Street, Soho—and formulated concerts in which their merits might be demonstrated. Thus in May, 1790, he arranged a concert at Hanover Square as part of a series run by Antonio Kammell, in which 'Clagett's [sic] Patent French Horn' was featured. The more effectively to do this he commissioned the composition of an *ad hoc Divertimento*

[1] Giovanni Battista Viotti (1753–1824), violinist and composer, made London his headquarters after he had found it prudent to leave Paris (where he was associated with the *Concert Spirituel*) in 1792. A frequent performer in Salomon's concerts, Viotti was expelled from England in 1798 on account of his alleged revolutionary tendencies. In 1801 he returned.

[2] Felix Janiewicz (Yaniewicz) (1762–1848), Polish violinist and composer, had studied in Vienna, meeting Mozart and Haydn there, before settling in Britain, where he was prominent in London, Liverpool and Edinburgh, and other northern cities.

[3] Franz Clement (1780–1842). Austrian violinist, who appeared in London as a boy prodigy. He played in Oxford in the second concert given in honour of Haydn's honorary Doctorate.

[4] George Bridgetower (1779 or 80–1860), son of an African father and a European mother, and a virtuoso violinist well known in Paris (*Concert Spirituel* in 1789) and in Vienna, where in 1803 he played the 'Kreutzer' Sonata with Beethoven. In 1813 he played in the Philharmonic Society's orchestra.

[5] Domenico Dragonetti (1763–1846), the greatest double-bass player of his age.

à 4 instruments, two violins, bass and horn, which was published in the same year by T. Skillearn. Three years later Clagget (whose brother, Walter, played most instruments and belonged to the Covent Garden and Haymarket orchestras) gave another similar concert at the King's Arms, Cornhill. By this time he was able to show a letter from Haydn commending his improvements to harpsichord and pianoforte.

THE BROTHERS WESLEY

The infant prodigy was always a potential investment, and one appeared after another. Apart from Mozart the one who showed the most musical consistency in later life was Samuel Wesley, who made his first London appearance in a supporting role to 'two French lads who played extraordinarily well on the violoncello'[1]. The advertisement in the *Public Advertiser* of May 20, 1777, read as follows:

> For the benefit of Messrs Rauffe, Two youths, the eldest not fourteen years old. At Hickford's Great Room, Brewer Street, this day at twelve noon precisely, will be performed a grand concert of Vocal and Instrumental Music.
> Under the direction of Mr Bach. The vocal parts by Signora Balconi, and Signor Savoi. The instrumental by Messrs Cramer, Fischer, Master, and Miss Weichsel, with concertos on the violoncello by Messrs Rauffe.
> End of Act II a young gentleman [Samuel Wesley] will perform extempore on the organ[2].

Two years later young Wesley and his brother Charles went into the Subscription Concert business on their own account, using for this purpose the largest room in their home in Chesterfield Street, but not to the general approval of the Methodist friends of their father. None the less a list of patrons which included the Bishops of London and Durham, the Earls of

---

[1] *Autobiography,* quoted in *Samuel Wesley, Musician,* J. T. Lightwood, London, 1937, p. 44.

[2] Wesley was eleven years of age, Charles Weichsell twelve, and his sister Elizabeth nine. The latter pair were the children of Karl Weichsell, a German oboist at the Haymarket. Charles was a violinist (later a composer), Elizabeth a singer and pianist. She became a notable soprano and married James Billington, the double-bass player.

9. Concert-room in the Augarten, Vienna, c.1800.

10. The Singakademie, Berlin, c.1830.

11. Consecration of the Building of the *Gesellschaft der Musikfreunde*,
Vienna.

12. Concert by Liszt, Berlin, 1842.

Dartmouth and Mornington, General Oglethorpe, the philanthropist, and the Danish and Saxon Ambassadors, was a sufficient warrant to proceed, and when the Bishop of London wrote praising the nature of the concerts and promising some pupils for Charles, Samuel Wesley senior, after reference to higher authority, felt justified in stating: 'I am clear, without a doubt, that my sons' concert is after the will and order of Providence. It has established them as musicians, and in a safe and honourable way.'

The programmes of the Wesleys' concerts[1] were conservative, reflecting those given in Bristol where they had hitherto lived, and the mainstays were Arne, Battishill, Boyce, Corelli, Cramer, Geminiani, Giardini, and Handel. But the young Wesleys were prolific as composers in their own right, producing sinfonias, concerti, quartets, organ voluntaries, and experimental works for two organs, and for harpsichord and organ. These concerts ran for four years, and the accounts add a delightful footnote to the intimacies of concert promotion at the time.

Working with some twenty-seven subscribers (1783) and a seasonal capital of eighty-one guineas therefrom the young Wesleys were well able to launch out with the aid of their expense accounts. Thus Sally's gown ($£1$ 1s 0d), Sally's shifts ($£1$ 1s 0d), Sally's gloves, Sally's powder (1s 0d) and Sally's hair-do (1s 0d and 1s 6d) were charged up; as were Sam's shirts ($£1$ 11s 6d) and Sam's watch (5s 6d). Sally's maid got two shillings for her duties in the concert-room, and on January 21, 1782, the miscellany of costs incorporated: tea (12s 6d), tea-pot (8d), lemons (1s 6d), sugar (3s 2d), cream (8d), cakes (6s 6d), wine (3s 10d), mats (3s 6d). Getting nearer to the business in hand there was a lamplighter to be paid 3s 6d, a constable 1s 0d, a porter 3s 0d, and candles were an expensive item at 14s 6d.

Samuel Wesley, when not at the harpsichord, led his orchestra, having a companion named Huxstable as his partner (10s 6d). The second violins were Higgins and McIntosh (10s 6d each); Archer was the viola player, also at 10s 6d, and there were two horns who having fewer notes to play received five

---

[1] Together with the accounts preserved in Brit. Mus. Add. MS. 35017.

shillings each[1]. Charles Wesley played the organ and harpsichord. When there were singers their fee was 2s 6d. In the last series of concerts, in 1783, there was a profit of £50 14s 6d, which went down into the books as 'Housekeeping'—a welcome item thus to be noted so far as the impecunious elder Samuel was concerned.

THE ANTIENT CONCERTS

The Wesley concerts—and Samuel junior was later to distinguish himself as the first English Bach scholar—looked backwards, but also in view of the characters of their own compositions, sideways. The conservative strain in English musical appreciation, however, was now being deepened under the influence of provincial oratorio festivals and by the Concerts of Antient Music.

This institution, stemming once again from the *Concert Spirituel*, was inaugurated by a committee of Lords temporal and spiritual in 1776, and since—for moral as well as musical reasons—most were confirmed Handelians the programmes given to Joah Bates (1776–1793) and to Thomas Greatorex (1793–1831) were dominated by that master's works. At the same time a wide range of other music, not less than twenty years old, was investigated, and the claims of Purcell, Morley and other madrigalists, some of the Italian masters of polyphony, and the greater Germans of the seventeenth and eighteenth centuries, were considered. To this extent the Antient Concerts played their part in promoting a knowledge of a wide range of music of the past. The performances were given in a room in Tottenham Street, to which King George III regularly took his family, until 1795. After nine years in the concert-room of the Opera House the Concerts were, in 1804, transferred to the Hanover Square Rooms. The Committee was

[1] Cf. the fees of players in London as quoted by Leopold Mozart, June 8, 1764: 'The first violin gets three guineas and so on; and all who play solos and concertos three, four and five guineas. The ordinary players receive each half a guinea and so forth. But, fortunately for me, all the musicians as well as the hall and everything also cost me only twenty guineas, because most of the performers would not accept anything.' The idea that professional musicians should be the only ones in the community to 'give their services' was tending to gain general currency, and was in a few years to cause controversy in the Philharmonic Society.

aristocratic and its members exerted the authority allowed to them by the accident of birth by taking it in turn to choose the programmes. In the end the underlying presumptions of the organisation destroyed it. In this destruction is symbolised the beginning of the long-deferred end of aristocratic privilege in British society.

> The principle upon which the royal and noble founders of this institution acted was to give no music by living composers. This ultra-conservative idea was intended to check the waywardness of modern ideas ... The subscribers had to wait for over thirty years after the death of Mozart before his name appeared in the programmes. The only exception made was in the case of Beethoven, for a piece of music by him was heard by the society in 1835, eight years after his death ... The last director was the Duke of Wellington (son of Lord Mornington), in 1848, the year in which the Society came to an end. It was killed by the too rigid pursuance of the principles which called it into being. It had grown too exclusive for a world in which all things are progressive. When the tide is at flood, things that were apparently stationary and solid are either swamped or swept away. Those who move not with the caravan are left to perish in the desert[1].

PROVINCIAL CONCERTS AND THE WEIGHT OF THE HANDEL TRADITION

In the provincial centres of Britain the main weight of opinion was firmly laid on the reputation of Handel, to whose general popularity the extraordinarily diversified list of subscribers to Randall's edition of 1760 bears testimony. In this enthusiasm the aristocracy agreed with the middle classes, and they, by the end of the century, with those of the workers whose religious connections had brought them into the environs of great music through occasional choral opportunity. By the early years of the nineteenth century the working-class choralists of the industrial north formed a decisive factor in regulating British taste along the line of piety long since drawn out of the Handelian canon by those with a vested interest in piety[2].

---

[1] *A Short History of Cheap Music*, London, 1887, p. 24.

[2] See Percy M. Young, *Die Händel-Pflege in den englischen Provinzen*, *Händel-Jahrbuch*, 1960, pp. 31–49.

Throughout this period there was also the Three Choirs Festival to emphasise the respectabilities—which were somewhat relieved by the 'miscellaneous concerts' interpolated between oratorios which were in due course to expand symphonically and secularly.

Since the eighteenth century saw the first major development of hospital building in Britain it was inevitable that oratorio should bear a principal part of the costs, and just as in Dublin and Newcastle so in Sheffield, Leeds, Liverpool, Birmingham, and many other towns oratorios or miscellaneous programmes of choice extracts were given in assembly rooms, churches, and theatres until such time as great auditoria primarily consecrated to this purpose should arise. In Sheffield, on August 15, 1795, one such programme given in St. James's Church was defined as a 'concerto spirituall'. Thus the spirit of Versailles was conveyed to Yorkshire.

FIN DE SIÈCLE

On the side the more progressive elements in provincial society emulated the Subscription Concerts of London. Thus in Leeds in 1763–1764 a series of twelve took place in the Assembly Rooms in Kirkgate, from October until April[1]. In Liverpool a Music Hall, seating 1300, was erected in Bold Street in 1786 and the annual series of twelve concerts was initially underwritten by three hundred subscribers, each donating two guineas[2]. In Manchester the Gentlemen's Concerts modulated from a tavern in the market place to a new and specially designed concert-room in Fountain Street, which, after taking two years to build, was opened in 1777. This room measured 81 by 30 feet and was said to have seated a regular audience of nine hundred, which on special occasions grew to twelve hundred. Amateurs and professionals happily continued to meet together and the main concerts were relieved by 'private' concerts, the informality of the latter eventually being stressed by a concession in the matter of dress. In the course of time decorum slackened and in 1803 the managers were obliged to request gentlemen not to

[1] See Thoresby Society Publications, xxviii, Leeds.
[2] *Liverpool Bulletin*, Vol. 7, 1959, p. 8.

attend in boots, to remove their hats, and to refrain from talking during the performances. The managers were disturbed when the latter request provoked some rude replies. Manners, it is reflected, were not what they were formerly[1]. In these concerts the programmes were similar to those of the Antient Concerts in London.

In smaller towns there were many musical clubs similar to that at Yarmouth visited by Charles Dibdin in 1788. But his *Musical Tour* (1787–88) hardly gives an encouraging general impression. In Ireland the great days were past, so that in Limerick in 1796 when a concert was given in the theatre at which the principals were Andrew Ashe[2] the Irish flautist, and Janiewicz, there was an audience of four: one gentleman in the pit, and, above, Lord Barrymore and his brother, and Richard Bellamy, a vicar-choral of St. Paul's Cathedral doing an Irish tour. For the rest the decline in musical standards in the Irish capital is rudely deplored in the anonymous *Concert Strictures revived*[3]:

> But cease thou haughty model of a city to boast of thy feeble attempts at musical entertainments—what though a Billington sings—and a *Castrato* presides at thy concerts—To the land of the Harp does the boasting belong—for *she* too has concerts—and there too—not disgraced by having enrolled among their directors a *mutilated Italian*—No—she exhibits to a *Knight*—a *Gentleman* and one *well-known* to the *Ladies* as something more than the mere *semblance* of a *man*.

Sir John Stevenson brought the Irish concert tradition to a sorry end, in arrangements of folksongs contorted by Tom Moore for suburban drawing-rooms, and in emasculated glees. The masters of Ireland, the significance of Dublin reduced by the Act of Union of 1800, approved such anaesthetisation of the native spirit in music, for Stevenson was:

[1] See Programmes of Gentleman's Concerts, 1799–1897, Manchester Central Reference Library; and *Remains of the Chetham Society*, LXXII, pp. 77–91. ('The Earlier Days of the "Gentlemen's Concerts".')

[2] 1759–1838: sometime flautist in the opera house in Brussels, at the Salomon concerts in London in 1791–2, where he played a concerto of his own. In 1816 Ashe succeeded Venanzio Rauzzini (1747–1810) in the direction of concerts in Bath. Ashe had married Rauzzini's daughter.

[3] Published, C. Lewis, 1805.

> By the College presented with Doctor's Degree,
> By the State dubb'd a Knight—for *composing a glee.*

Field, Balfe, and Wallace, inheritors of an earlier and more vigorous tradition, had to seek other fields than those of their native Erin in which to dispose their talents.

In Scotland, too, the tradition dimmed. The Aberdeen Concerts came to an end in 1800, and in Edinburgh the St. Cecilia's Hall, its primary purpose exhausted, passed to the Baptists in 1802, and to the Freemasons seven years later. In all these cases the cause of the collapse was the lack of performing ability on the part of the gentlemen members.

Professional Organisation

THE GEWANDHAUS CONCERTS

*B*Y THE END of the eighteenth century the shift of emphasis within the field of music was complete—even though vestigial influences from the past remained. The main impulses—despite the English and German oratorio cults—were secular, finding outlet in the opera-house and the concert-room; the noble patron, even though taking an unconscionable time entirely to quit the scene, had for the most part given way to collective sponsors—sometimes aristocratic, sometimes bourgeois, often both; the ranges of sonority attainable through the now comprehensive orchestra suited general aspirations in aesthetic philosophy and, insofar as nationalism became a positive issue, politics; finally, the amateur musician was now entirely outpaced by the professional. As in other departments of society, therefore, organisation became increasingly important, and in the nineteenth century the first, consistent, large-scale, organisation of musical activity took place.

Progress in this direction had taken place previously, but only spasmodically. Nevertheless, the major developments of the nineteenth century were the consequence of what had gone before; and nowhere was this more clearly shown than in Leipzig, where the *Grosses Konzert* had been established in 1743. This organisation grew into the most significant of its kind. Under the professional leadership of Mendelssohn it brought into being the first great concert orchestra and Mendelssohn himself may be regarded as the first virtuoso conductor. What was more significant was the acceptance of the idea of public responsibility for the Gewandhaus concerts.

The founder of the modern tradition in Leipzig was Johann Adam Hiller (1728–1804), whose early education was in Dresden. Having been a pupil in the Kreuzschule he looked for further opportunity for experience and found it in the Gymnasium in which Rector Baumeister had founded a new-style Collegium Musicum. The Rector's intention was to improve the musicianship of his pupils and he held two meetings weekly, in a class-room. Sensing a possible deficiency in this school ensemble, or Collegium Musicum, Hiller bought a second-hand double-bass for eighteen groschen, and thus obtained entry. After studentship in the University of Leipzig Hiller took a tutorial appointment, in 1754, to Heinrich Adolph Brühl von Martinskirche. He was the younger brother of Count Hans Moritz von Brühl, the Saxon representative at the English Court, who subscribed to the concerts of Charles and Samuel Wesley (see page 151). In 1758 Hiller's duties took him to Leipzig and here he set about repairing the ravages inflicted on cultural life by the Seven Years' War. Helped by the local players and the youthful Corona Schröter[1], or Elisabeth Schmeling, Hiller revived the meetings of the *Grosses Konzert* by copious doses of Hasse, whose music Hiller came to know in Dresden, and Handel.

In 1763 the concerts were re-named *Liebhaber-Concerte* and Hiller was accepted as their director. The meetings took place in the *Drei Schwanen*; in the course of a year there were twenty-four concerts, for which the subscription was nineteen thalers; and the orchestra comprised eight first and eight second violins, three violas, two 'cellos, two double-basses, two each of flutes, oboes, bassoons, and horns, with lute and harpsichord[2]. Hiller himself was a singer and his equal enthusiasm for vocal as for instrumental music led him to reorganise the choral activities of Leipzig, to which end he anticipated his Berlin

[1] 1751–1802: she was actress and composer as well as singer. In the latter capacity she appeared in London between 1772 and 1776. Invited to Weimar by Goethe, she became known for her settings of his lyrics, among which was one of *Der Erlkönig*.

[2] J. Waldorff, *Geheimnisse der Polyhymnie*, Berlin, 1963, p. 206. On the necessity for retaining the original equality of first and second violins for modern performance of music of this period the reader is referred to the excellent article 'Authenticity?' by R. C. Saxby, *Musical Times*, November, 1963, p. 791.

colleagues by founding a school for singing in 1771. Combining his forces he undertook large-scale oratorio performances, of Handel, Graun, and Hasse. It was thus that the problem of a suitable auditorium became urgent. As an institution the *Grosses Konzert* officially ended in 1778, and for the next few years Hiller carried on his concert-giving activities as best he could. But in 1780 the municipality intervened with a proposal to design a new concert-room in the Gewandhaus, a building otherwise used by the cloth-merchants for the transaction of their business. The architect of the new room was Dauthe, and the wall-paintings were by Oeser. When it was ready—the first programme containing works by Christian Bach and Reichardt was given on November 25, 1781, Hiller was delighted:

[Previously] the concerts in Leipzig—as well as being otherwise susceptible of improvement—lacked a spacious and well-appointed auditorium. Councillor [Wilhelm] Müller, of the War Department, the Lord Mayor, who was unequalled in his zest for extending and beautifying [the city] initiated the scheme for building a new concert-room in the Gewandhaus. After Michaelmas, 1781, this was ready and at once taken over. My already existing institute was now in the hands of twelve directors responsible for the musical arrangements and policy, and I received 400 thalers annually. This concert-giving body—its concerts were public— established its activities in the new room. During the first winter the chief singers were the two Podleska sisters[1] from Bohemia. Then they were given an engagement by the musical establishment of the Duke of Kurland at Mietau where I accompanied them in the summer of 1782[2].

In the third concert of the first season of Gewandhaus concerts Anton Stamitz appeared as concert-director, and a symphony of Haydn was included for the first time. The organisation of the concerts was effectively in Hiller's hands, even though he was technically responsible to Müller and the

[1] Pupils of Hiller. Two other sisters of this family also came to Leipzig to sing, and in 1832 all four defrayed the cost of a memorial to Hiller near to the Thomaskirche, of which he became Cantor in 1789.

[2] *Johann Adam Hiller*, No. 1 of *Lebensläufe deutscher Musiker von ihrem selbst erzählt*, ed. Alfred Einstein, Leipzig [1915], pp. 28–29. Hiller's autobiography had first been published as an appendix to *Lebensbeschreibungen berühmter Musikgelehrten und Tonkünstler neuerer Zeit*, Leipzig, 1784. This was a collection of such autobiographical pieces as had been published periodically in Germany since Mattheson's *Ehrenpforte*.

committee of twelve. While he remained as leader the composers whose works were most often chosen were Christian and Emanuel Bach, Dittersdorf, Josef and Michael Haydn, Carl and Anton Stamitz, Gluck, Graun, Galuppi, Hasse, Sacchini, Traetta, Abel, Boccherini, Cimarosa, Jommelli, Pergolesi, Piccinni, Salieri, Grétry, and Hiller himself. On July 24, 1782, a symphony of Mozart was played in the Gewandhaus. This was the first opportunity the Leipzigers had of hearing a work by him[1].

Hiller was a vigorous influence in the musical life of Leipzig, a modernist in many ways but with a concern for the broader issues of appreciation and education. He was a populariser and his efforts to place choral music equal in esteem with orchestral led him to make strange editions of classical choral works which frequently paid scant respect to the original. At the same time he did leave the Leipzigers (as well as citizens of other cities) with the firm idea that Handel was a great German composer; in so doing he furnished the inspiration for the significant Handel revivals of the nineteenth and twentieth centuries in Germany. Hiller produced *Messiah* in Berlin Cathedral in 1786, and in the University Church in Leipzig in the two years following, on which performances, in accordance with the then German doctrine of justification by words, he wrote a *Nachricht von der Aufführung des Händelschen 'Messias' in der Domkirche zu Berlin* and *Drey kurtzen Aufsätzen, bey Gelegenheit des zu Leipzig aufgeführten Händelschen 'Messias'*! Hiller's other writings on Handel and other of the 'older' composers were invaluable foundations of later criticism, musicology, and practice.

In the latter respect Hiller took less account of 'authenticity' than of the traditions particularly derived from the august institution of the Thomanenchor. This body, founded in the thirteenth century, has at all times been a source of pride to Leipzig and since its close connection with the secular music of the city as early as the year 1519 there has always been assured a reciprocity between choral and instrumental music. This

---

[1] Mozart gave an 'Academy' in the Gewandhaus on May 12, 1789, the programme including two symphonies, one piano concerto, and arias sung by Josefa Dušek (1754–1824), a Bohemian soprano, and wife of Frantisek Dušek: see Paumgartner, *op. cit.*, p. 410.

reached its peak of accomplishment in the time of Sebastian Bach. But the Thomanenchor was subsequently firmly associated with the *Grosses Konzert*; with the *Liebhaberkonzerte* (Hiller was allowed eighty thallers for twelve choristers, within the grant shown on p. 159); and then with the Gewandhaus concerts. The fact that Hiller having moved from the one body to the other ensured that the connection between the two was strengthened, and—despite the formation of a Sing-Akademie, after the Berlin model, under Johann Philipp Schulz, conductor of the Gewandhaus from 1810 to 1827—the Thomanenchor took an important part in oratorio performances to the time of Mendelssohn and beyond.

When Hiller transferred to the Thomaskirche in 1789 his Gewandhaus duties were taken over by Johann Gottfried Schicht (1753–1823), who had frequently appeared as solo harpsichordist (pianist) under Hiller, and he maintained Hiller's catholic policy. Thus while he resuscitated the motets of Bach (of which he published an edition in 1802–1803) he also nurtured the triple cause of Mozart, Haydn, and Beethoven, whose symphonies and concertos were soon accepted as the basis of a concert programme. Schicht succeeded Hiller at the Thomaskirche in 1810, and during the next seventeen years, under Schulz, the programmes showed a commendably wide range, adding Spohr, Spontini (Generalmusikdirektor in Berlin from 1820), Cherubini, Boieldieu, Rossini, and the London-based Muzio Clementi to the already existing list of the 'classics', and introducing Weber, as composer and pianist, to the Leipzig audience. After Schulz came Pohlenz, to whose credit was the performance of Wagner's C Major Symphony in 1833 and Mendelssohn's 'Hebrides' Overture one year later. It was under Pohlenz that, on November 24, 1831, the jubilee of the foundation of the Gewandhaus Concerts was celebrated.

Christian August Pohlenz (1790–1843), admirable as a singing-teacher and as a general musician, was not adept at organising orchestral performance. Indeed the on-the-spot direction was entrusted to Mattäi, the leader, and Pohlenz would only intervene when choral music was produced; he would, for instance, take over for the last movement of the Ninth Symphony of Beethoven with chaotic consequences[1].

[1] Richard Wagner, *My Life*, London 1911, I, p. 69–70.

In an age when the standard of orchestral virtuosity was rapidly rising against the challenge of the 'new music', when critics, especially in Germany, were becoming more sensitive to details, and when there seemed a need to counter the attractions of lighter music and to wean the teen-agers from the even then persistent and adult-annoying guitar[1], the conservative Pohlenz was hardly ideal. In 1835, therefore, negotiations took place to translate him full-time to more congenial fields of endeavour. In his stead came Mendelssohn.

Mendelssohn looked on his appointment to the Gewandhaus as his great opportunity.

> Its advantages were similar to those of Düsseldorf, the place not being a government appointment subordinate to any official authority, but a free association, formed for the purpose of promoting good music, and desirous of engaging a director able to use the best means towards the realisation of that purpose. Leipzig, too, was a middle-sized German town, and the life there suited Felix very well . . . The Gewandhaus concerts had existed for fifty-six years, and were thus a long-consolidated establishment. Such union may produce remarkable results, far superior to anything at Düsseldorf, where many things of musical importance were still in their very first period of development. Regular businesslike rules and forms were in existence, each had his own sharply defined department, conflicts about competency could not occur; and Felix, to whom the vague, wavering state of affairs in Düsseldorf had been a real infliction, felt most agreeably impressed with the difference in that respect which he met with at Leipzig[2].

Mendelssohn was the new broom but he had considerable tact. He maintained a happy relationship with his predecessor (whom he appointed as professor in the Hochschule für Musik on its foundation in 1843), even though Pohlenz sighed for the more leisurely days of the past[3]. He contained the leader within his proper field of playing and directed the concerts, more or less in modern manner, from a conductor's desk, and, through the *Leipziger Allgemeine Musikalische Zeitung* and Schumann's *Neue Zeitschrift*, persuaded the public that this was a good thing. Having established his authority as a conductor, however, Mendelssohn exercised it fairly loosely. Thus after setting

[1] H. C. Worbs, *Felix Mendelssohn Bartholdy*, Leipzig, 1958, p. 242.
[2] Sebastian Hensel, *The Mendelssohn Family*, London 1881, I, p. 333.
[3] Wagner, *op. cit.*, p. 124.

the tempo of a movement he would give up using the baton and in moments of excitement would applaud the music. By his skill and enthusiasm he removed his players, whose skills he was always ready to acknowledge, from their former lethargy, and induced them to play allegro movements at a reasonable speed[1]. He paid more attention to the details of a score than was previously done, and his sister Fanny observed as follows of a performance of the Ninth Symphony at Düsseldorf in 1836: 'This gigantic Ninth Symphony, which is so grand, and in parts so abominable, as only the work of the greatest of men could be, was played as if by one man; the finest *nuances*, the most hidden meanings, were exposed to perfection; the masses fell into shape, the symphony became comprehensible, and then it was really exquisitely beautiful . . .[2].' Mendelssohn, one of the most personable young men ever to stand on a rostrum, and well blessed with a talent for public relations, established the real authority of the orchestral conductor, whose pre-eminence dates from October 4, 1835, when Mendelssohn undertook his first concert with the Gewandhaus. The programme was: *Calm Sea and Prosperous Voyage*, Mendelssohn; the scena by Weber for Cherubini's *Lodoïska*, Spohr's Eleventh Violin Concerto, and for the second part, Beethoven's Fourth Symphony.

Thus, having set a pattern for 'symphony concerts' which has been more or less maintained to the present day, Mendelssohn endeavoured to take into account the broad taste of his audiences as well as his own inclinations. Oratorios continued in full spate, and Mendelssohn as composer added to their number. Chamber music and piano recitals were interspersed among the larger events. And while Mendelssohn furthered the claims of Schubert and Schumann, and a host of young composers from other lands who flocked to Leipzig during his reign, he did not disdain to entertain his patrons with fantasias on themes from popular operas—by Rossini, Auber, or Meyerbeer. In 1840–1841 he paid tribute to the past in four 'Historical Concerts', devoted respectively to Bach and Handel, Haydn, Mozart, and Beethoven. Four years later, under pressure from the Prussian court, Mendelssohn handed over the Gewandhaus

[1] Letter to his family, of November 6, 1835.
[2] Hensel, *op. cit.*, II, p. 8.

appointment to Niels Gade, a Danish protégé[1], and went to Berlin as Kapellmeister. In a decade he had brought the Subscription Concert into the nineteenth century, had made the Gewandhaus the cultural centre not only of Leipzig but also of Europe, and had shown that the best music was no more to be considered as a province reserved for princes and the nobility. But this had long been inherent in the musical life of Leipzig[2].

DECLINING STANDARDS IN ENGLAND

On the personal level, through the family connections of the House of Hanover, through the continuing absorption of German musicians into every branch of British musical life, and through an implicit pride in economic prosperity and the collective ability to employ and to enjoy the best in European musical culture, English and German musical organisations maintained a certain reciprocity. So that Mendelssohn, who moved from one country to the other with some regularity, may be seen as a kind of Englishman extraordinary. A large number of Mendelssohn's works bear English dedications, and among those on a larger scale the first (or thirteenth) symphony in C minor was composed in 1824, at the invitation of the Philharmonic Society of London, and *Elijah*, more than twenty years later, came at the behest of the Birmingham Festival. By this time, 1846, the British pattern had settled down: orchestral music was mostly in London, elsewhere there was a diet, to become progressively more dull, of oratorio. In so far as European music was concerned, however, the foundation of the Philharmonic Society[3] was as significant a step as the modernisation of the Gewandhaus.

While the Salomon Concerts were maintained at their first excellence London was able to enjoy at least reasonably high

[1] Gade (1817–1890) became in 1850 conductor of the Musikforeningen (Music Society), founded in Copenhagen in 1836. He reformed the orchestra and brought into the Danish repertoire many works, familiar in Leipzig, which had not hitherto been heard in Denmark.

[2] Mendelssohn's work in Leipzig is admirably displayed in Worbs's book; see 'Der Gewandhaus Dirigent', pp. 134–180.

[3] There was a previous Philharmonic Society in London; an amateur orchestra, sometime led by Michael Festing, which met at the Crown and Anchor, and supplied the players for Handel's *Esther* at the Academy of Music performance in 1732.

standards. But the pressure of free-lance work on the one hand and the dilution of orchestras on the other militated against any kind of continuity or progress. It has already been seen that Haydn on one occasion took exception to casual arrangements that were, in fact, and long remained, general. Moreover the public was fickle. Referring to the Subscription Concerts inaugurated by Abel and Bach, Slingsby's *Musical Biography* remarked, 'After having for many years conducted these concerts with credit and reputation, the public at length grew tired of them, and the proprietors were compelled to withdraw themselves, with the loss of a great sum of money[1].' Samuel Wesley indicates the kind of behaviour that added other hazards to direction. 'The performers on wind instruments,' he wrote,

> are subjected to several unexpected causes of failure. I remember the Anecdote of an envious musician, a Hautboy player, who being jealous of a brother performer on the same instrument placed himself directly in front of him at a public concert when he was just about to execute a concerto; at the commencement of which he slyly drew a lemon from his pocket, and then cut it in half with his penknife: of which the immediate consequence was that a juicy sympathy excited in the mouth of his rival (who had unluckily witnessed the operation) so filled up and choked the reed in the hautboy, that he became utterly incapable of articulating a single passage in the piece[2].

Orchestral players were given to comedy when there was opportunity. Robert Lindley (1776–1835), the great 'cellist, once insisted on protection by umbrella against the leaks in the roof of St. Andrew's Hall, Norwich, while he played a concerto. Discipline in the free society clearly left something to be desired, in contrast with the sterner precepts to which the court bands on the Continent were accustomed, or, indeed, in the military music in England, which had taken a more orderly place in affairs since Frederick, Duke of York, returned from his military education in Germany in 1787 and brought back a

[1] II, p. 343.
[2] Wesley's lectures, British Museum Add. MS. 35015, Lecture No. 4 f. 62v, 63r–v.

complete band for the enhancement of English loyalty through Teutonic strains[1].

If orchestral playing was in many ways casual there was also a somewhat easy attitude towards composers' intentions. Thus,

> ... certain invaluable works originally constructed for a full Band have been very ingeniously contracted for the convenient Accomodation of small musical Parties; — and among them let me instance twelve delectable Symphonies of Haydn which have been reduced from the score with extraordinary ingenuity and accurate judgement, by the late accomplished and energetic Master of his Art, John Peter Salomon, and nicely adapted for two violins, tenor, bass, flute, and a supporting accompaniment on the piano forte[2].

For amateurs such reduction was welcome; but when it bred an indifference to the new tonal values the arrangement was baneful.

FOUNDATION OF THE PHILHARMONIC SOCIETY

Dissatisfaction with the existing state of affairs at the beginning of the nineteenth century was felt by a number of leading professionals, among them Salomon, who towards the end of his life was planning an Academy of Music in conjunction with William Ayrton (1777–1858), one of the first regular professional writers on music in England. This concept coincided with the one floated by J. B. Cramer, Philip Corri, son of Domenico and brother-in-law of Jan Ladislav Dušek (1766–1812)[3] and

---

[1] Frederick engaged flutes, trumpets, trombones, and serpent, which he added to the normal English military ensemble of twenty hautbois two clarinets, two horns, and four bassoons. For more or less exotic purposes three negroes were employed to cope with tambourines and Turkish bells (see W. T. Parke, *Memoirs*, II, pp. 239–40). See also H. G. Farmer, *The Royal Artillery Concerts* (1810–1911), for an interesting development of orchestral from wind-band music, and for programmes of the symphony concerts instituted by the Royal Artillery, at Woolwich, at the beginning of the nineteenth century.

[2] Wesley, *ibid.*, f. 225v.

[3] Bohemian composer, sometime a pupil of C. P. E. Bach, in Hamburg, and known as a symphonist in most of the European capitals. Dušek fled from Paris at the time of the Revolution and took refuge in England. Having failed in a music-business enterprise undertaken with Domenico Corri he escaped his creditors by going once again to Hamburg where he managed to engage the interest of Prince Louis Ferdinand, whose tutor he became.

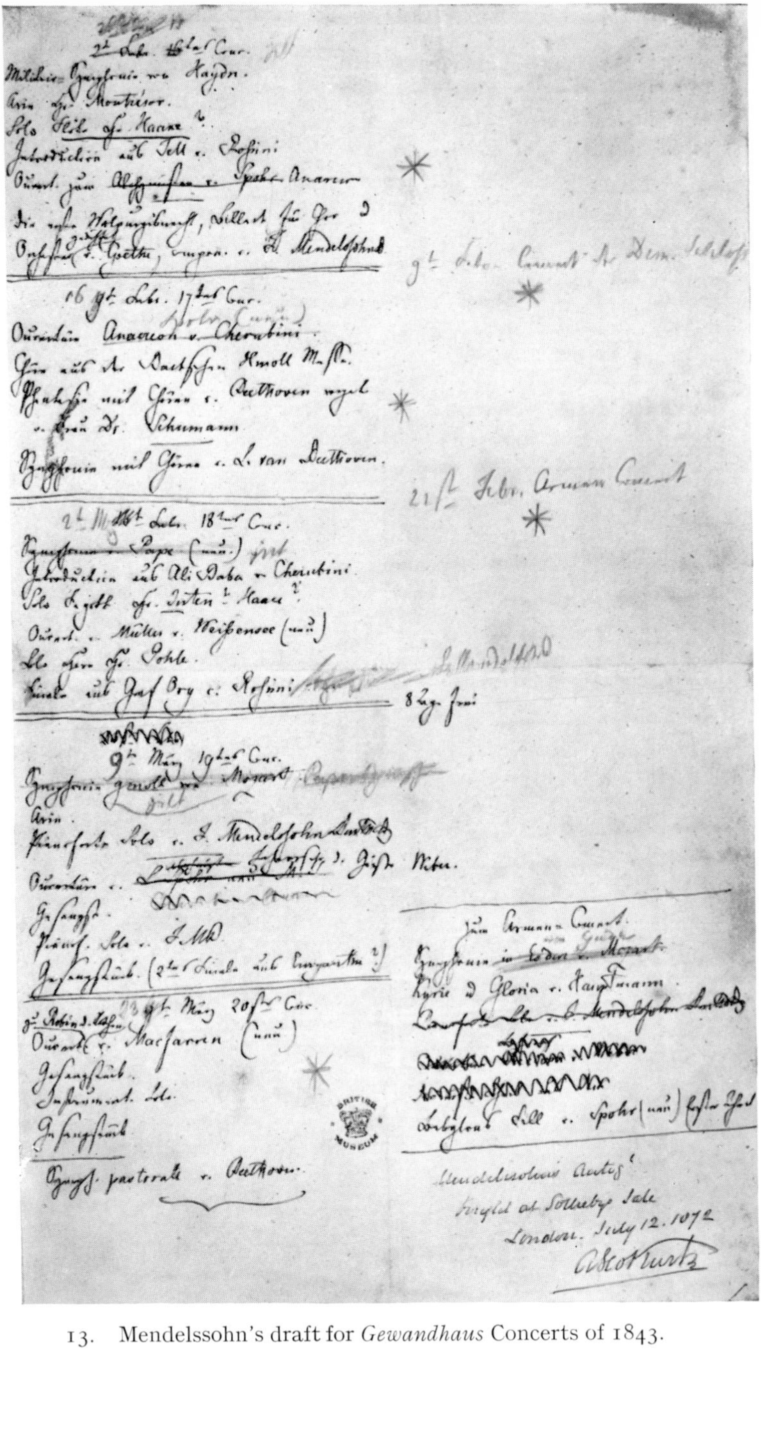

13. Mendelssohn's draft for *Gewandhaus* Concerts of 1843.

14. Berlioz as conductor, 1847; caricature by J. I. Grandville.

15. String Quartet at the Musical Union.

William Dance, grandson of Sir George Dance, the architect, and a leading London violinist. This trinity issued a circular inviting those interested in the furthering of the interests of instrumental music to meet at Dance's house on January 17, 1893. The scheme was launched, it was stated, with the intention of 'restoring to the world those compositions which have excited so much delight, and rekindle in the public mind that taste for excellence in instrumental music which has so long remained in a latent state'. The aims included performance of instrumental music 'in the most perfect manner possible', and the inclusion of vocal music only when the proper orchestral accompaniments should be provided[1]. Thus the promoters looked at the decline that had taken place since Haydn was in England, and there were, as Samuel Wesley testifies, sidelong glances at the growing fossilisation of the programmes of the Antient Concerts. Within two months a new series of Philharmonic Society subscription concerts, eight in number, was launched at the Argyll Rooms in Regent Street. Salomon led the orchestra, and Muzio Clementi played the piano, the operations being thus directed by a dual system of control that lasted until Spohr, who especially admired the Philharmonic string playing, arrived in England in 1820 to demonstrate the advantages of a single conductor, unhampered by direct instrumental responsibility[2]. The members of the new Society worked on a co-operative basis, each paying a subscription of three guineas annually (associates two guineas)—and none deriving any profit. This arrangement in a few years led to a good deal of acrimony, and to a further stage in the proper emancipation of music as a profession.

---

[1] There was, however, another factor, which illustrates the then relative balance between the two main departments in English music: '. . . . Vocal music forms a part of the concerts, not as belonging to the objects of the institution, but as being necessary to make them attractive to a public audience . . .' George Hogarth, *Musical History, Biography and Criticism*, London, 1838, II, p. 268.

[2] 'I took my place, with the score before me, at a desk specially set up in front of the orchestra, drew my baton from my pocket and gave the signal to begin. Shocked at such an innovation, some of the directors wished to protest. However, when I asked them at least to give it a try, they consented.' See *The Musical Journeyings of Louis Spohr*, trs. Henry Pleasants, Oklahoma, 1961, pp. 204-6.

The founder members of the Society were Cramer, Corri, Dance, Clementi, Ayrton, William Shield (1768–1829), a northerner and a former pupil of Charles Avison, J. J. Graeff, Henry Bishop, Benjamin Blake, the pioneer viola player[1], Salomon, Charles Neate, who met Beethoven and studied with Winter in Vienna, R. H. Potter, George Smart, F. Cramer, Thomas Attwood, who had had lessons from Mozart at the instance of the Prince Regent, Giovanni Battista Viotti, the currently famous violin virtuoso, Frederick Hill, the flautist, and member of a famous family of instrument-makers, Moralt, viola player and related to a Munich family of musicians, George Griffin, who composed a piano concerto in 1797 into which he introduced 'The Blue Bells of Scotland', James Bartlemon and Charles Knyvett, singers and promoters of the Vocal Concerts initiated in 1791 in conjunction with Samuel Harrison, Louis (Ludwig) Berger, a Berliner, pupil of Clementi and master of Mendelssohn, Charles Ashley, a 'cellist, a founder of the Glee Club in 1793, and for twenty years in such financial embarrassment that he lived under the control of the King's Bench Prison, Benjamin Cooke's son, Robert, who drowned himself in the Thames a year after the foundation of the Philharmonic Society, Yaniewicz, the younger Samuel Webbe, Vincent Novello, William Horsley, W. Sherington, and Andrew Ashe, already mentioned on page 155.

The associates included Samuel Wesley, Cipriani Potter, to become the second Principal of the Royal Academy of Music in 1832, as well as Bridgetower and other well-known instrumentalists. The first Secretary of the Society was Ayrton, who was succeeded by Dance in 1815. Clementi, R. H. Potter and Thomas Attwood each served for a year in this office, and in 1821 Dance again took over, to remain as Secretary for eleven years, during which time he had to steer the Society across a crisis of some magnitude.

The Philharmonic Society—like the London Symphony Orchestra almost a century later—was at its inception the result of professional competence on all levels, artistic, administrative, and financial. It avoided entanglement with dilettante

[1] Blake was a member of George III's band and also of that of the Prince Regent (George IV), whose private music was the most creditable side of his otherwise disorderly career. He inherited his father's musical interest after the most agreeable German manner (see Adam Carse, in *M. & L.*, xxvii, 1946, pp. 147 *et seq.*)

advisers and governors, and, taking its stand on Mozart, Haydn, and Beethoven, propagated the cause of 'modern music' with an eagerness hardly ever paralleled in England. In 1814 the Society gave the first English performance of the *Eroica* symphony.

BEETHOVEN AND THE PHILHARMONIC SOCIETY

Beethoven's name dominated the scene until his death. In 1815 Charles Neate visited him in Vienna and offered £75 for an exclusive interest in three overtures to be specially written for the Society. Beethoven sent the score of an already existing work, to the chagrin of his prospective patrons. Overlooking his temperamental disabilities and their own disappointment the Society gave first English performances of the Fifth and Seventh Symphonies, and of the *Fidelio* overture, in 1816 and 1817, and in the next year commissioned two symphonies and also invited the composer to visit London, on advantageous terms. The matter lapsed for a time, but in 1822, after Ferdinand Ries had acted as intermediary, £50 was offered for the exclusive rights of performance in the forthcoming Choral Symphony[1], which, after being given in Vienna, received its English première under Smart on March 21, 1825. On this occasion Smart, batonless, was at the pianoforte, and the text was given in an Italian translation. Two years later, after the Society had again raised the matter of an English visit by Beethoven, the committee sent a donation of £100 towards the now dying master, 'to be applied to his comforts and necessities during his illness'. The Viennese dilettanti took a poor view of charity thus being dispensed from London.

In the early days of the Society, Cherubini, Spohr, Moscheles, and Liszt appeared as composers and executants, and in 1829 Mendelssohn appeared for the first time, to conduct his Symphony in C Minor. For this performance Mendelssohn replaced his original Minuet and Trio with an orchestral version of the Scherzo from the *Octet* (Op. 20). In that year the Argyll Rooms

---

[1] On the presentation copy (now on loan in the British Museum) Beethoven added this inscription:

Grosse Sinfonie geschrieben für die Philharmonische Gesellschaft in London in his own hand.

were destroyed by fire and the concerts were transferred to the King's Theatre, until, in 1833, they were homed in the Hanover Square Rooms.

A CRISIS

The success of the Philharmonic Society was spectacular, and Spohr commented on the difficulty of accommodating all those who wished to attend the concerts. But success was not easy to maintain, and for some time the affairs of the Society ran dangerously close to the rocks. To many professionalism was anathema, and the idea that musicians should be prepared to work for nothing is a principle in English society not even yet quite buried. The crisis of the early years was epitomised by an anonymous correspondent to the *Harmonicon* who was answering a somewhat reactionary letter in the same journal. He wrote as follows on August 19, 1828:

> ... The members of the new union had inveterate habits and obstinate prejudice to encounter; they had private interests opposed to their project, and, starting as they did entirely on a risk, and not at all anticipating the extraordinary success by which their endeavours were speedily crowned, they agreed, both for themselves and such other professors as they could persuade to assist them—the wind instruments excepted, which were paid—to contribute their services under a condition of receiving no sort of remuneration for their labours; considering this resolution as the best guarantee they could give of the disinterestedness of their views, and the most likely means of attracting the notice of those whom they wished to wean from the trashy music then prevailing.
> On this plan the Society flourished for three years, and as the expenses were small and the receipts large, a considerable sum was accumulated. Nevertheless, at the end of the season of 1815, personal differences broke out among the members, and an opposition concert, under the name of *The Professional*, was carried on for one year by the schismatics. But the attempt proved as abortive as it had been ill-judged, and the deserters were glad in the following season to flock again to the standard they had abandoned.
> This temporary alienation of some of the performing members made it imperative with the directors to engage other assistance

upon the usual professional terms, which, as a matter of course, led to the payment of all who formed the orchestra. This change in the constitution of the Society had drawn many bitter laments from those whose judgments are led astray by high-sounding words, and who do not consider that the springs of human nature act as powerfully in artists of any descriptions, in despite of their love of glory, as in other people; and among the number that sadly deplore, and take deeply to heart, this alteration, I think I may reckon 'Old Subscriber'. But, let me assure him, as well as all who feel as he does, that, but for the abrogation of the law concerning gratuitous service, the Society could not have been kept together another year. The object for which personal sacrifice had been made was attained—public taste was invigorated and refined, and that very public would soon, and of their own accord, have protested against the impolicy, as well as the injustice, of any longer suffering professional men to exercise their talent and exhaust their strength, without the prospect of that reward, which, however enthusiasts may declaim, is the surest stimulus to continued exertion.

... The existing proprietors might at once have distributed among themselves the whole of what had been gained; and this moral as well as legal right to have appropriated the produce of their own speculation and efforts, no one could fairly have disputed. But, instead of this, they determine that, of the fund created, and remaining from season to season when all expenses are discharged, a proportionate part shall be paid to the representative of every member on his decease: thus keeping the bulk of the accumulation untouched for many years, and therefore applicable, to the last shilling, to the purpose of the institution, and holding the Society together by one of the strongest bonds of union that can be devised, till the death of all its present members at least. Without some *vinculum* as this, there would have existed continued danger of jealousies, jars, and divisions. We have already seen that these did actually take place when the strong tie was wanting; for musicians belong to the *genus irritable*, and I have no reason, after some experience, to think that they are more blessed with high-mindedness than the learned professions; they are about as capable of resisting such tempting prospects of profit as might possibly have seduced them from the Philharmonic ranks as a barrister in a moderate practice is of refusing the bench—or the rector of a parish of saying *nolo episcopari*, when a good bishopric is placed within his grasp. No, sir, the members of the

171

Philharmonic Society are like most other men: indeed, in this instance, they have acted much better than members placed in very exalted stations have done, are still doing, and will long continue to do, when exposed to the allurements of a good bait.

THE PROTECTION OF BRITISH MUSIC

The Philharmonic Society is one of the great foundations in British music, and its influence on music in general has proved not inconsiderable. It is, however, possible that although a pioneer organisation in a European context it came twenty years too late in the local setting. In the Bach–Abel–Salomon days, there was a genuine and strong orchestral tradition. By the time of Queen Victoria's accession to the throne in 1837 the twin theses that oratorio represented all that was best in musical culture and that the British were a singing nation had been united. The Antient Concerts set a metropolitan standard of respectability that had already taken firm root in the provincial festivals and had stimulated the middle-class, and amateur, Sacred Harmonic Society, founded in 1832. On the activities of this body, its home being in Exeter Hall, Mendelssohn had set his oratorial seal in 1837 when he attended the first London performance of *St. Paul*. The Sacred Harmonic Society (which left a valuable library to the Royal College of Music after its closure in 1888) did, however, serve to nourish the enthusiasm of one of the promoters of musical appreciation for the next generation. Sir George Grove, seventeen years of age in 1837, and already stimulated by Clarke-Whitfield's edition of Handel and by Ayrton's *Musical Library*, let it be described in his biography how in that year he and his sister set out from their home in Clapham for Exeter Hall. 'The house-key was hidden under the gate and supper left out for them on their return, which was seldom before eleven for they footed it both ways.' It was then that Grove began to appreciate the effectiveness of the propaganda for choral music. He reported how a friendly policeman thus addressed him, as he set out for Exeter Hall; 'Well, sir, some likes pianny, and some likes the flute, and some likes various sorts of instruments; but for me, sir, I like the wocal. Indeed, sir, I may say I'm a *hog* at the *wocal*.'

172

As has been seen the Philharmonic Society nearly foundered when a realistic appraisal of professional circumstances was made. Beneath this ran egalitarian ideas that can also be recognised in the public exposure of the unsatisfactory contractual arrangements imposed on orchestral players at the King's Theatre. The French Revolution and the Napoleonic Wars bore other fruit. Chauvinism showed up in English music and a consequent xenophobia. This led to curious and conflicting conclusions: that foreign musicians were superior to native, but that their morals were unsteady, so that it came to be accepted that all musicians, and most music that was not controlled by biblical words, tended to immorality; that English musicians didn't have a fair showing, and that, for the honour of the nation, they should; but that, by and large, music was not of much significance anyway. Feeling that the Philharmonic Society was displaying dangerously outward-looking tendencies in some particulars 'a numerous class of persons who are anxious to see native talent encouraged' took advantage of the cessation of Harrison's and Knyvett's Vocal Concerts and got up a series of British Concerts in 1823, the conductors being George Smart, Thomas Attwood, and Henry Bishop. The leading composer produced by this enterprise was James Calkin whose string quartets were England's answer to Mozart, Haydn and Beethoven, but whose symphony, after rehearsal by the Philharmonic Society, was not considered good enough to be played in public.

It was in that same year that the Royal Academy of Music (its charter as such being granted seven years later) was set up under the reign of Lord Burghersh. The hopes of many centred in 'Old Musician's' letter of January 13, in the *Harmonicon*, which took it that the intention of the institution was 'to render the annual importation of foreign performers, of all descriptions, for the use of our theatre, concerts, schools, etc, unnecessary'. On April 24 a concert, to raise funds for the Academy, was given in the King's Theatre, at which the *pièce de résistance* was Crotch's oratorio *Palestine*. The programme book contained a policy statement at which the *Harmonicon* glanced sourly, and looked dubiously toward a future brighter than the brief past. 'But the first step towards amelioration must be, to eject from its lists any person whose profligate character is likely to contaminate the morals of the pupils, or to bring disgrace upon those to whom the general management is entrusted.'

In 1834 further steps to protect the native interest were taken by the foundation of a Society of British Musicians, whose preamble has the merit of being, apparently, permanently relevant.

> In an age like the present so zealous in exertions for the advancement of liberal arts and sciences, and in a metropolis so abundant in institutions to promote that desirable object, it is an extraordinary fact, that British music alone has escaped attention—British musicians alone have hitherto been destitute of the advantages such institutions are calculated to afford. While the Royal Academy of Arts, and various other establishments, have shed their fostering influence on painting, sculpture, and the tributary arts, the British musician has been left to his unaided endeavours to combat the unjust prejudices of the unthinking, and to compete with the composers of Continental Europe, provided as they are with every assistance necessary for the development of their genius and the display of their talents. The overwhelming preponderance of foreign compositions in all musical performances, while it can scarcely fail to impress the public with the idea that musical genius is alien to their country, tends also to repress those energies, and to extinguish that emulation in the heart of the youthful aspirant, which alone lead to pre-eminence[1].

English music thus stepped uneasily into the new age.

PARIS—CONCERTS DU CONSERVATOIRE

The main stream of concert organisation in Leipzig progressed according to one pattern, in London to another; in Paris yet another. Here two factors supervened to alter the existing conventions. These, so far, were strongly and exclusively aristocratic, and were overturned by the events and consequences of the Revolution (in honour of which and the Republic numerous composers produced prototype ideological essays)[2]. In 1795 a free school of music, or Conservatoire, was est up, after two decades of lobbying on the part of interested

---

[1] Hogarth, *op. cit.*, II, p. 270.
[2] See Knepler, *op. cit.*, I, p. 111 *et seq.*

parties. The Conservatoire, of which Bernard Sarrette (1765–1858) was Director until 1815—when the monarchy returned in the person of Louis XVIII and royalists paid off old scores—was a State institution, and in 1800 its standing was confirmed by the appointment of Gossec, Méhul, Lesueur, Cherubini, and Monsigny, as Inspectors of Tuition. Sarrette laid the foundations of the Conservatoire with great administrative ability; in addition to supervising the building of premises, and the inauguration of public rehearsals as an incentive to students, he also established, at the State's expense, the Prix de Rome. In 1815 Sarrette was succeeded by François Perne (1772–1832), a scholar whose chief practical interest was in vocal music. After seven years as Director Perne was followed by Cherubini, whose twenty-year tenure of office was notable in all ways, not least of all because it was under his protection that Habeneck was able to found the *Société des Concerts du Conservatoire* in 1828.

After the cessation of the *Concert Spirituel* in 1791 similar concerts were given, under the direction of Jean-Jacques Grasset (1769–1839), under the name of the *Concert de la Rue Cléry*. For this an orchestra of twenty-four players was retained, and made a speciality of the symphonies of Haydn. It was in the Rue Cléry concerts that the first symphony of Anton Reicha (1770–1836), the future teacher of Liszt, Gounod, Berlioz, and Franck, was given. A change of room in 1801 brought this sequence of concerts to an end. The *Concert des Amateurs* was still maintained and a letter of October 10, 1802, from the Directors to Haydn indicates the popularity of that master in France at the time:

> The six months which have elapsed since our concerts of the last winter have not been able to make us forget the success which we gained by performing your sublime compositions, nor the promise you were kind enough to give us, that you would go to the trouble of writing a symphony for us, to the execution of which we would devote the care proportionate to our gratitude ... Consider, Monsieur, how many people you would delight if you were to respond to this universal enthusiasm by offering to the public, as the overture of our next series, a new *chef d'œuvre* which would reassure them, and no less ourselves, as to the state of your health[1].

[1] Quoted from H. C. Robbins Landon, *op. cit.*, p. 59.

Haydn was unable to comply with this request and the health of the *Concert des Amateurs* fell into something of a decline, although artificial respiration to the cause was applied in the amateur concerts held at the Tivoli d'Hiver and at Vauxhall, and by *L'Athénée musical*, founded by Hippolyte Chelard, winner of the Prix de Rome in 1811, and patronised by the Prefect of the Seine.

In 1803 François Habeneck, of German birth but educated at the Conservatoire, entered the field of orchestral direction, in the amateur concerts known as the *Concert Français* and given in the theatre of the Conservatoire. Habeneck (whose father was a military musician in a French regiment) was a first-rate orchestral leader, and he showed his talents particularly in the symphonies of Beethoven, which he was the first to introduce to Paris. It was the *Concert Français* which gave him the first opportunity, and in 1805 he moved to professional orchestral circles by taking charge of the resuscitated *Concert Spirituel* (which, however, never regained its former pre-eminence), with which he continued his championship of Beethoven, against much opposition, and also of Étienne Méhul (1763–1817), the most progressive French composer of that age and one who in orchestral imaginativeness anticipated and influenced Berlioz.

It was against this background that Habeneck proposed the Société des Concerts du Conservatoire, as an organisation of professional competence, adequately supported, and a focal point for orchestral music in the nineteenth century. Habeneck had been encouraged in his ambition by the enthusiasm engendered by his celebration of St. Cecilia's Day, 1826. He had then invited the orchestral players from the opera to lunch—with their instruments. Before eating they rehearsed the *Eroica* with such thoroughness that it was almost four o'clock when Habeneck called out: 'Au nom de Beethoven reconnaissant, vous êtes priés de vous mettre à table pour diner.' 'Il etait temps,' commented Elwart, 'car les instruments à vent surtout étaient sur les dents, et le contre-basse commençait à pousser des cris de cannibale[1].'

The first concert of the Société took place in the afternoon of March 9, 1828, in the theatre of the Conservatoire. The

[1] *Histoire de la Société des Concerts*, etc., Paris, 1860, p. 62.

orchestra—a significantly large one—was composed of fifteen first violins (Habeneck conducting from the first desk), sixteen second violins, eight violas, twelve 'cellos, eight double-basses, four flutes, three oboes, four clarinets, four bassoons, four horns, two trumpets, four trombones (one doubling with ophicleide), timpani, and harp. The programme was:

Eroica Symphony	Beethoven
Duet from *Semiramide*	Rossini
Horn Solo—composed and played by Meifred[1]	
Violin Concerto	Rode[2]
Air	Rossini
Chorus from *Blanche de Provence*	Cherubini
Overture—*Les Abencérages*	Cherubini
Kyrie and Gloria from 'Coronation' Mass	Cherubini

From this it will be seen that the form of the *Concert Spirituel* (this title, indeed, was applied to three concerts of the Société in 1830), with its quota of religious, choral music, was well fixed in the French system, Revolution or no Revolution. But the highly professional nature of the undertaking and the acknowledgment of the claims of modern music made a tremendous impact, that was summarised by Fétis in the *Revue Musicale* of March 16, 1828: 'le neuf mars, 1828,' he wrote, 'sera inscrit comme un beau jour dans les fastes de la musique française, et comme l'époque de sa régéneration.'

POPULAR AND PROMENADE CONCERTS

Habeneck and the Conservatoire between them provided the inspiration and the means whereby orchestral music in Paris should reach a high degree of perfection; and they also laid the basis of a popular appreciation of music. On this side, the devolution of military music with open-air concerts in the Champs-Élysées, under Philippe Musard, and the spectacular cornet playing of Dufrêne, brought a new dignity to the music

[1] Pierre-Jean Meifred (1790–1867), a founder member of the Société des Concerts du Conservatoire, and a champion of the cause of the valve-horn. His performance at the Society's first concert was the first on this instrument in public in France.

[2] Pierre Rode (1774–1830), French violinist of international repute; together with Kreutzer and Paganini one of the founders of modern violin technique. He composed ten violin concertos of high quality.

of the streets and underlined a healthily vulgar trait in French music that found later expansion in Berlioz, Gounod, and César Franck. A conductor of the Musard tradition—specialising both in 'light' and 'serious' music—and one who made the art of showmanship a necessary part of the business was Louis Antoine Jullien (1812–1860), whose influence, however, was to be more strongly exercised in London and in New York. Of more integrity was Henri Justin Valentino (1785–1865), who had conducted at the opera with Habeneck, and after being expelled from that post during the Revolution of 1830 was glad to be rehabilitated by an invitation in 1837 to conduct a series of concerts intended to have a wide appeal. It was Valentino who first conducted the symphonies of Beethoven outside the Conservatoire. But his popular classical concerts—the first of their kind—were premature, and came to an end in 1837. Two years later, however, *Promenade Concerts à la Valentine* were given in the Crown and Anchor Tavern, in the Strand, London, and complementary but competing *Original Promenade Concerts à la Musard* in the English Opera House. Thus, in fact, came the first impetus towards the most esteemed of latter-day English institutions—from France[1]. Another conductor associated with Habeneck (his associate conductor at the Conservatoire) was Théophile Tilmant (1799–1878), who in the *Gymnase Musical* founded in 1835, astonished and delighted by the fire and brilliance which he brought from his players: 'Il essaya des combinaisons d'instrumentation plein d'audace et de nouveauté.' It was Tilmant who first conducted Berlioz's *Harold in Italy*.

A PHILHARMONIC AND OTHER SOCIETIES IN VIENNA

That composers increasingly aimed at broader horizons is clear from the nature of music itself and from the co-operative and corporate institutions which gradually took over the task of patronage. Insofar as it was the city most prominently associated with Mozart, Haydn, and Beethoven, Vienna

---

[1] Advertisements exhibited at Fishmongers' Hall, London, in June–July, 1904 and detailed in *An Illustrated Catalogue of the Music Loan Exhibition*, etc., London, 1909.

occupied a position of considerable power. With regard to public concerts, however, Vienna, proud of its imperial status, was somewhat laggardly. The Augarten Concerts which, in 1789, came under the direction of Ignaz Schuppanzigh (1776–1820)[1], and in 1813, under that of a court functionary assisted by Paul Wranitzky, continued with their high level of intention until about 1830, when, in common with similar undertakings in Britain, they succumbed to the pressure of contrary entertainment of less idealistic character. Orchestral playing fell on lean days for another reason. After 1813 economy led to the dissolution of many private orchestras—those of Esterházy, Schwarzenburg, and Lobkowitz remaining in revised form—and their substitution by chamber ensembles, which, however, gave an impetus in another direction. Edward Holmes reflected thus on Viennese musical standards in his *A Ramble among the Musicians of Germany* (1828):

> The flippancy of taste displayed by the more fashionable concertgoers in Vienna may be imagined from an exhibition of instrumental playing with which they were entertained on one occasion when I was present, the prominent parts of which were variations for the violin, performed by Madame Paravicini, and the first movement of Hummel's pianoforte concerto in B minor played by Frederic Wörlitzer, of Berlin, a boy thirteen years old. The lady's violin performance required much politeness and self-command to restrain laughter, it was so extremely bad and particularly in some rapid *staccato* passages near the bridge, where the defiance of tone was droll; the boy, though well tutored, got through his task without conveying the slightest pleasure. Both these performers seemed to attract in proportion as the individuals were unfit to manage their instruments—the lady to *fiddle*, or the boy to play on the pianoforte.

But it was in the Augarten, where the programmes began at the unconscionable hour of 7.30 a.m. that the break-through to a wider appreciation was readily achieved so far as Austria was concerned. Mozart was honoured there; and so too was Beethoven. His first five symphonies, and his first three pianoforte

---

[1] Leader of a famous quartet of his own, and also of that maintained by Prince Rasumovsky, and the first to play quartets of Beethoven and Schubert. As a conductor Schuppanzigh insisted on 'clarity and precision', especially in the 'most difficult' symphonies of Haydn and Mozart (*Allgemeine Musik-Zeitung*, quoted in Kobald, *op. cit.*, p. 134).

concertos, for instance, were regular pieces in the repertoire; while it was in the Augarten that Bridgetower and Beethoven gave the first performance of the 'Kreutzer' Sonata[1].

As the Augarten concerts declined, however, another society was beginning to evolve. Franz Lachner (1803–1890), a friend of Schubert, was appointed assistant conductor at the Kärntnertor Theatre in 1826, and a year later succeeded Thaddäus Weigl in the senior position. This he kept until 1834, when he moved to Mannheim. Seeing the quartet evenings of Schuppanzigh, Böhm, and Janza, the various private concerts, and the mixture of *Concerts Spirituels* and *Gesellschäftskonzerte*, that distinguished the middle and upper layers of the Viennese musical scene, Lachner also saw the possibility of centralising this skill and enthusiasm into regular concerts from which the orchestral players themselves might derive more consistent benefit. In 1833 four subscription concerts were given, by the chorus and orchestra of the Kärntnertor Theatre in the Redoutensaal, but with Lachner's departure the first season of that venture was also the last.

Eight years later the German conductor and composer Karl Otto Nicolai (1810–1849) became first conductor at the Kärntnertor Theatre. With a considerable experience of the musical life of Berlin behind him he was more than ready to welcome proposals that Lachner's project should be revived. At this juncture Nikolaus Lenau, the poet, August Schmidt, editor of the *Allgemeine Musikzeitung*, Alfred Becker, Count Laurencin, Karl Holz, second violin in Schuppanzigh's quartet, and others, lent vigorous support. The influential voice of the *AMZ*—by now the musical journals were becoming increasingly effective in focusing taste throughout Europe—ushered in the new undertaking:

At a time when concerts in Vienna are on a high level this journal has the pleasant duty to acquaint the public with a concert announcement which, because of the names of its promoters as well as the programme, gives the assurance of great distinction in every respect. All the orchestral players from the Royal Opera House, with the respected Director, Georg Hellsmesberger, at their head, are formed into a great 'Philharmonic Academy', under

[1] See A. W. Thayer, *Ludwig van Beethovens Leben*, Berlin, 1866–79. II. p. 229.

Kapellmeister Nicolai. The concert will take place in the large *Redoutensaal* on the Sunday after Easter (April 3rd), at mid-day, and will present only classical music in its most attractive form.

In the event the first concert of the Vienna Philharmonic Society took place on March 28, 1842, at 12.30 p.m. The programme was as follows:

I

1. Symphony No. 7 in A   Beethoven
2. Aria from *Faniska*
   (sung by J. Staudigl)[1]   Cherubini
3. Concert aria 'Ah perfido'   Beethoven
   (sung by Frau von Hasselt-Barth)

II

4. Overture *Leonora* No. 3   Beethoven
5. Concert aria (not detailed)
   (sung by Jenny Lutzer, with violin obbligato by
                                     Josef Mayseder[2])
6. *La Romanesca*, 16th century melody
   (played as a 'cello solo by François Servais[3])
7. Duet from *Medea*   Cherubini
   (sung by Frau von Hasselt-Barth and Franz Wild[4])
8. Overture [Die Weihe des Hauses]   Beethoven

During the next season Nicolai achieved one of his great ambitions, to give a worthy performance of the Choral Symphony (previously given on March 29, 1840, by the *Musikfreunden Wien*). Aided by Hasselt-Barth, Dietzl, Kraus, Staudigl, and the opera chorus, and having devoted thirteen rehearsals to the project, he accomplished this on March 19, 1843. On six concerts during that season there was a profit of eight thousand gulden. According to the best capitalist principles, then, the Philharmonic Society was justified, and the

[1] Joseph Staudigl (1807–1861), the great bass of the Kärntnertor Theatre: in 1846 he visited England and created the title part of Mendelssohn's *Elijah*.

[2] 1789–1863, violinist and composer, who was the second violin in Schuppanzigh's quartet, and had made his debut as virtuoso in the Augarten in 1800. After 1837 he would not appear in public, concentrating on composition, in which he specialised in chamber music.

[3] 1807–1866: Belgian 'cellist and composer, who played a concerto of his own at the Philharmonic Society in London on May 25, 1835.

[4] Tenor singer at the Kärntnertor Theatre, and highly regarded throughout Europe.

181

cause of classical music assured. Nicolai conducted the Society from 1842 to 1847 (when he went to Berlin), with an intermission in 1844–1845. In this year Georg Hellsmesberger (1806–1873), a school-fellow of Schubert, a pupil of Böhm, and the future teacher of Joachim and Leopold Aueur, officiated. Hellsmesberger again took over in 1847, and in the next year his son, also Georg (1830–1852) reflected the tensions of the period in his *Grosse Fest-Ouverture . . . zur Feier des Wiener Bürger Concert's am 25ten März, 1848*. After Hellsmesberger the conductors of the Philharmonic were Ludwig Wilhelm Reuling (1849), Heinrich Proch (1850–1854), and Carl Eckert.

Eckert (1820–1879), born in Berlin and a student at Leipzig under Mendelssohn, accumulated a great deal of practical experience before he was invited to Vienna in 1853 to conduct the court opera. He had worked in Berlin, had been accompanist at the Italian opera in Paris, and to Henriette Sontag on her American tour of 1851 before being appointed conductor of the Italian opera. Eckert's predecessors in Vienna had all been composers as well as conductors, and some much more skilled in that faculty. He too was a composer, but his talent in this respect was far outstripped by his competence in orchestral direction. He it was who made the Viennese Philharmonic Orchestra the first such body in the international field. He it was also who broadened the programmes, by introducing, for example, the sacred arias of Stradella, the operatic arias of Handel, and the instrumental works of Bach into the concert repertoire. On December 12, 1856, Bach's *Toccata in F*, orchestrated by Heinrich Esser, was given its first performance in transcription. Esser also orchestrated, and popularised, the *Passacaglia in C Minor*.

The Viennese Philharmonic Society was the most conspicuous symbol of the emancipation of music from its aristocratic nursery; it was also the culmination of a half-century or more of experimentation in instrumental music, in the cultivation of which the Viennese school was supreme. At the same time choral music was not neglected in Vienna, being entrusted to the *Gesellschaft der Musikfreunde*, founded in 1812 as a result of the enthusiasm created by performances of Handel's *Alexander's Feast* in that year. This society flourished under the patronage of the Archduke Rudolph, and oratorio performances on a vast

16. The Music Fund Hall, Philadelphia.

17. Concert Room in the Hungarian Academy of Music, Budapest.

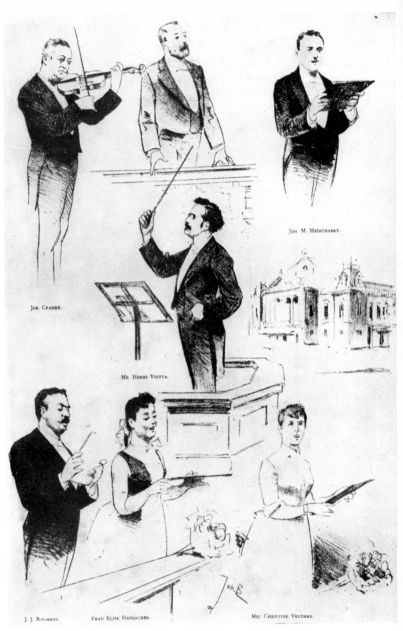

Jos. Cramer.

Joh. M. Messchaert.

Mr. Henri Viotta.

J. J. Rogmans.   Frau Elise Harlacher.   Mej. Christine Veltman.

18.   First concert in the Concertgebouw, Amsterdam.

scale—with one thousand performers—took place in the Riding School.

In 1836 the Gesellschaft founded a Conservatorium, later to become a world-famous seminary for the training of musicians. In emulation of this association others were founded in Austria, principal among which were the *Musikverein für Steiermark* in Graz (1815), the *Verein zur Aufnahme der Ton- und Redekunst* in Innsbruck (1818), and the *Gesellschaft der Musikfreunde* in Linz (1821). So in ancient cities whose musical traditions were established in deference to the musical requirements of the privileged the influence broadened.

11

Expansion

TOWARDS A COMMON CULTURE

*I*N THE FIRST PHASE of stabilisation of the orchestral concert these main trends may be seen: a further development of international collaboration, an increasing control by the middle classes, an appreciation, gradual but unmistakable, of the standing of the orchestral player, a zeal for general musical education, and a collateral demand for the higher training facilities that a high school of music could provide. From time to time stronger nationalist ambitions obtruded, and the evolution of a new, corporately conscious, working class in industrial communities hinted at possibilities of still further development. These latter, however, lay some way in the future, across the divides of 1830 and 1848.

The concert, as an institution, was, like music itself, conditioned by the circumstances of history, but also it could stand away from reality in the first degree to emphasise a more valid conception of reality, at least in a philosophic sense. Thus Haydn spread a beneficent influence across the whole of Europe, and further afield, bringing together the contrary impulses of Hungary, Germany, and Austria, and synthesising them in a form amenable to mankind as a whole; while Beethoven's acceptance, particularly by the French during the Napoleonic era and a period of French aggression, was a superb realisation of his own libertarian and fraternal aspirations. The institutions described in the previous two chapters, although the most important of their kind, were by no means the only ones of their several orders. But they exerted a powerful influence, first by compelling imitation, second by providing a ready stock of executant musicians, whose mobility was a contributory factor in the extension of a common musical culture.

184

MUSIC AND CHARITY

In spite of the orchestral tradition established in London the English provinces mainly endeavoured to come to terms with the moral attitudes enshrined in the tacitly accepted premises that music existed either to support the doctrines of the Established Church, by way of Handel's biblical works, or to raise funds for necessary charities. This attitude was not, however, entirely idealistic. Unlike German towns those of Britain, court-less, were deficient in the trained personnel now necessary for the proper production of contemporary music. Thus choral music, which could be encouraged on account of its low cost to the community, became increasingly important; for it was supported by ecclesiastical foundations—parish churches and, somewhat later, dissenting organisations—and the large numbers involved formed a valuable connection with the not actively musical middle classes whose subscriptions were the guarantee of any extension of medical—rather than musical—services. Behind English provincial music lay, of course, the image of the Three Choirs Festival, the Handel Commemoration, and the annual concerts for the 'Royal Society of Musicians and their distressed families', into which series the Commemorations did in fact fall.

The Birmingham Festival (dating from 1768, enlarged in 1799, and triennial), divided between the Theatre Royal and St. Philip's Church[1] was in aid of the General Hospital[2]; the Leicester Festival (1827), in St. Margaret's Church and the New Assembly Rooms, was on behalf of the 'Infirmary, Lunatic Asylum, and Fever House of Recovery'; the Norwich and Norfolk Festival (held irregularly since 1770, but put on a triennial basis in 1824), in St. Andrew's Hall, was for the benefit of the Norfolk and Norwich Hospital; the Yorkshire Musical Festival (founded in 1791), in York, in the Minster and the 'Concert Room built for the purposes of such Musical Festivals as may be held for the Benefit of the Charities'[3], for the York County Hospital and the General Infirmaries of Leeds, Hull, and Sheffield. The Sussex Festival of 1828 took place in St.

[1] The 'New Town Hall' was first used in 1834.

[2] Between 1768 and 1874 the hospital benefited to the extent of £102,781.

[3] Title page of programme of evening performance for Second Festival of 1825.

185

Peter's Church, Brighton, in which town the residence of the Prince Regent had left something of a courtly tradition in a permanent musical establishment, and was in aid of the funds of the Sussex County Hospital. All such occasions had their roots in eighteenth-century practice, but were made more ambitious, and they became increasingly dependent on assistance from London. From such occasions derived the impetus to build concert halls; not so much for the sake of music as for the sustenance of charities.

PERSONNEL AND PROGRAMMES

These Festivals—as also the more independent Gentlemen's Concerts of Manchester and Liverpool (where the foundation-stone of St. George's Hall, to replace the Music Hall that had been erected in the city in 1786, was laid in 1838) relied on local amateurs and professionals, such as there were, all of whom, however, were taken in hand by the peripatetic principals from London. Thus Francis Cramer, Weichsel, Mori[1], and Moralt (violin), R. Ashley and Joseph Calkin (viola), Robert Lindley and Dragonetti, as well as Charles Nicholson[2] (flute), Gratton Cooke[3] (oboe), Thomas Willman[4] (clarinet), John Mackintosh[5] (bassoon), Giovanni Puzzi[6] (horn), Thomas Harper[7] (trumpet), J. Smithies[8] (trombone), would be found as a *corps d'élite* at any festival during the reign of William IV; while the conducting, still from keyboard or violin desk, was entrusted to Thomas Greatorex (1758–1831)[9], Cramer[10] or Sir George Smart[11] (1776–1867).

[1] Nicholas Mori (1797–1839), pupil of Barthélemon and leader of the Philharmonic Society orchestra.

[2] 1795–1837: born in Liverpool, where his father was a flautist.

[3] 1809–1889: son of the Irish singer and composer, Tom Cooke (1782–1848).

[4] c. 1783–1840: member of Opera and Philharmonic Orchestras, and ranked by Fétis as the equal of Berr and Bärmann, the German clarinettists.

[5] 1767–1840: Scottish virtuoso, with a European reputation.

[6] 1792–1876: one of the greatest horn players of his age.

[7] 1786–1853: of Worcester.

[8] Editor of trombone parts for *Messiah*.

[9] 'Dr Camidge (assistant conductor) presides at the Organ; and Mr Greatorex at the Piano Forte', York Programme, 1825.

[10] Who was the 'leader' at the Secular Concerts at Leicester in 1827, Greatorex controlling the oratorios

[11] 'Conductor, Sir George Smart, Who will preside at the Organ, built expressly for the Festivals by Mr Gray of London'. Programme of Festival Performance of *Messiah* (arr. Mozart), Norwich, 1830.

The programmes of these Festival occasions suffered from one defect inherent in their charitable purpose: they were designed with a view to their box-office appeal, and the musically progressive were, therefore, held back by the non-musical. Thus, to take an example, the evening concert of September 4, 1827, at Leicester contained popular arias and duets from operatic works by Rossini, Lebrun, Sacchini (as well as the overture to *La Gazza Ladra*), Guglielmi, Nicolini, and Meyerbeer; songs by William Knyvett (he was also a conductor at this period), Bishop, Arne, Pepusch, Lee, Castelli; a glee by Callcott; virtuoso trivialities, by Hoffman (a violin concerto played by Kiesewetter), and Puzzi (he played his own fantasia for horn); and a trio for violin, 'cello and double-bass, for Cramer, Lindley and Dragonetti, attributed to Handel and Martini. On the more positive side there were excerpts from Mozart, the *Anacréon* overture of Cherubini, and Beethoven's First Symphony.

Concerts with items of merely sensational character fitted into the scene more than intermittently, and the coinage of British musical life began seriously to be debased, despite the valorous efforts of the Philharmonic Society. So, for instance, a 'Grand Dramatic Concert' took place on July 2, 1838, in which attention was principally concentrated on the 'first appearance of Mr Henry Herz on the English stage', superintending a performance of Czerny's *Concertstücke* for eight pianos and twelve harps. Among the team of pianists was William Sterndale Bennett, one of the main hopes of English music. Herz was one of the less successful pupils of the Paris Conservatoire; Louis Antoine Jullien (1812–1860), was another. Both were showmen; both were popularisers.

MORE PROMENADE CONCERTS

In 1845 Jullien conducted *concerts monstres* at the Royal Zoological Gardens, attracting crowds of up to twelve thousand to hear quadrilles, polkas, galops, and 'works from the great masters'. The *pièce de résistance* at this time was 'Suona la tromba', from Bellini's *I Puritani*, arranged for twenty cornets, twenty trumpets, twenty trombones, twenty ophicleides, and twenty serpents. Nevertheless Jullien introduced fresh audiences to Haydn and to Beethoven, and in 1846 organised a Beethoven Festival, followed in due course by Mozart and Mendelssohn commemorations. In 1848, at Drury Lane Theatre, and assisted by four regimental bands, Jullien took up the idea of Promenade Concerts, and having successfully proved their viability met with competition two years later in the somewhat misleadingly titled 'Grand National Concerts', the promoters of which attempted to seduce away all Jullien's players. The conductor of these concerts was the Irishman Michael Balfe (1808–1870). The 'Grand National Concerts' lasted for one season and Jullien was left free to pursue his aim, in which, although criticised by the knowledgeable, he largely succeeded. The *Musical World* of 1850 acknowledged that he was 'the first to attempt the popularisation of the highest class of orchestral music in this metropolis'.

It is sometimes represented that Jullien was a prime cause of the debasement of English musical taste. This is not fair. The mixture of the run-down 'Gardens' song, the second-rate Italian opera aria, and the instrumental show-piece, the new vanities of singers able in the ballad age to command high fees and even royalties from composers, and the growing detachment of the English bourgeoisie, all contributed. So from the Oxford University Festival of 1831 there may be quoted one item from a 'Miscellaneous Concert': 'Scena—Signor de Begnis— *I Violini*—Sacchini (In imitation of a Fanatical composer giving direction to the Orchestra at the first Rehearsal of his New Composition).'

WALES AND THE EISTEDDFOD

During the first part of the nineteenth century English music steered an uncertain course through the opulencies of the period, with English composers featuring less prominently in programmes than at any time since the inception of public concerts. But in Wales a movement was astir which might have saved British music as a whole from a long night of near despair so far as creative activity was concerned. The Eisteddfod, suppressed in the sixteenth century and tentatively revived in the eighteenth (Llandegla 1719, Bala 1760, Llangollen, Corwen, and Bala, 1789), returned to the main stream of Welsh cultural life.

But the English nobility used their powers of patronage to ill effect. Lip service was paid to the cultural genius of the Welsh nation, but the Marquess of Bute, the greatest landowner in the Principality, saw to it that outside the competitions the tastes of the fashionable prevailed, and the concerts which formed an important part of the Eisteddfod were turned over to Braham, Mrs Knyvett, Mrs Bishop, and Miss Stevens, great singers with notable deficiencies in taste, and Welsh musical culture was flattered and deceived by Teutonised ballads centred on such appealing themes as *Glyndwr's War Song*, the *Maid of Llangollen*, and *Prince Madoc*. The struggle of the Welsh people to build a musical tradition was against overwhelming odds, and in the end victory (at least for the time being) passed to the big battalions. Welsh music fell under the sovereignty of the German *Hochschule für Musik*, and there was not sufficient native experience to stand up against it.

GERMAN SCHOOLS OF MUSIC AND NEW ORGANISATIONS

The Leipzig Hochschule was the most influential of the German academies and acted both as accelerator and as brake. But the stabilisation of music in German life itself went on methodically and efficiently through a period in which first Weber and then Wagner, not to mention Mendelssohn and Schumann, in whom national pride was never disguised, completed the rout of Italian opera in central Europe. In 1811 a school of music was set up in Prague (then considered as within the German sphere of cultural interest) as an offshoot from the *Verein zur Forderung der Tonkunst in Böhmen*, presided over by the Prince Ferdinand Lobkowitz. Three years later a musical academy was tentatively established in Dresden under Morlacchi and with the consent of the Russian governor, Prince Repnin: in 1856 this became a national institution, and, like all German schools of music, handsomely subsidised from State funds. The Munich Konservatorium opened in 1846, and that of Köln four years later. In the meantime more and more concert organisations arose from older tradition, so that a series of Museum Concerts were founded in Frankfurt by Nicolaus Vogt in 1808 (these were later transferred to the magnificent auditorium of the *Saalbau*), a Philharmonische Gesellschaft was formed in Hamburg under the chairmanship of a leading banker of the city, Rudolph Petersen (a *Sing-Akademie* had existed in Hamburg since 1819), and a *Musikverein* was established in Mannheim. In 1818 the Lower Rhine Festival had come into being in emulation of the Thuringian Festival held at Erfurt in 1811—as a union of the musical interests of Düsseldorf, Elberfeld (soon to be replaced by Köln), and Aachen. The first director of the Festival was Nobert Burgmüller, who was responsible for the performance of the Ninth Symphony at Aachen in 1825. The Festivals at Düsseldorf in 1833 and at Köln in 1835 were directed by Mendelssohn.

MUSIC AS A PART OF SOCIAL ACTIVITY

In the years between the Congress of Vienna in 1815 and the Revolution of 1848, life in Germany, the thirty-nine states not yet secure in the intention towards political unity, was pleasant, and culture as a whole lay under the massive protection of Goethe. Music during this era was built into the lives of the urban communities more than anywhere else in Europe. Edward Holmes paints a charming picture of the public gardens music of Dresden in 1828[1], contrasting the simplicity of manners there with the sophistication of England, where 'the caresses of the fashionable' were so much more important:

> As all the actors, singers, and artists of the city frequent this garden it is neither an unpleasant nor disagreeable occurrence to find oneself seated next to some person who the evening before was filling you and a whole room of company with admiration and pleasure. The applause of the public does not spoil the *bonhommie* of the man, and the repulsiveness of an overweening conceit is unknown . . .
>
> The most noticeable music here given was some of the sinfonias of Beethoven and Haydn—the overtures to *Fidelio* and *Anacreon*, Mozart's finale to *Don Juan* and *Figaro*, ably adapted . . . by Meyer, brother of the celebrated composer of that name. I will not say that this music was so dashingly played as it might have been by our own Philharmonic orchestra, but it was complete enough for those who enjoy the display of an author's mind more than the

[1] *A Ramble, etc.*, pp. 200 ff.

pride of perfect *fiddling*. Our artists play too well, which is a paradox of which the initiated will require no explanation ...

The music in this garden is played in a kind of open summer-house, and the performers do not scruple during the pauses to avail themselves of certain ham sandwiches and sundry bottles of wine, thus repairing dilapidations of their spirits, and keeping up excitement. I found here a man, named Stephan, a good trumpeter, who had lived for many years at Brighton in the private band of the Prince Regent, but who preferred Dresden in spite of more work and less pay. England he thought a dear country, for, said he, 'I must pay six-and-twenty pounds a year for my leetle house'. Stephan said something more about his wife not liking our climate; but I saw plainly that he loved sociality and thought our Sundays rather dull.

A little more than twenty years later, however, the situation was greatly altered and the tensions of the then situation produced this alteration in the Anglo-German cultural equation:

The hospitality which England is now showing to foreign artists is unprecedented. In addition to the refugees who have established themselves among us permanently, we hear so constantly of fresh arrivals, that it may be said there is scarcely any one of continental celebrity who is not to be found in London. As this is a branch of 'free trade' not likely to be reciprocated, it puts the generosity and forbearance of our native artists to a somewhat severe trial; yet seeing that the thing is inevitable, it is well to submit with a good grace. Meantime we are certainly gainers with improved and augmented resources of music.

It is impossible to reflect on the changed condition of musical affairs in Germany without sympathy. Establishments broken up, salaries suspended, and old grey-headed artists within armchair days revolving speculations of flight to America ... We remember well when strolling in the shady retired walks of the English garden at Darmstadt ... that we encountered one of the orchestra walking home under the trees with his violin case in his hand. This appeared to us the *beau-ideal* of musical existence[1].

This exodus of musicians was to have important consequences, not only in other parts of Europe, but also in America.

[1] From his unsigned article, 'The Musical Season' in *The Musical Times*, May, 1852, by Edward Holmes: the Darmstadt occasion is described in *A Ramble, etc.*, p. 48.

EFFECTS OF EUROPEAN UNREST ON
AMERICAN MUSICAL LIFE

Two great revolutionary movements, that which led through the War of Independence to the signing of the Declaration of 1783 which brought the United States of America into being as a nation, and that which convulsed Europe in 1848, form the limits of the first period of the development and emancipation of American music. During this period the democratic ideals of America and the accumulating wealth and consequent opportunities that stemmed therefrom were magnetic to many in Europe whose inclinations were adventurous and or in the van of social-philosophic progress. American music hitherto had European practice as its point of departure, but with a potent Puritanism acting as one distinctive influence and an absence of aristocratic patronage formulating another. In Boston, New York, and Philadelphia, as well as in smaller communities, music, under strict regulation in this particular, was ancillary to religious doctrine, stern, uncompromising, psalmodic, but, basically popular; it was a branch of learning, one of the sciences developed in the Old World to be further developed and extended in the New; it was a potential means of individual and national self-expression, and it possessed incentive virtue.

Francis Hopkinson (1737–1791), scholar, lawyer, statesman, and a signatory of the Declaration of Independence, was a native of Philadelphia and his musical interests formed one important centre of accomplishment and intention. He regularly entertained musicians at his house and organised public subscription concerts. He was also a composer, and in 1788 he issued his *Seven Songs, for the harpsichord or forte piano*, dedicated to George Washington. In his Preface he observed:

> However small the Reputation may be that I shall derive from this Work, I cannot I believe, be refused the Credit of being the first Native of the United States who has produced a Musical Composition. If this attempt should not be too severely treated, others may be encouraged to venture on a path, yet untrodden in America, and the Arts in succession will take root and flourish amongst us ...

Hopkinson represented one wing, the intellectual; in Boston there was, on the other hand, William Billings (1746–1800).

He was a tanner, self-taught, and possessed of a prophetic zeal, who provided, in his psalms, and less frequent secular pieces, a necessary connection with the fundamentals of life and thought in the emergent nation. Billings was also active in forming and directing choral societies, which were to play a large part in disseminating interest in the classics of sacred choral literature.

Native composers were necessarily infrequent, and for some time to come the provision and execution of music in the American cities was mainly by immigrant musicians, who, however diverse in antecedents, notably combined to produce a new synthesis of ideas that issued eventually as distinctively American.

Concert life in Boston was of old standing, and some continuity of organisation was maintained by Josiah Flagg (1728–1794) and William Selby (1738–1798), the latter a former London organist, enthusiastic for choral music, especially that of Handel. Among Selby's no longer extant compositions were a number of which the titles at least spoke of his newly assimilated nationality. These included Odes, *in honor of George Washington* and *on the Anniversary of Independence*. Another favourite work, played many times by its composer under Selby's dispensation, was John Berkenhead's *Demolition of the Bastile*, for harpsichord or pianoforte. Programme music and ballads were insinuated into concert programmes partly on account of their frequent topicality and partly because, as in England at an earlier date, anti-theatre legislation made it necessary to disguise dramatic productions by veneering them with instrumental and vocal items. Particularly was this the case in Philadelphia, where the Quakers were insistent on the observance of such legislation from 1778 until the end of the century. The effects of revolution and war being more keenly felt in Philadelphia and New York than in Boston, there was more leeway to be made up in those cities, but it was not long before Subscription Concerts were instituted.

SUBSCRIPTION CONCERTS—PHILADELPHIA, NEW YORK, BOSTON

In New York the initiative came from William Brown, flautist and composer; in Philadelphia from John Bentley. Both men were in uneasy association for a time in Philadelphia, where they were also joined in management by Henri Capron, a Frenchman, presumed to have been of the family of Nicolas Capron, a pupil of Gaviniès and a noted violinist at the *Concert Spirituel*. In 1786 a benefit concert for Henri Capron took place in Philadelphia, at which Alexander Reinagle (1756–1809) made his first appearance in America. Reinagle, brother of Joseph Reinagle, 'cellist in the Edinburgh St. Cecilia's Hall and the London Salomon Concerts, had wide experience before emigrating, having been a pupil of Raynor Taylor (a Chapel Royal chorister and musician at Sadler's Wells) and one of the second violins at the Handel Commemoration of 1784. Reinagle took an active part in the direction of the Philadelphia City Concerts, where in 1791–1792 he was partnered by John Christopher Moller, and the programmes mostly reflected current European tastes. But as a composer Reinagle declared his allegiance in a number of occasional pieces, of which the best known were the ballad 'America, Commerce and Freedom', and the *Federal March* of 1788. Raynor Taylor followed his pupil to America in 1792, bringing another in the person of a Miss Huntley, a burlesque singer, with whom Taylor put his expertise to profitable use in presenting parodies of Italian opera. Finding this less profitable the more he practised it, Taylor moved on to Philadelphia from Annapolis, and undertook the general occupations of a contemporary English musician. He was organist, teacher, composer, and impresario. In 1814 he played the organ at the newly opened Vauxhall Garden in Philadelphia, and six years later was a prime mover in the foundation of the Musical Festival Society in the city, which important body built its own Concert Room in 1824.

In 1792 there was a considerable exodus from London, and in September the *New York Daily Advertiser* announced the arrival in the United States of James Hewitt, Jean Gehot, B. Bergmann (violinists), William Young (flautist), and a 'cellist named Phillips. They were 'performers of music from the Opera House, Hanover-square, and professional Concerts under the direction of Haydn, Pleyel, etc, London'. This quintet of musicians, assisted by New York colleagues, signalised their arrival in the New World in a concert at Corre's Hotel, where they played works by Haydn, Pleyel, Stamitz, and by Phillips, Hewitt, and Gehot. Phillips followed convention by performing his own 'cello concerto. Hewitt produced a 'Battle' Symphony, for which there was ample precedent, and Gehot an overture in twelve sections descriptive of the voyage from England to America. One other Englishman of some importance came to America in the same year; George Gillingham—like Gehot a first violin in the Handel Commemoration—who was to lead Reinagle's orchestra in Philadelphia, and, like his other fellow-countrymen, to take part in the general organisation of concert life.

Towards the end of the century concerts went into relative decline, as prohibitions regarding the theatre were relaxed and a new era opened in the field of drama. New York particularly had reached saturation point in respect of subscription concerts and musicians began to look for opportunity elsewhere. Among them was Peter von (previously van) Hagen, of Dutch extraction, a pianist, conductor, composer, teacher, music-seller, and publisher. Von Hagen's wife was also a pianist and teacher, and their son, also Peter, a violinist. Their concerts in Boston were largely for the sake of publicity and exhibited promising pupils, whose efforts, it was hoped, would lead to a more general cultivation of domestic music-making. Among the performers at the von Hagen concerts, however, were two artists of quality, Gottlieb and Catherine Graupner.

BOSTON SOCIETIES

Gottlieb Graupner, oboeist and double-bassist (1767–1836), Hanoverian by birth, had spent five or six years in England (it is supposed that he, too, took part in Salomon's Haydn concerts) before sailing to America. For a time he lived in Charleston, South Carolina, playing the oboe in the theatre orchestra and occasionally appearing as soloist at benefit concerts. In Charleston he met Catherine Hillier, an English actress and singer, and in 1796 they were married. After moving about for three years they settled in Boston, where they readily became involved in the musical and theatrical life of the town. Graupner was a patient and successful teacher, and his formation of a Conservatory in 1801 in which his wife, Filippo Trajetta (1777–1854), an Italian, and Francis Mollet, a Frenchman, taught, was an important stage in the development of musical culture in Boston. Even though this institution was short-lived it stimulated another attempt at group-practice in 1813, and led to the eventual Boston Academy of Music which was incorporated in 1833. Graupner possessed business acumen as well as doggedness and also set up a publishing house through which he introduced to New England the most respected items in the European repertoire, from the works of the first Stamitz to those of Weber. After a decade of endeavour Graupner was able to found a Philharmonic Society. This functioned at first as a private society, but by 1817 had blossomed into a mixed professional and amateur orchestra competent to join with the Handel and Haydn Society of Boston in oratorio performances that immediately captivated the interest of the Bostonians. The oratorios were given in the Boylston Hall, capable of seating an audience of eight hundred, the orchestral concerts—promoted at regular intervals by the Philharmonic alone—in a hall in Pond Street and later in the new Pantheon. The Philharmonic faced many difficulties, lack of sufficiently expert players and dependence on visiting artists or more or less gifted amateurs, and lack of a sufficient variety of music, being conspicuous. But Graupner's persistence carried this body—largely with a repertoire to which he had accustomed himself as a young man—through many crises until it was integrated with the Handel and Haydn Society. This latter controlled the major concerts in Boston across the remainder of the first half of the nineteenth century, and in 1847 appointed its first professional conductor, Charles Edward Horn, the Anglo-German composer of 'Cherry Ripe'. Soon after this the Germania Orchestra (1849–1854) and the Mendelssohn Quintet Club (f. 1849) were established in Boston.

PHILHARMONIC SOCIETY OF NEW YORK

While Boston was developing its own institutions, so also was New York. James Hewitt had founded a Philharmonic Society, the Germans their Concordia, a choral body of forty singers, while in 1801 a third such body appeared under the name of the Euterpean Society. Of these societies the most important was the Concordia, directed by Daniel Schlesinger (1799–1839). Schlesinger, a piano pupil of Ries and Moscheles, came to New

York in 1836 and made a great impression both as a pianist and a conductor of the Concordia. After his untimely death in 1839 a memorial concert was given, the programme including Schlesinger's overture written for the Philharmonic Society of London and two movements from his piano quartet. Taking part in this concert were the Concordia and an *ad hoc* professional orchestra. From this sprang the idea of a permanent orchestra and through the exertions of Ureli Correlli Hill (1802–1875), a violinist and former pupil of Spohr in Kassel, the pianist William Scharfenberg (1819–1895), a German whom Hill had met in Kassel, and Henry Christian Timm (1811–1892), also a German and a pianist, a Philharmonic Society of New York was inaugurated on December 7, 1842, at the Apollo Rooms.

The programme was:

Symphony No. 5	Beethoven
	(Conductor, Hill)
Scena from *Oberon*	Weber
Pianoforte Quintet in D Minor	Hummel
Overture to *Oberon*	Weber
	(Conductor, D. G. Etienne)
Duet from *Armida*	Rossini
Scena from *Fidelio*	Beethoven
Aria from *Il Seraglio*	Mozart
Overture in D	Kalliwoda

In the first season three concerts were given, the conducting being shared between Hill, Timm, W. Alpers, Alfred Boucher, and George Loder. Thus there came into existence the third permanent and professional concert orchestra in the world, the only older ones being those in Leipzig and Vienna. It is not altogether surprising that the first Philharmonic Society of New York Orchestra was comprised largely of German players.

CONSIDERATION OF NATIONALISM

Human nature in itself does not vary greatly in fundamentals, so that a study of the capacity for musical appreciation, even according to the most scientific principles (so far as these can be established) generally shows what is intuitively, or empirically accepted; that there are those who are sympathetic, those who are antipathetic, and those who are indifferent to music. Arguments based on an inherently greater musicality in one nation than another are fallacious. The significant word is opportunity. And it is opportunity that caused the facile assessments of the nineteenth, and probably the twentieth, century. The Germans (and the Austrians), because of conditions which have already been outlined, built music into their way of life, and having done this found it a valuable faculty for promoting an internal sense of social solidarity centred on bourgeois standards and an appeal to national pride, and also for propagating German ideals elsewhere. The focal point of German music was the symphony, and in an age of expansion the symphony—and its cognate and derivative forms—expanded. The Revolution of 1848 came and went. Some musicians also went; so too did other representatives of the intelligentsia. But the hopes of the revolutionary year, and of the brief Frankfurt Parliament, were dissolved into political reaction and into a nationalism that was itself diverted in the direction of imperialism. German music, in itself a source of pride, became a symbol of continuity—hence the image-building applied to the old masters—and of unity: the concert thus became a solemnity. In the neighbouring countries that had long fallen under the German–Austrian cultural hegemony the middle classes, like the aristocracy, were orientated, by the adoption of language and by the processes of education, to Germany and to Austria; but in the countries on the eastern frontiers the forces of nationalism were too strong to be entirely defeated. National ideals showed through, in Russia, Bohemia, and Hungary, as in Italy, in opera; national theatres, at first a compromise, led to the endowment of national orchestras, and these, by the end of the century, had become a means of presenting special appeals to the outside world.

Relatively secure in the political sense and, as a nation, affluent beyond former understanding, the British, who had accustomed themselves to the idea that music was primarily a matter for resident, or visiting, Germans, Italians, or Frenchmen (to which conclusion they had been influenced by the European connections of the monarchy and by the rigorous view of entertainment imposed by the Established Church), relegated music to a position of secondary or tertiary importance. During the Victorian era the composer, unless he

19.   Queen Victoria at the People's Palace.

20. Opening of the Queen's Hall.

conformed to the dictates of commerce and produced ballads (more profitable to the singers and to the publishers than to himself), or unless with docility he scattered canticles and cantatas among the Anglican faithful, came off badly. If he wrote a concerto or an overture he took it to Leipzig for a first performance, hoping that in due course the increasingly con-servative Philharmonic Society would consider it[1]. In the great age of private initiative, however, there were numerous instances of its application to musical organisation, with often stimulating results. And when social consciences were pricked by the evidence of social inequality, or injustice, there were those who sought to express a conviction that music was rather nearer to being a necessity than a luxury through the extension of musical activity. The notion that great literature should be generally available, which found expression both in the issue of cheap books by publishing houses and the provision of libraries, in some cases was accompanied by a similar idea in respect of music. The fountain-head of the dogma was the Shelley–Lamb–Vincent Novello circle, which, on the publishing side, promoted the foundation of a great publishing house. The house of Novello exercised its own influence on the concert life of Britain during the second half of the nineteenth century.

SIGNIFICANCE OF THE ORCHESTRAL CONCERT

Among other factors which brought the orchestral concert into high prominence after the midway point of the nineteenth century was reached were these: the cult of the virtuoso, the educative potentialities within this medium, and the simple

---

[1] Bennett was a particular beneficiary of the Gewandhaus, where his overture *The Naiads* and his Piano Concerto in F Minor both had first performances, in 1837 and 1838. The situation remained depressing for the native composer. Thus F. H. Cowen could comment in 1895: 'Certainly, English music is performed a great deal more than it used to be, but I think there is plenty of room for improvement still. . . . the reason is to be found in the fact that the field is very limited. Take the symphony, for instance. No publisher would pay a good price for a symphony, because there are so few chances of having it performed. Fortunately for me, the Scandinavian Symphony was published in Vienna, and, in consequence, it has gone all through Germany, and, in fact, all over the Continent. There are, probably, fifty orchestral societies on the Continent to one in England. If a publisher saw his way to sell a hundred full scores of his symphony, he would be much more likely to pay a decent price.' Interview in *Strand Musical Magazine*, Jan.–June, 1895, p. 250.

wish not to appear inferior to others. In so far as the virtuoso was concerned his cult was a continuation of what was both familiar and, apparently, necessary. Although the singer still compelled attention in the nineteenth century, the pianist had become his near rival if not sometimes even superior in popularity, while the conductor—the supreme magician in the public eye—was beginning to outstrip both. In the Baroque and classical periods public music still generally affected relatively small associations, and, while there was a growing literature of the art, the problems attendant on musical invention or reproduction could be discussed more or less intimately. In the nineteenth century audiences were larger, and, since knowledge for the sake of knowledge was not held in disdain, there was an apparent need, to be met by the programme note. Of this the originator, as has been seen, was Reichardt; and it was a surprisingly long time before his lead was followed at all widely. The competitive element—still playing its part in international cultural behaviour—arose quite simply: the Bostonians and Philadelphians, for example, saw that an orchestra existed in New York, and took it as a civic indignity that they did not possess one of like standing. One aspect of the competitive spirit derived from certain historical accidents. The nineteenth century, an age of active nationalism, was happily placed to catch a crop of centenaries that could focus new attention on some parts of the concert repertoire and could show means whereby this repertoire could be enlarged.

THE SUPREMACY OF LEIPZIG

The enviable musical situation in which Leipzig found itself in the middle of the nineteenth century was due to a confluence of circumstances: to the tradition inherited from Bach, which branched out into scholarship while remaining fixed in civic esteem; to the pedagogic opportunities newly developed; to an established literature ancillary to concert performance, which took on a renewed lease of life under the inspired leadership of Robert Schumann; and to the inspiration of Mendelssohn, whose skill was applied to all departments of musical life, and whose catholic tastes, and equal respect for the old and the new, were responsible for widely ranging programmes. Mendelssohn gave the first performance of Schubert's 'Great C Major' Symphony in 1839. In the next year Schumann's first symphony was heard. While the 'Historic Concerts', devoted to Bach and Handel, Haydn, Mozart, and Beethoven, took place in the 1840–1841 season, Berlioz and Schumann took pride of place two years later. After Gade's brief conductorship in Leipzig the direction of the Gewandhaus—the orchestra at that time numbering about fifty-six players—was entrusted to another of Mendelssohn's protégés, Julius Rietz (1812–1877).

Rietz, a Berliner and a former pupil of Zelter, came to Leipzig from Düsseldorf, where he had also succeeded Mendelssohn in controlling both the ecclesiastical and the secular music of the city. He remained in Leipzig for twelve years, distinguishing himself in many fields. He promoted the interests of Berlioz, who conducted movements from *Harold in Italy* and *Faust* and the *Carneval Romain* overture at a concert on December 1, 1853, and of Brahms. The latter played his D Minor Piano Concerto in the Gewandhaus on January 27, 1859, without, however, persuading the audience that this was truly in the great tradition. Rietz came to conducting through the 'cello, on which he was an expert player, and thus set a precedent. He was a composer (his E flat symphony becoming a hardy annual in the German repertoire), a teacher, and an editor, whose scrupulous endeavours on behalf of Bach, Handel, Mozart, Beethoven, and Mendelssohn on the one hand, and Breitkopf and Härtel on the other, put him in the debt of every musical society in Europe for many years to come.

Rietz was succeeded by another musician of versatility in Carl Reinecke (1824–1910). Reinecke, whose compositions found some favour in England in an era in which a German composer was generally held to be incapable of error, was in office at the Gewandhaus for thirty-five years, until 1895, and while the classical composers formed the staple of the programmes Mendelssohn, Schumann, and Brahms were ratified in status as their worthiest successors. The first performance of Brahms' violin concerto, with Joachim, a frequent performer at the Gewandhaus over many years, was in 1879. During Reinecke's conductorship newer music was represented by Dvořák, Saint-Saëns, Rubinstein, Bruch, Grieg, Tchaikovsky, and Strauss, most of whom came to conduct their own works. On the other hand there were, once again, specialised concerts, such as the series of 1865–1866, based on a panorama of works from the sixteenth to the nineteenth century, or the French and Italian concerts (from *c.* 1550–1850) of the 1875–1876 season. In 1870 Reinecke was in charge of the Beethoven Centenary Concert, and eleven years later the festivities which marked the hundredth birthday of the Gewandhaus Concerts. This was an incentive to build a new concert hall, more fitted to the needs of the nineteenth century, and the work was entrusted to the Berlin architects Martin Gropius (1824–1880) and Heinrich Schmieden (1835–?). A classical, academic building, the new Gewandhaus was superbly designed for its purpose, and the reputation of its acoustics still acts as a criterion[1]. The large concert room accommodated an audience of one thousand seven hundred, the smaller, chamber-music room about a third of that number. The new Gewandhaus was opened on December 11, 1884, with Beethoven's *Die Weihe des Hauses* overture, a spoken Prologue (written by Rudolf von Gottschall), Bach's D Minor Toccata and Fugue (played on the new Walcker organ), Mendelssohn's Psalm 114, and the Choral Symphony. In the following March two ceremonial concerts, the second given by the court orchestra from Meiningen under Hans von Bülow, closed the old Gewandhaus. In 1892, the year in which Mendelssohn's statue (destroyed by the Nazis) was erected, Reinecke presided over the last commemorative occasion of his reign: the hundred and fiftieth anniversary of the *Grosses Konzert.*

THE CRITIC AS ARBITER OF TASTE

The extent to which music itself and attitudes to music are affected by critical journalism is debatable. What lies beyond debate is the capacity of the Press to arouse attention. Berlioz, Wagner, Schumann, and, somewhat later, Mosonyi of Budapest, were the principal musician-journalists of the Romantic era, and, while in each case they were defending their own positions, they spread an interest in music beyond the confines of opera-house, concert-hall, or church. In so far as they were progressive

---

[1] See T. Somerville and C. L. S. Gifford, 'Tonal Quality in Concert Halls', in *Mus. Times*, Sept., 1963, pp. 618 ff.

they may be said to have indicated in no uncertain terms the claims of contemporary music, and to have stressed the relationship between music and life. This, broadly speaking, may be said to have been the purpose of Romantic music.

Eduard Hanslick (1825–1904) was a writer of a different kind, detached from the practice of music, inclined to regard it as a thing-in-itself, and to pontificate from premises erected on an arbitrary system of abstract aesthetics. Hanslick, born in Prague and introduced to music by his parents, by Jan Tomašek, the leading Bohemian composer of his day, and by Johann Friedrich Kittl (1806–1868), conductor of the orchestra of the Prague Conservatorium, arrived in Vienna in 1846. His career as a music critic began when August Schmidt invited him to contribute to the *Wiener Musikzeitung*. During the next fifty years Hanslick, a formidably fluent, engaging, but provocative critic, built for himself an unassailable reputation in Vienna and further afield, and for many his utterances came to have the force of law. Hanslick's position was never in doubt. An idealist, he looked backward rather than forward, and assumed that the classical composers of Vienna especially had set standards beyond which progress was, to say the least, problematic. 'The most recent example of [Wagner's] reforms does not represent an enrichment, an extension, a renewal of music as did the art of Mozart, Weber, and Schumann. It is, on the contrary, a distortion, a perversion of basic musical laws, a style contrary to the nature of human hearing and feeling. One could say of this tone-poetry: there is music in it, but it isn't music[1].' Hanslick was resolute against Wagner, but also against Berlioz and Liszt; his later antipathies included Bruckner and Richard Strauss. On the other hand he consistently championed Schumann and Brahms. What Hanslick sought was 'nobility': what he abhorred was self-advertisement, and a conscious appeal on the part of composer or performer for easy applause. In an age of ferment Hanslick was not alone in thus seeking an 'ennoblement' of music, but he was the most persuasive and influential, and the later tyranny of the so-called classical, and the division of music into compartments, may be seen in large

---

[1] E. Hanslick, *Vienna's Golden Years of Music, 1852–1900*, trans. and ed. H. Pleasants, London 1951, p. xvi.

part as derived from his views. On the other hand the appreciation of technical standards which took place in Vienna in his day also owed something to his critical presence.

RENEWAL OF STANDARDS IN VIENNA

When Hanslick arrived in Vienna he reported musical life as being at a low ebb. The values which predominated lay in the Viennese Waltz, Italian Opera, and virtuoso recitals. The concerts of the *Gesellschaft der Musikfreunde*, and the *Concerts Spirituels* which were held in 1819–1848 in the church of St. Augustine, were uninspiring and marred by dilettantism. The *Tonkünstler-Gesellschaft* considered its duty done by annual performances of *The Seasons* and *The Creation*. In the period between the departure of Nicolai and the coming of Eckert the Philharmonic Society concerts lost their initial impetus and brilliancy of execution. The state, then, was one of decline, and the prevalence of triviality was the starting-point of Hanslick's critical campaign and provided a foundation for his aesthetic dogmas. That Vienna renewed its eminence in music was in fact in large measure due to Hanslick's reverence for proper authority. The revolution of 1848 provided incentive for a new way of thinking. Patriotism, the strongest note in that revolution, inspired a xenophobic outburst, and the Italian opera season of 1848 had to be cancelled. This outburst was due to 'a general trend toward all that was German—manners, politics, art'. Thus the position of the symphony—a German–Austrian creation—was enhanced and also the standing of the conductor who could most effectively bring symphony to life through the potential of the orchestra. There was another reason—'less conspicuous, but [which] played an undeniable part. It was of a democratic nature. Italian opera was regarded as an exclusive artistic expression of anti-German, and specifically aristocratic, entertainment'[1]. The result of this latter motivation was the ready acceptance, in Vienna, of Brahms, and the subsequent, if somewhat delayed, apotheosis of Bruckner—despite the opposition to this composer by both Hanslick and Brahms.

The improvement of the concerts in Vienna during the second half of the nineteenth century was, not surprisingly, due to a

[1] Hanslick, *ibid.*, p. 9.

succession of notable directors, to an elimination of unprofessional management, and to the provision of adequate accommodation. In 1831 a *Musikvereinsaal* had been built to replace the old, cramped, *Zum rothen Igel*, but as the orchestras increased in size (that of the Philharmonic coming up to eighty members) this also proved inadequate. In 1870 the third *Musikvereinsaal*, with a large hall for an audience of fifteen hundred, and two recital rooms, was erected. This was a notable period of building in Vienna (the Opera House was finished in 1869), and the architect of the *Musikvereinsaal* was Theophil von Hansen (1813–1891), a Dane, who was also responsible for the Parliament Building.

The Philharmonic Society Orchestra (all the players belonged to the Opera) was conducted by Eckert from 1854–1860, after which it came under the direction of Felix Dessoff (1835–1892), a notable exponent of Beethoven. Dessoff, a former student at the Leipzig Hochschule under Rietz, spent fifteen years as conductor of the Opera and of the Philharmonic. He also taught at the Conservatorium and in his pedagogic capacity was called upon to examine Bruckner in 1861. He agreed with his colleagues, Herbeck and Sechter, that Bruckner (whose music he never felt himself able adequately to understand) should have been examining the examiner. Through Dessoff's sympathy for the new as well as for the old, Wagner, despite Hanslick, was eventually accepted in the repertoire of the Philharmonic, which he conducted in 1872 and 1875. In 1863 Brahms's second Serenade was given its première at one of the Society's concerts, as were the Haydn Variations in 1873. In 1863 Brahms, disappointed at being passed over for the conductorship of the Hamburg Philharmonic Society in favour of Julius Stockhausen, was glad to accept that of the Wiener Singakademie (f. 1813), a post which he occupied only for a year, but which gave him the opportunity to take root in Vienna. In 1872 he became director of the *Gesellschaft der Musikfreunde*, which had been under professional direction since 1851.

The previous conductors of the *Gesellschaft* concerts were Joseph Hellmesberger (1828–1893), son of Georg, who befriended Wagner in Vienna in 1863[1], Johann Herbeck (1831–1877), Bruckner's most loyal sponsor, and, for one year only,

[1] *My Life*, II, p. 849.

Anton Rubinstein. The first recognised peak of achievement by the *Gesellschaft* was in 1861, in the performance of the *Missa Solemnis* under Herbeck. In the following year the *Singverein*, the choir of the *Gesellschaft* formed in 1858, gave the first Viennese performance of the *St. Matthew Passion*. In 1876 the *Gesellschaft*, whose programmes were complementary to those of the Philharmonic, gave the première of Brahms's first symphony, the second being undertaken two years later by the Philharmonic, now under Hans Richter.

Richter succeeded Dessoff in 1875 and proved himself the first truly international specialist conductor. Born in Hungary, Richter was educated in Vienna, where his mother (who sang the part of Venus in the first Viennese performance of *Tannhäuser* in 1857) was a celebrated singing-teacher. He was a violinist and a horn player, and for a time played in the orchestra of the Kärntnertor Theatre. Recommended by Heinrich Esser, he went to Lucerne to act as Wagner's amanuensis, from which commitment he passed to the conductorship of the Court and National Theatre in Munich for a year. Between 1871 and 1875 Richter was in charge of the national opera in Budapest, and in the later year his appearance as conductor in Vienna stimulated such enthusiasm that he was given the succession to Dessoff. A stern disciplinarian, a musician of fixed views (which overlapped those of Hanslick, except in respect of Wagner), Richter inculcated authority into his players, so that the Viennese were assured that in classical music Richter's presence was a guarantee of authoritative interpretations. Richter took the Philharmonic Orchestra to Salzburg in 1877, after which its participation in the Mozart Festival became customary, and to Budapest in 1879. In the meantime, however, he had been introduced to the concert life of England, where later he was to make a special contribution. For some time the musical affairs of England had pursued an unpredictable and somewhat unruly course.

PROGRESS AND REACTION IN LONDON

During the 1840's the periphery of London concert music was well occupied; by the miscellaneous concerts at Hanover

Square organised by Cipriani Potter[1], Henry Blagrove[2], or Michael Costa[3]—the orchestra on these occasions being a mixture of Opera and Philharmonic players in a free-lance capacity; the chamber music recitals undertaken by Charles Neate and, from 1845 when he founded the Musical Union, John Ella (1802–1888); by the oratorios, appealing to a wider public than the orchestral and chamber performances, given by the Sacred Harmonic Society which had been founded in 1833; and by a considerable variety of 'Grand Concerts' by which the virtuosi kept their names before the public. The most noteworthy out-of-the-run concert of a special virtuoso order was that conducted by Berlioz in Drury Lane Theatre on February 7, 1848. The programme included *Harold in Italy*, *Carneval Romain*, and the first two acts of *Faust*. A fillip to chamber music was given in 1845, when a Beethoven Quartet Society was established in London, as a result of the Beethoven Festival in Bonn that year, which was attended by Queen Victoria and the Prince Consort[4]. In the 1849–1850 season an attempt was made by the violinist John Willy (1812–1885) to popularise chamber music by low-cost performances in the recital room of the St. Martin's Hall (to be formally inaugurated in 1850 by John Hullah). 'What the Sacred Harmonic has done for choral music, and Mr Jullien for orchestral,' commented the *Musical World*, 'Mr Willy has begun to do for the music of the chamber.' Willy, himself a violinist, also got together an *ad hoc* orchestra for the London Wednesday Concerts (1848–1852, at the end of which period they had deteriorated into ballad concerts) at Exeter Hall. These too were aimed at the less wealthy and admission price ranged from one shilling to seven shillings in contrast with Philharmonic charges of four guineas for eight concerts, or one guinea for a single concert. While such efforts were being directed towards a new kind of audience John Hullah, singing-teacher and pioneer of mass-teaching methods, for his part was trying, by more direct methods, to educate the audience of the future.

[1] One of the attractions of Potter's 1840 concerts was 'One of S. Bach's Pedal Fugues with Signor Dragonetti'.
[2] 1811–72: violinist, one of the first pupils of the Royal Academy of Music, a member of Queen Adelaide's private band (1830–7), and founder of a quartet of which the other members were H. Gattie, J. B. Dando, and C. Lucas.
[3] 1808–84: Anglicised Italian musician, knighted in 1869.
[4] See Elwart, *op. cit.*, p. 344, etc.

The centre of activity, however, was still assumed to be the Philharmonic Society, which in the space of thirty years or so had developed the inertia that feeds on social success[1]. Conservatism was so strong that, despite Spohr, it was not until 1846 that a conductor, as distinct from a first violinist or pianist director, was appointed. This was Costa, hitherto a conductor of opera. The repertoire was conventional, with the main places occupied by selected symphonies of Haydn, Mozart, Beethoven, Mendelssohn, and Spohr, supplemented by overtures by Weber and Cherubini, and popular Italian opera arias and minor miscellaneous pieces selected for their display value. In 1852 dissatisfaction with the existing state of affairs found expression in a joint enterprise by Frederick Beale, music publisher, and Henry Wylde (1822–1890), pianist and composer. Between them they launched the New Philharmonic Society, which continued as pace-maker to the Philharmonic until 1879. The prospectus of the new society read as follows:

> The growing taste for the Arts, more especially for music, in this country, demands a new institution where the greatest works by the greatest masters of all ages may be heard by the public at large . . . Exclusiveness, the baneful hindrance to all progress of Art, will not be tolerated in this society . . . by the performance of new works a laudable curiosity is gratified, on the other hand encouragement is given to unknown and aspiring talent . . . The New Philharmonic does not entertain the opinion acted upon by an elder institution, that no schools but those which may be called classical are to be considered as capable of affording pleasure and that the works of such schools can only be enjoyed by a select few amateurs and artistes.

The New Philharmonic took up its quarters at Exeter Hall, undercut the Philharmonic by pricing tickets between two shillings and sixpence and ten shillings and sixpence, and engaged Berlioz, who had spent a somewhat frustrating period in London in the winter of 1847–1848, and had written of London musical life during the Great Exhibition year (1851) in

[1] '. . . to such an extent have the Philharmonic conferred their favours on dullness, to the exclusion of all that is good, great, or excellent, that the Society is becoming a worthless vessel manned with decrepit mariners, and o'erloaded with useless ballast.' Leading article from *Musical Periodical*, 1839, quoted in Ella: *Record of the Musical Union*, 1845, p. 7.

Les Débats, as its first conductor. The opening concert, on March 24, showed the progressive intention by presenting the 'Jupiter' Symphony, excerpts from Gluck's *Iphigenia in Tauris*, Beethoven's triple concerto, Weber's *Oberon* overture, and Berlioz's *Romeo and Juliet*. In the second concert the new music of England was represented by a piano concerto by Wylde and by an operatic masque by Edward Loder[1]. In 1853[2] the New Philharmonic gave the first London performance of Wagner's *Tannhäuser* overture, and the Philharmonic, by now determined to lose its reactionary reputation, riposted with Schumann's first symphony. Both works got a bad press, and *The Times* managed to work into its notice an unflattering comment on native music. The symphony, it said, 'made a dead failure and deserved it. Few of the ancient "Society of British Musicians" symphonies were more incoherent and thoroughly uninteresting.'

Internal dissensions and a loss of revenue on the 1854 season led to the resignation of Costa from the Philharmonic and, after attempts had been made to procure Berlioz (already under contract by the rival society), Wagner was invited to undertake a season. Wagner's conducting, resulting in 'coarse, monotonous, uniformly loud, and at the same time rigorously frigid performance', according to the *Musical World*, was not greatly appreciated, but his choice of programmes, which included works by Charles Lucas[3], Cipriani Potter[4], and George Macfarren[5], as well as, of course, of specimens of his own music, was commended by the progressive and thus it was easier for Sterndale Bennett, who became conductor of the Philharmonic, to break lances in championship of his old friend Schumann. In 1858 Clara Schumann appeared at a Philharmonic concert, as also at the New Philharmonic—where she played Robert's

---

[1] 1813–65: a pupil of Ferdinand Ries at Frankfurt, Loder's primary interest was in music for the theatre. His *The Brooklet* (Wilhelm Müller's *Wohin*, as set by Schubert) is still occasionally to be heard.

[2] For Berlioz's comments on the feverish state of musical life in London in this year, see *Berlioz in London*, A. W. Ganz, London, 1950, p. 175.

[3] 1808–69: succeeded Potter as Principal of the Royal Academy in 1859. Wagner conducted Lucas's *Sinfonia in B flat, No. 3*, at the fourth of his concerts.

[4] Symphony in A Minor, at the fifth concert.

[5] The Overture *Chevy Chase*, which had been played at a Gewandhaus concert in 1843.

piano concerto, at the Musical Union, and at Sterndale Bennett's private soirées.

Meanwhile Jullien, interrupting his Covent Garden concerts with a lengthy visit to America, was achieving great success with his Promenade Concerts. Spectacular—Jullien dressed for the part and only conducted Beethoven in white gloves, ceremonially handed to him on a silver salver—with an immense variety of tone-colours derived from the two worlds of orchestral and military band music, and with programmes that swept from Mozart and Beethoven at one extreme to the *Fall of Sebastopol*[1] at the other, these concerts promised to furnish a permanent foundation for a truly popular cult of music; but in 1856 Covent Garden was burned down, and Jullien's career thereafter declined both rapidly and disastrously.

MANNS AT THE CRYSTAL PALACE— AND PROGRAMME NOTES

As a result of the Great Exhibition of 1851, however, there was another possible auditorium in London, to be more exact at Sydenham, where the Crystal Palace had been moved. In 1854 concerts by a wind band, conducted by August Manns (1825–1907), a former German band conductor, took place. Two years later, after a string ensemble had been added, from 'double-handed' wind players on the strength plus a few supernumeraries, a Mozart centenary concert was projected at Crystal Palace, and this was the origin of the series of Saturday concerts that were to play a conspicuous part in English musical life for nearly half a century. It was the first Crystal Palace concert that stabilised the analytical programme note, and brought into prominence the most distinguished author of such notes of the nineteenth century: George Grove (1830–1900).

[1] This quadrille sequence of five movements was a piece of programme music fit to end all programme music: in the last movement the music indicated 'the deafening noise of exploding mines, the row of cannons, the whistling of the bullets, the hurtling of the shells, the rattling of the drums, the shrill sound of the trumpets, the ships blown in the air, the cries of the fugitives and the shouts of the victors', culminating in *Partant pour la Syrie* and *God Save the Queen* (programme note). Performances of this work led to rough-house displays by gangs of toughs, which in turn led to police-court proceedings. See Henry Davison (compiler), *From Mendelssohn to Wagner*, London, 1912, pp. 201–2.

Grove did not invent the programme note. As has already been seen Reichardt probably deserves the initial credit, while John Ella at the Musical Union, John Thomson at the first Reid concert in Edinburgh on February 12, 1841, John Hullah at the historical concerts at Exeter Hall, Wylde at the New Philharmonic, and Thomas Bowlby in respect of *The Fall of Sebastopol* at Jullien's concerts, all provided sporadic literary asides to music. But Grove found the formula, blending biography and dissection, which has proved to be most acceptable to the professional and the amateur musician alike; a formula that is, for practical purposes, the one in current use at the present day.

'The analytical programme', said Grove in a speech in 1850, 'originated entirely from the suggestion of a friend. We were going to celebrate the birthday of Mozart in 1856, when the Crystal Palace music was just beginning to struggle into existence, and Mr Manns said to me how much he wished that I would write a few words about Mozart himself, and about the works to be performed. I tried it, and that gave me the initiation; and after that, as the Saturday Concerts progressed, I went on week after week. I wrote about the symphonies and concertos because I wished to make them clear to myself, and to discover the secret of the things that charmed me so; and then from that sprang a wish to make other amateurs see it in the same way . . . '

The incentives to inspire the amateur in Victorian England were powerful, springing from self-esteem, national pride, and a desire to be on terms of parity with the leading European musical countries, on the one hand, and from a wish to escape from the spiritual traumas inflicted by an industrialised and increasingly materialistic society on the other. The Victorian conclusion to these several impulses, under the influence of mythological premises concerning the ultimate origins of music and the moral dogmas that were publicly preached, was, on the whole, that music should be imported and imposed: the idea that native self-expression should be nurtured was too often ignored. Paradoxically it was the German directors of English concerts who did most for native composers, and of these Manns was the most generous. 'When I began my work in 1855 at the Crystal Palace,' he said, 'I could scarcely find half a dozen English composers whose works were suitable for the grand

Crystal Palace Saturday Concerts. The catalogue of music performed at those concerts since 1855 contains the names of three hundred and forty-three composers, of whom no fewer than one hundred and three were born and trained in England.' Among these composers were Sterndale Bennett, Sullivan, Parry, and Stanford, of the Establishment, and Henry Leslie[1], J. F. Bennett[2], Ebenezer Prout, F. H. Cowen, Frederick Corder, G. A. Macfarren, Hamish McCunn, Alexander Mackenzie, Frederic Cliffe[3], Henry Gadsby[4], and Edward Elgar, whose scores arrived on Manns's desk more fortuitously. Manns, who conducted at the provincial festivals and organised the great Handel jamborees at the Crystal Palace in which the northern choirs were invited to take part, was indeed one of the greatest influences on British music. Without his refinement of the popularising projects of Jullien the Promenade Concerts of Newman and Wood would have been without proper foundation; without the impact made by his personality, and by his disciples, further movements within the field of education would have lacked force; had it not been for his championship of the British composers the latter might well, for practical purposes, have ceased to exist.

ST. JAMES'S HALL

Another factor bearing on the general expansion of the metropolitan musical life during the latter half of the century was St. James's Hall, in Piccadilly. This was the result of complaints at the inadequacy of the existing halls for contemporary needs and the initiative for its erection came from the publishing houses of Beale and Chappell and Co, who formed a company

[1] 1822–96: a pioneer in amateur music, who founded the Henry Leslie Choir (with the first intention of cultivating madrigals) and in 1863 was the conductor of the Herefordshire Philharmonic Society.

[2] 1837–1906: student in Leipzig where he appeared as pianist at the Gewandhaus, and a prolific composer of unpopular symphonic and popular choral music.

[3] 1837–1931: born in Bradford, where he astonished his acquaintances by performing the whole of the '48', he became a teacher at the Royal College of Music. His Symphony in C Minor (Op. 1) was rejected by the Leeds Festival Committee but on being played at the Crystal Palace, on April 20, 1889, created a considerable impression.

[4] 1842–1907: Manns put his *Columbus* for male voices into a Crystal Palace programme in 1881.

to promote it. The architect was Owen Jones (1806–1889), who had been responsible for some of the detail of the Crystal Palace, and he designed an auditorium capable of seating an audience of about two thousand: beyond this was a recital room, and a suite of necessary ancillary offices. St. James's Hall was opened in March, 1858, with a concert in aid of the Middlesex Hospital, and in the course of the next year Arthur Chappell, of the publishing house of that name, established a series of Popular concerts ('Monday Pops', after 1865, in alternation with 'Saturday Pops') with the dual intention of helping to pay the running costs of the hall and also aiding the general movement towards the democratic emancipation of great music. Phenomenally, the Popular concerts were of chamber music, and the artistes who performed for the shilling-a-time audiences included Charles Santley, Louis Ries, Alfredo Piatti—who performed at the first and also the thousandth such concert on April 4, 1887—Joachim and Clara Schumann. This enterprise was commemorated by Robert Browning in *The Founder of the Feast*.

Thanks, then to Arthur Chappell, thanks to him,
Whose every guest henceforth not idly vaunts,
Sense has received the utmost Nature grants,
My cup is filled with rapture to the brim,
When, night by night—ah, memory, how it haunts!
Music was poured by perfect ministrants,
By Hallé, Schumann, Piatti, Joachim.

It was also memorialised by W. S. Gilbert in *The Mikado*:

The music-hall singer attends a series
Of masses and fugues and 'ops'
By Bach, interwoven
With Spohr and Beethoven,
At classical Monday Pops.

The vogue for chamber music thus established (Ella also transferred his Musical Union to St. James's Hall, where it functioned until 1880) was one of the most striking features of London musical life during the last part of the nineteenth century, and when the Popular concerts came to an end in 1898 an epoch during which the most aristocratic form of music had been brought into the broader esteem closed.

Although St. James's Hall was a great asset when it was built, organisations were generally reluctant to change their habits, and it was not until 1869 that the Philharmonic Concerts found a home there. Ten years later the most ambitious orchestral undertaking so far envisaged was added to the engagements of the Hall. This was the series of St. James's Hall Concerts, which soon became more generally known by the name of their conductor, Hans Richter.

Richter had conducted in the eight Wagner concerts of 1877 in the Albert Hall[1] and then expressed a wish to return to London. The opportunity came ten years later, and the agent largely responsible for his return was Hermann Francke. On Monday, May 5, 1879, Richter presided over an orchestra of one hundred and ten players, led by Francke, for his first St. James's Hall concert. The soloists were Clementine Schuch-Proska, from the Royal Opera in Dresden, and George Henschel; the programme containing the *Kaisermarsch*, excerpts from *Tannhäuser*, *Die Meistersinger*, *Die Fliegende Holländer*, by Wagner, from Mozart's *Die Entführung aus der Serail*, Schumann's *Manfred* overture, and Beethoven's Seventh Symphony, was entirely German. Yet Richter it was who perceived the real genius of Elgar, whose *Enigma Variations* were given their première at a Richter concert in St. James's Hall on June 19, 1899. From London Richter moved to Manchester, where he conducted the Hallé Orchestra until 1911. Richter's contribution to the technical side of British music was great. Apart from his enthusiasm for Elgar he kept the repertoire mostly within the ranges of German taste, but in respect of Beethoven and Wagner (his own insight into the former was affected by his close personal acquaintance with the latter) he intensified understanding by the scrupulous care paid to the scores, while his former experience as an orchestral player earned respect from his players, and thus the whole standard of orchestral performance was enhanced. 'Richter,' said one violinist, 'taught the fiddles in British orchestras to use uniform bowing. We must thank him for *that*.[2]'

---

[1] Built between 1817–71, under the general direction of H. G. D. Scott (1822–83).

[2] Percy A. Scholes, *The Mirror of Music, 1844–1904*, London, 1947, I, p. 385.

On the credit side immigrant European musicians (mostly, but not entirely, German), raised executant standards in Britain, both by example and by teaching, there being few large towns at the end of the century without a few music-teachers of foreign birth. On the debit side native creative aspirations were either suppressed or else directed towards the narrowly academic ends held as ideal in the major German teaching establishments. The situation in the United States was not dissimilar.

THE AMERICAN SITUATION IN THE LATER
NINETEENTH CENTURY

In 1848 a complete orchestra arrived, refugee-wise, in New York. On October 5, it was announced in the *Tribune* that after the performance of the play, *Lady of Lyons*, at William Niblo's Astor Place Theatre, there would be a 'Grand Instrumental Concert by the Germania Music Society, consisting of twenty-five performers, from Berlin, directed and conducted by Herr Lenschow'. A few days later the Germanians, now so termed, set out on a series of concerts of their own promotion. The programmes, aimed at the general public and its supposed taste, or lack of taste, included popular dances, polkas, and waltzes, selections from the currently favoured opera composers, pot-pourris, and realistic—mostly military—programmatic works. In these, inevitably punctuated by firearms, fireworks, even fire-engines, audiences had good reason vicariously to applaud the old Mannheim masters, from whom came the commanding effects of *crescendo* and *decrescendo*. The Germanians, however, sensitive to more enlightened standards of appreciation, also played the works of Mozart, Beethoven, and Weber, and in a peregrinatory career through the major American cities that lasted until their disbandment in 1854 found most response in Boston. It was here in 1852–1853 that they gave twenty subscription concerts, in the course of which six symphonies by Beethoven, two by Mozart, and one each by Haydn and Mendelssohn, were played, as well as the Finale of *Tannhäuser*, the latter being heard, with some incredibility, for the first time in America.

Carl Lenschow left the Germanians in 1850 and settled in Baltimore. His successor was Carl Bergmann, the 'cellist, who after being occasional conductor of the New York Philharmonic Society in alternation with Theodor Eisfeld, became its director in 1866, a post which he maintained until 1876. The flute player of the Germanians, Carl Zerrahn (1826–1929), stayed in Boston, where he remained a highly important influence in the city's music until his death. Between 1855 and 1863 he conducted various orchestras designated Philharmonic; for nearly half a century he was in charge of the Handel and Haydn Society; he directed the concerts of the Harvard Musical Association, and conducted the Worcester, Massachusetts, Festivals, for thirty years. Of the other immigrants of 1848 Eisfeld, formerly conductor of the Court Theatre in Wiesbaden and of the Concerts Viviennes in Paris, and Otto Dresel (1826–1890), pupil of Hiller and Mendelssohn, and friend of Robert Franz, broadened interest in chamber music in New York and Boston respectively, thus giving a new dimension to American appreciation.

While the one side of concert life was thus being strengthened, virtuosi of one sort or another, almost all visitors, were exposing the less experienced among Americans to the allurements of the spectacular. Ole Bull, Jenny Lind, Henrietta Sontag, Henri Herz, Sigismund Thalberg, all made considerable profits out of one-night stands—Jenny Lind, indeed, was said to have collected 175,000 dollars in two seasons—and were followed by a tribe of other performers. In 1853 Jullien arrived with a number of 'the most distinguished Professors, selected from the Royal Opera Houses of London, Paris, Vienna, Berlin, St. Petersburg, Brussels, etc' and let the Americans see all his tricks.

'Monsieur Jullien,' said the New York *Courier and Enquirer*, is a humbug; which may be news to our readers, but it is not news to M. Jullien. Let us not be misunderstood. M. Jullien is not a pitiful humbug, or a timorous humbug, or worse than all, an unsuccessful humbug; he is a splendid, bold, and dazzling successful humbug; he who merits his great success almost as much as if he had not employed the means by which he has achieved it. The discipline of his orchestra is marvellous. He obtains from fifty strings a pianissimo which is scarcely audible and he makes one hundred instruments stop in the middle of a fortissimo which seems to lift the roof, as if a hundred men dropped dead at the movement of his hand.

There was another point. Jullien invited works from American composers, and if possible played them. Thus William Henry Fry (1815?–1864), a composer of more valour than discretion, more ambition than ability, and with a vigorous pen which he used in the native interest, having written four symphonies found one of them—the *Santa Claus* Symphony—on Jullien's list. The critics did not like it, but the acrimonious public correspondence that ensued invited the participation of George F. Bristow (1825–1898), composer, conductor, director and violinist of the Philharmonic, and a patriot. Feeling ran high between Bristow and his fellow directors of the Philharmonic, who felt that Bristow's strictures on their un-American proclivities were unjustified. In consequence Bristow resigned from the Society, but after a year's absence returned, considering that while he could as conductor of his own Harmonic Society encourage the interests of American composers the well-being of the Philharmonic was, taking the long view, of supreme importance.

It was at this juncture that there appeared the first American conductor competent by other standards. This was Theodore Thomas (1835–1905). The Thomas family came to New York in 1845, from the neighbourhood of Hanover, and within the next year or so Theodore was exhibited as a prodigy violinist. At the age of sixteen he was frequently playing at a first violin desk in various orchestras, and five years later organising concerts of chamber music. In 1867 he turned conductor, undertaking fifteen concerts at the Irving Hall with his own orchestra, the first being on May 13. The programme on this occasion included the overture to *Die Fliegende Holländer* (which brought harp and cor anglais into an American orchestra for the first time) and Liszt's arrangement of Schubert's 'Wanderer' Fantasia, with William Mason as pianist. The Steinway Hall being opened in 1866, Thomas transferred there, with five concerts annually. This number was dictated by circumstance, for Thomas recognised that competent performance depended on permanence of personnel and employment, and the only way in which this could be ensured, if at all,

217

was on a peripatetic basis. This was not the most satisfactory arrangement, but there was no alternative, short of the kind of subsidisation commonplace in Germany but less acceptable elsewhere. While thus arranging his own affairs Thomas was conducting the Brooklyn Philharmonic, at first in conjunction with Eisfeld, and after 1866 independently.

His most striking early achievement, however, was in the field of the popular concert, in which Thomas may be said to have practised a moderate de-jullienisation. In 1865 there were thirty-two concerts in the Belvedere Lion Park. In 1866–1867 he conducted one hundred and eighty-seven in Terrace Gardens. In the following year he took a lease from the restaurateurs and set up in Central Park Garden, which he rapidly turned into 'the most interesting and important music center in the city and nation'. In seven years he gave one thousand, one hundred and twenty-seven orchestral concerts and, weaning his audiences from the merely trivial, introduced complete evenings of Mozart[1], Beethoven, Schubert, and Wagner, all the symphonies of Schumann, the works of Berlioz, Liszt, and (specially congenial to Thomas) Brahms.

Thomas's programmes were, indeed far more progressive than those of the London Philharmonic Society at the same time. Having established contact with Chicago (in which city the tentative Philharmonic set up in 1854 collapsed after encountering the standards presented by Thomas) he was invited to transfer his popular concerts from New York to the Exposition Hall of Chicago. In the meantime he was appointed to organise the Cincinnati Festival—the consequence of the festivals of German choral societies that had taken place since 1869—and other important commitments followed in Philadelphia and New York. During this period, however, he was often at odds with the commercial backers whose attitude to music, whether in the concert hall or in the conservatory, was conditioned by the inviolability of the profit motive. (A College of Music was founded in Cincinnati in 1878, from which Thomas resigned after a year's direction for this reason.) Nonetheless, largely

---

[1] E.g. Introduction and Fugue in C Minor; Masonic Funeral Music; 'Concertone' for two solo violins, solo oboe, 'cello obbligato, and orchestra; overture to *Figaro*; 'Jupiter' symphony; Concerto for flute, harp, and orchestra; *Rondeau de chasse*.

through his persistence with his own orchestra. Thomas was making progress: he was recognised as the leading exponent of orchestral music in the country, and in 1880 was, for the second time, given charge of the New York Philharmonic.

This orchestra had fallen on evil days against the competition of the recently formed Symphony Society of New York (1878), of which the conductor was Leopold Damrosch and Thomas's own orchestra. Thomas remained at the head of the Philharmonic for twelve years, restoring its standards and also breaking new ground by providing concerts for young people. An attempt to do for opera what he had done for the orchestral concert brought him to a state of financial disorder, but a condition of personal disillusionment with the uncertainties of American musical life was eventually relieved when, in 1891, the Chicago (later Symphony) Orchestra was founded on the solid basis of well-backed promissory notes from fifty prosperous citizens. Their faith in Thomas was not misplaced, and during his fourteen years' tenure of office, the Chicago Orchestra became the most prominent in the country. This was due to the quality of the playing, but also to the imagination which the conductor brought to the task of programme-building. Here he was a firm supporter of the claims of American composers, and his lively interest in a wider field was shown by his promotion of the works of Elgar.

Thomas made the American symphony orchestra. His accomplishment was thus generously recognised in 1870 by Anton Rubinstein in a letter to one of the Steinways:

> I have found in America something which I least expected to find. I had no idea that such a new country had an orchestra like Theodore Thomas's. Never in my life ... have I found an orchestra that was as perfect an organisation as Theodore Thomas has created and built up[1].

He also made the American audience. He civilised taste and he civilised manners, which if no worse than in Berlin or Vienna according to Hanslick's strictures, were not very creditable.

[1] 'Thomas and Central Park Gardens', in *Music Quarterly*, *XXVI*, 1940, p. 149.

Not a work passes without some scathing rebuke from him to those ill-bred and ignorant people who keep up a continual buzzing during the performance of the music to the annoyance of decent folk[1].

Thomas was a pioneer, and it is not surprising that often his way was difficult. His ultimate success, the result of idealism backed by extraordinary tenacity, was, however, not only in his own endeavours but also in those of others who took him as their model. The most notable extension of Thomas's ideas regarding orchestral music was in Boston, where in 1881 the Boston Symphony Orchestra was founded[2]. The promoter of this was Major Henry Lee Higginson, who having fully endowed the organisation ran it according to his own ideas. His philosophy in the matter was simple. 'Higginson, who had been a music student in Vienna, was well aware what a paternalistic government could accomplish. However, in this country, according to his creed, this function should devolve upon paternalistic capitalism, through the efforts of those who had been financially successful[3].' On the practical side the conditions were equally clear. These included full-time service (with permission to give private lessons in free periods), adequacy of rehearsal, and a cautiously progressive basis for programme selection. 'I do not,' said Higginson, 'like Wagner's music and take little interest in much of the newer composers, but I should not like to bar them out of our programmes. People of education equally objected to the later compositions of Beethoven as those of a lunatic. Possibly they were right. But, of course, anything *unworthy* is to be shut out.'

In so expressing himself (in the statement of aims issued as preliminary to the foundation of the Boston Symphony Orchestra) Higginson laid down a pattern of words which had been accepted by many among the newer patrons of music; and neither to the advantage of music itself nor its audiences. The crucial word is 'unworthy'.

---

[1] *Dwight's Journal of Music*, July 10, 1875.

[2] The first conductor was George Henschel, who was followed by Wilhelm Gericke in 1889, and he by Nikisch, who remained in Boston until 1893.

[3] John H. Mueller, *The American Symphony Orchestra*, Bloomington, Indiana, 1951, p. 80.

12

Music for the People

*J*N 1845 BENJAMIN DISRAELI published *Sybil*, and there-in was set forth the sharpest and plainest description of the two nations that comprised the English people: 'the rich and the poor'. Before this time, although a division in music was tacitly accepted—'Gentlemen's Concerts' making an effective frontier in the field of instrumental music—the barriers were not absolute. For the music of the Gardens and oratorio performances, especially in the north of England, were widely appreciated, without any suggestion that one kind of music was fit for some and another kind for others. The merits of the music of the Gardens, in its heyday at least, was that it was comprehensive, ranging from symphonies to ballads. The pattern was, as has been seen, transferred to the concerts of Jullien and of Manns, and, at the end of the century, to the Promenade Concerts begun by Henry Wood, in the newly built Queen's Hall, in 1895. But since the British middle-class, varied in circumstance but uniform in apparent respectability, was large, the popular side of the concert tradition increasingly drew its clientèle from this class. It should be made clear, however, that any such circumscription was alien to the philosophies of Jullien, Manns, or Wood, whose concern was that music should not be exclusive.

LIVERPOOL PHILHARMONIC

Apart from the stimulus these conductors afforded to other concert-giving agencies, they also assisted the revivification of amateur instrumental music (that has been seen to have been at a low ebb at the beginning of the nineteenth century) and many Philharmonic Societies sprang up in all parts of the country. After the manner of the eighteenth century they included a few professional players, but mostly comprised reasonably well-informed amateurs. One such society, which was later to achieve considerable eminence, was the Liverpool Philharmonic Society, which gave its first quarterly performance, in Mr Lassell's Saloon, Great Richmond Street, on March 12, 1840. Lassell was in an authentic line; he was a dancing-master. The conductor was John Russell, and the programme—clearly designed to appeal to all tastes—was:

I

Overture [?] (first time in Liverpool)	Kalliwoda
Glee	Bishop
'Fire, fire'	Morley
Round—'The Sun has been long on old Mont Blanc'	
	Bishop
The Music in 'Macbeth'	[?] Matthew Locke
Finale—Chorus, 'Bright Orb'	Bishop

II

Overture, *La Fiancée* (first time in Liverpool)	Auber
'Fair as a bride' (William Tell)	Rossini
'Flora gave me fairest flowers'	Wilbye
Sextet	Onslow
Trio, *Azor and Zemira*	Spohr
A Glee and a Chorus	Bishop

In 1846 the foundation stone of a Philharmonic Hall was laid, and three years later the building (which was burned down in 1933) was ready for occupation. By this time the Society's orchestra had much increased in strength and comprised ninety-six players, of whom the majority were professional. The appeal of the Society, however, whether in its 'Full Dress' or 'Undress' Concerts (the prevalence of those described by the first label in England until well into the twentieth century is a good indication as to the type of audience expected) was to the prosperous bourgeoisie of Merseyside. To make the point quite clear the programmes carried this legend:

No gentleman above twenty-one years of age residing or carrying on business in Liverpool, or within ten miles thereof, and not being an officer of the Army or Navy or Minister of Religion, is admissible to the Boxes or Stalls at the Philharmonic Society's Concerts, unless he be a Proprietor, a member of a Family residing at the home of a Proprietor, or has his name upon the list of Gentlemen having entrée exhibited in the corridors.

And so it was with other similar, if less ambitious, societies.

THE APPROACH TO THE WORKING CLASSES IN VICTORIAN ENGLAND

The working classes were confined to choral music (although after 1845 the brass band began to assume importance in industrial England). At their skill the critics were often surprised. For their benefit a number of selfless practitioners—Joseph Mainzer, a refugee from Germany and the author of *Singing for the Million*, John Hullah, the first seriously to take in hand the musical training of teachers, and John Curwen, a Methodist minister and the chief promoter of the system of *sol-fa*—laboured with astonishing success.

At the same time the independent movement for adult education was touching the intellectual fringes of musical appreciation. There were two reasons for this. On the one hand, as in the case of other voluntarily supported charities (and education was regarded as a charity), musical performance was a means of raising funds: thus, as early as May 10, 1832, there was a concert to raise funds for the London Mechanics' Institute, at which 'W. Sterndale Bennett, a pupil of Mr W. H. Holmes' played. On the other the natural instinct of the working people for music, of which the public-houses provided disconcerting evidence, was a means whereby their attention could be turned into other channels. William Gardiner describes how the Strutt family, Derbyshire cotton magnates, remarkably introduced orchestral music under competent supervision into their mills at Belper[1]; and in his autobiography, Thomas Cooper of Lincoln details the development of choral and orchestral music in the Mechanics' Institute in Lincoln[2]. Mainzer was a god-send (as were also Hullah and Curwen), and classes based

---

[1] William Gardiner, *Music and Friends, 1838-53*, pp. 511-12.
[2] Thomas Cooper, *The Life of Thomas Cooper, written by Himself*, 1872, p. 107.

The subject of music in adult education in the Victorian era is dealt with by Reginald Nettel in *The Englishman makes music*, London, 1952.

on his methods were set up in many institutions, especially in London, the Manchester region, and Scotland.

But such propagation of music was less concerned with establishing an amenity than extending the principles of social reclamation and reform. In an expansionist age, in which newly chartered cities vied with each other in the erection of public monuments, Town Halls were built. Being intended for various purposes the concert facilities they afforded varied, but in all cases the high moral support which was expected by the city fathers to derive from music was symbolised in great organs. Sometimes the intention was more specifically stated, as in Bradford, where it was hoped cheap concerts might 'draw away the votaries of the beershops and the public houses'. When the Lancashire and Cheshire Philharmonic Institute issued a report on July 7, 1845, it was hoped to 'rescue music from the gin-shops, the proprietors of which were using it as a bait for custom'. The Irish priest and temperance advocate, Father Mathew, coined a phrase which, intelligible in its context, has tended to overhang the intentions of all subsequent musical do-gooders. 'Our teetotalers,' he declared at Cork in 1842, 'will all become pupils, and, their affections being purified and exalted, they will never again be enslaved by the gross passion of intemperance.'

HALLÉ ORCHESTRA OF MANCHESTER

It was shortly after this that music in Manchester took a new turn with the arrival in the city of Charles Hallé (1819–1895), who was appointed to take over the direction of the existing orchestral society of the Gentlemen's Concerts from January 1, 1850. Hallé, German by birth and a pianist who had attracted the favourable notice of Spohr in Kassel, had played in London with success for a number of years before the events of 1848 led him to make his permanent home in England. Having carried on his orchestra in Manchester for some time the Art Treasures Exhibition held in the city in 1857 provided the opportunity to plan more ambitiously. The orchestra was enlarged and strengthened, and the concerts of 1857 were so fruitful of promise that Hallé was loth to disband his team. In 1858, therefore, he, like Theodore Thomas in America, took the initiative of giving a series of Subscription Concerts, which he hoped might be self-supporting. The first was on January 30, in the Free Trade Hall[1]. At the end of sixteen concerts Hallé found that he had a paying proposition: the profits on the season amounted to half-a-crown. Taking encouragement from this he continued, and, with a sideways look at the democratic principles that were in evidence around him, insisted on the provision of cheap seats, at a shilling each, for the less prosperous.

The programmes were as lively as any to be heard in London, embracing the established classics, but also the new music of Sterndale Bennett (Pianoforte Concerto in F Minor) and Gade (Symphony in C Minor), as well as 'Old Jacobite Songs' such as could awaken ancient memories in Manchester, and Liszt's arrangement of the 'Hungarian National March' (always marked, 'by desire'). This latter was held in high affection in a city in which Liberalism was in the ascendant, and where the recent Hungarian War of Liberation had found many friends for the Magyar cause. The extent to which Hallé succeeded in his undertaking was indicated in the *Musical World* of January 14, 1860:

'Mr Charles Hallé's Manchester concerts are becoming the vogue with all classes, from the rich merchant and manufacturer to the middle-class tradesmen and bourgeois, and from the middle-class tradesmen and bourgeois to the respectable and thrifty, albeit humbler, artisans.'

MUNICIPAL ATTITUDES

Concentration on the respectable, thrifty, humble artisan was splendid; but no attempt was then made to explain why he should not enjoy music to the same extent as his social superiors. The zest for choral music was separated from a

[1] Built to the plans of Edward Walters between 1853 and 1856.

The programme for January 30, 1858 was: Overture, *Der Freyschütz*, Weber; Andante in A flat (Symphony in E flat), Mozart; Concertstück in F Minor (played by Hallé), Weber; Symphony No. 1, in C, Beethoven: Overture, *La Sirène*, Auber; Ballet des Sylphes, *Faust*, Berlioz; Selection, *Il Trovatore* (arr. M. Baetens), Verdi; 3 Songs without Words (played by Hallé), Mendelssohn; Overture, *Le Siège de Corinthe*, Rossini.

Reserved seats 2/6; Unreserved seats in the Gallery and Body of the Hall 1/–; Subscription for eight concerts £1.

general sense of appreciation, and since it inevitably came to be regarded as *sui generis*, and socially confined, it also came to be considered as of inferior musical standing: a conclusion of which the effects have lingered on. The patron saint of the artisan choralist was Handel, and since the narrower reflections of divines and doctors of music had taken strong hold, the heresy that the primary purpose of music was to improve morality was accepted in the lower échelons of society (insofar as the matter received attention) and grew into a myth. The myth was assisted by the triennial rites accorded to Handel at the Crystal Palace, where, from 1857 until 1926, oratorios were given by three to four thousand performers, among whom large contingents of singers were drawn from the chorally strong provinces. These performances, conducted successively by Costa, Manns, Cowen, and Henry Wood, were of immense social and musical importance, both adding to and detracting from the native musical tradition. The chief item to be noted on the debit side was the consistent alienation of the largest sections of the community from other kinds of music, from which stemmed the conviction that missionaries should set to work to reclaim the lost souls for Mozart and Beethoven. A further proposition appeared. Music along these lines was profitable; there was, therefore, no reason why *laissez-faire* economic principles should not be allowed to work, thereby relieving authority of any further demands on its collective conscience. Thus it was that concert halls in Britain, and music in general, fell outside the legislation that brought Art Galleries and Public Libraries into the field of public responsibility.

BIRMINGHAM

Having accepted a missionary intention as a unique part of the English Victorian musical scene it remains to see this in operation. In 1879 the Birmingham Musical Association was formed by Jesse Collings and other citizens. 'We will,' it was stated, 'make Birmingham's music a blessing to the town: we will have cheap concerts (tickets sixpence and threepence—not more), we will educate the people to understand music; we will learn as to what is being done at home and abroad; we will have a band, a school of music, and a library.' Sol-fa classes were established, choral activity was managed by A. R. Gaul[1] and Rowland Winn, while C. S. Stevens, leader of an amateur orchestra, supervised the instrumental side. At first the concerts (depending on a good deal of altruism on the part of professional musicians) were well patronised, with average audiences of 2616. For four seasons all went well, but in the fifth, a decline of interest reflected in the adverse balance of four hundred pounds on the year's working, led to abandonment of the pristine idealism and retreat to the safer territory of the ballad concert.

EDWARD DE JONG IN MANCHESTER

At about the same time as the Birmingham venture was begun an ambitious scheme of cheap concerts was formulated in Manchester by the Council of the Working Men's Clubs Association. The scheme was federal, uniting various functions of similar character that were given in outlying parts of the city. The programmes were of 'good music'—from oratorio and cantata, with interspersed solo items. As in Birmingham the audiences were large. To explain this is not difficult, for alternative forms of recreation were rare. In 1882 the Council appointed a musical director, in the person of Edward de Jong.

Here again the musical culture of northern England was linked, albeit tenuously, with the great tradition of northern Europe. De Jong was a Dutchman, expert in a number of instruments and something of a composer, who had been one of the first students at the Konservatorium in Köln and a favoured pupil of Hiller. His principal accomplishment was the flute, and after further study in Leipzig and a period of freelance playing in Europe he arrived in London in the early eighteen-fifties with one shilling and sixpence in his pocket. An application to Jullien brought him an engagement in Jullien's band, on tour, and in 1857 he met Charles Hallé, who was looking for players for his Art Treasures Exhibition orchestra. Hallé offered de Jong a job, and a year later he became the principal flautist in the Hallé Orchestra, which he remained for thirteen years. About 1870 de Jong branched out as conductor and, building up

[1] 1837–1913: a composer of (largely) sacred music that was among the worst of its kind and enjoyed great popularity.

his own orchestra of sixty players, gave fortnightly Saturday concerts in the Free Trade Hall.

> Coincidentally with the above, Mr de Jong has directed for the last five years a series of 'Workmen's Concerts' which are given alternatively [sic] with the series just mentioned. These have proved an immense success, and every night tax the extraordinary capacities of the Free Trade Hall to their utmost extent. Seldom is there present . . . an audience of fewer than four thousand persons, whose appearance and demeanour bear comparison with those of the frequenters of the highest class of concerts[1].

The concert manners of the working classes compelled such attention from sceptical observers that it is small wonder that in due course the idea of culture became repellent to the intended beneficiaries. The *Musical Times*[2], in describing de Jong's concerts, could not refrain from drawing attention to the unexpected propriety of the audiences:

> The character of the music is mainly popular and vocal, varied by selections performed by military bands and instrumental solos, while local choral societies lend their aid for the performance of glees, choruses, part-songs, and other concerted music. The soloists are generally local professionals, and the bands are those of the garrison. All performers are paid for their services, and the pecuniary result is very satisfactory, the net receipts thus far more than covered the expenses of the concerts. It is pleasant to add the experience of the Director . . . that 'the behaviour of the audience has always been most orderly; they listen most attentively, and their discretion in applause is most wonderful'.

The premises implicit in such attitudes (which may be discovered in relation to other branches of culture) have, of course, underwritten many estimable ventures which have, however, eventually collapsed under the weight of bourgeois patronage imposed by them, or changed their character. As it happened, at the time when de Jong's concerts flourished there was in Manchester yet another attempt to spread the virtues of the arts. This, conceived at once more modestly and yet more broadly, was one of the most interesting attempts in the late Victorian

[1] From a biographical notice in *Illustrated Sporting and Dramatic News*, Nov. 1885, reprinted in *Manchester Faces and Places*, II, No. 5, Feb. 10, 1891. pp. 73–5. Charges for admission ranged from 4d to 1/–.

[2] 'Music for the People', August 1885, pp. 456–9.

era to bring art into relationship with the facts of industrial life. That part of Manchester known as Ancoats, it was said, 'has been a veritable Klondyke for over fifty years. The gold, however, has gone, but the debris, human and otherwise, was left. How to raise things up to a better level was the problem that faced all of us who thought about things at all, human and social[1].' The writer of this was Charles Rowley (1839–1933), a native of Ancoats, a graduate of evening continuation classes, and a passionate follower of William Morris. Inspired by the revolting conditions then obtaining in Manchester, and by Christian Socialism, Rowley became a City Councillor in 1875. So far as he was concerned improvements in cultural life must come at the same time as those in sanitation and general living conditions, and he campaigned on a broad front.

PIONEER WORK IN ANCOATS

In addition to arranging exhibitions of pictures, and flower shows in Ancoats, Rowley also saw to it that concerts were given in the parks (some of which in due course the municipality took over). in 1889, out of these and other social and intellectual activities, the Ancoats Brotherhood was formed. The members were given the opportunity of hearing lectures—by Oliver Lodge, Walter Crane, William Morris, Bernard Shaw, G. K. Chesterton, Hilaire Belloc, and members of the teaching staff of Owen's College—and music by such artists as Charles Hallé, Neruda, Leonard Borwick, Ludwig Straus, and the Brodsky Quartet. 'The generosity of musicians,' wrote Rowley[2], 'is notorious, and we have tapped it abundantly. Our afternoons have become famous for the quality of our talking, our music, our power of silent listening, and our excellent enthusiasm.' There was, he said, the atmosphere of a salon; but the salon was based on a workman's cottage, at 78 Canning Street, Ancoats, Manchester.

The work of the Ancoats Brotherhood (which continued until the Second World War) in respect of music led Richter to contribute an article on the subject to a Viennese journal; but the principles and practice were most adroitly summarised by Bernard Shaw:

[1] *Manchester Evening Chronicle*, April 16, 1912.
[2] *Ibid.*

Ancoaters who are by nature recalcitrant to Bach and Beethoven simply do not join the Brotherhood, just as the same sort of people in the richer classes do not go to the Symphony concerts, but to races and shoots. The Brotherhood automatically selects from the population of Ancoats the people who need and appreciate music and literature as naturally as others need and appreciate bull dogs and tobacco. The proportion of these is quite as large as, possibly larger than, the proportion in Mayfair ... When Rowley says, in effect, to the Brotherhood, 'You shall not wallow in Beethoven all the afternoon; you must have a tonic; you must wake up and think about public affairs and about the soul of your country between the quartets': he is precisely right. The result justifies him, his people are cultivated but not demoralised[1].

PEOPLE'S PALACE

In the East End of London the fervour for cultural self-help, particularly developed by Octavia Hill through the Kyrle Society, found its most notable musical expression in the Popular Musical Union founded in 1882, 'for the musical training and recreation of the "industrial classes" '. The concerts at the People's Palace, in the East End of London, continued until 1935, but the amount of success achieved in respect of their initial intentions must remain problematic. Bernard Shaw noted the real desiderata after one of his visits:

On Saturday evening, during one of my East End expeditions, I discovered the People's Palace, which consists of a board with an inscription to the effect that if I choose to produce £50,000, the palace will be built for me forthwith. This rather took me aback; for I had thought that the palace was an accomplished fact. But no: there was a huge concert-room, a reading room, and shanties containing a bath, a gymnasium, and a restaurant, also a little clubhouse, but no palace. In the concert-room some unfortunate artists were bawling ballads in the vain hope of gaining the attention of an immense audience. But the thing was impossible: the place was too big. Hundreds of young people loafed and larked, or stared and wandered in and out, at the end of the room. I thought of the late Edmund Gurney—of his useless big book to prove that Wagner's music was wrong and his invaluable little

---

[1] 'The Tyranny of Ancoats', *Manchester Guardian*, reprinted in the *Ancoats Recreation Brotherhood Programme*, 1923–4.

plea for an orchestra for the East End. One hundred and twenty good players, under an able conductor, could make that concert-room useful. They would cost money, too; but why not stick up a board and ask for it?

But there is another way of getting music afoot there. Why not buy first-rate wind instruments; engage a really competent, instructor-bandmaster; and then invite the East End to come in and play for itself. There is plenty of musical talent knocking about misused or misdirected among the wage-workers. I have often heard a knot of East End amateurs with a few brass instruments helplessly making the most hideous discord, because they had never been taught to tune their slides or warned against the impossibility of making up a band with a fortuitous concourse of deadly weapons tuned to different pitches and only agreeing in the single point of having been purchased at a pawnbroker's. With properly assorted instruments and a little simple instruction, these enthusiasts would have made excellent music. The proletarian bands of the industrial north and of the Salvation Army prove it[1].

RESPONSIBILITIES

In the Renaissance and Baroque eras there was virtually no barrier between the composer and his audience, since, within the then narrower confines of public performance, the members of the interested public knew the general principles on which the composer's expression was based and were acquainted in a practical way with the means at his disposal. This is not, of course, to say that every composition met with approval, or that there were not cases of misunderstanding. Bach, for example, was not quite everybody's cup of tea; Handel was sometimes thought to err on the side of excessive noise; the Earl of Kelly upset his fellow Scots by his modernity; Beethoven was an occasional stumbling block to some. But to suggest, as is frequently done by various defenders of new faiths, that all composers who essayed novelty of expression were inevitably subject to contumely and accused of deliberately laying perplexities before their mystified auditors is quite untrue.

It is only since the beginning of the nineteenth century that the great division between creative musician and audience has

[1] May 13, 1889, *London Music in 1888–9*, London, 1937. For other references by Shaw to the same subject see pp. 95, 109, 238, 248.

been erected. The reasons have been exposed. In brief recapitulation they are: the increase of scientific and technical skills (in the widest sense) which has destroyed the competence of the well-informed citizen in a number of fields and reduced his function to that of a specialist in one; the consequent development of instrumental, vocal, and compositional virtuosity to such an extent that an amateur is isolated—in which case he falls back on that part of tradition that he can feel himself to comprehend because, in an ideal sense maybe, it falls within his own potential; the exhibitionist qualities of title-ridden and programmatic music which invites admiration rather than, as was the implication of 'classical' music, participation; and the necessary stabilisation of the concert as an institution, together with the sophisticated organisation that has developed about the composer and his interpreters a *mystique* acceptable to, but in another way also discouraging to, the audience. In the Romantic period the tenets of institutional religion were beginning to be discarded. The opera house provided one form of substitute, the concert hall another. Going to a concert was, and often still remains, a ritual observance.

The malaises of the situation at the end of the nineteenth century—in so far as England was concerned—were exposed by Shaw in every page of his criticism. He was concerned not with the intrinsic quality of music *per se* but with its special significance and social function. Thus, as expressed in relation to the Ancoats Brotherhood, music had to be practised, to be thought about, and then, so to speak, to be put into action. Shaw, preaching in a philistine society, was necessarily obliged to follow such apparent utilitarianism, for it was only by bringing pressure to bear on what had now become the educative aspect of music that any kind of official support (in the form of words only, as a rule) could be compelled. By that time the very virtues of the British concert tradition, of independence and self-help and frequent openmindedness, had become an impediment. In Europe civic and State funds were available for public music, because the paternalist system had, for its own ends. shown the way.

In 1845 John Ella observed that the *Monstre Concerts* in Paris were under the control of the Minister of Fine Arts. 'It were advisable,' he added, 'that a similar power existed in

London, to save the arts from degradation.' He further campaigned for the erection of a proper concert hall in London, which was worse off than the northern cities in this respect, considering its population and the wealth of concert activity, and hardly adequately supplied even after the building of St. James's Hall. Ella further complained of the general high cost of concerts in London, stating that it was a disgrace in 1851 that the only regular orchestral concerts were those of the Philharmonic Society, whereas in Paris there were those of the Conservatoire, the Union, the Saint-Cécile, and the Philharmonic at one quarter of the London price of admission.

Round the corner resided the spirit of communal responsibility, and the prospect—so alarming to Major Lee Higginson—of public maintenance. The question of State subsidies for concerts did not come out into the open until the very end of the century. In 1896 a Mr Whatley W. Ingall, with the approval of George Grove and Hubert Parry—who was 'very anxious to see something of the kind started'—proposed that the local orchestras should be supported by a special local rate. He approached the Prime Minister of the day (Lord Salisbury) who could not 'look upon the maintenance of an orchestra as an expense which could be legitimately defrayed out of the local rates', and the Duke of Devonshire, Lord President of the Council, to whom 'the scheme did not appear of a practical character, or one which the Government could consider'. On the other hand Mr Joseph Chamberlain 'true to radical principles . . . did not see any objection to giving power to local authorities to contribute money for the purpose named[1].'

A little more than twenty years later the General Purposes Committee of the City of Birmingham—the Chamberlain radicalism in local affairs now being prescribed by Neville and orchestral music having been carried on by W. C. Stockley and Swinnerton Heap—reported that it was ready to proceed with a scheme to support a municipal orchestra. Thus was symbolised the inevitable transference of patronage in a modern society; but, however admirable the conduct in this particular of the rulers of Birmingham, their action had been anticipated in almost every large city on the continent of Europe.

[1] *Musical Standard*, February 5, 1898.

Modern Times

ORCHESTRA AND CONDUCTOR

*J*N THE COURSE of the century and a half which passed between the recognition of orchestral music in the acclamation of Corelli as composer and director and the death of Mendelssohn, the principal architect of the balanced programme, the symphony orchestra came to maturity. Existing in its own right—even though connection with an opera house was not uncommon—it constituted a focal point for musical experience. It met the call of the new era. The orchestra became a medium for the expression of heroic, national, romantic ideals; it was there to convey the varied moods of pride—in national achievement or economic and industrial expansion—that spread across the middle ranges of European and American society in the latter part of the nineteenth century; in so far as it could draw attention to the glories of a supposedly golden past through production of the symphonies of the classics—Mozart, Haydn, Beethoven, it could counteract any decline in spiritual conviction. The symphony orchestra came to pre-eminence not fortuitously, but according to a reassembling of both social and musical factors. Having arrived it provided a challenge; to players and conductors, to establish standards of technical excellence, and to composers to make the best use of the opportunities now available. There was, of course, a further challenge; to communities to provide their own orchestras, which had in the past been the more or less casual result of aristocratic patronage.

Some part of this, since change is always gradual, has already been seen, in Paris, Leipzig, Vienna, London, New York, Boston, while the possibilities of accepting this form of music in a more plebian setting have also been made apparent. The full story of the transition of concert music from the nineteenth to the twentieth century, however, centres on the foundation of a number of other organisations; on the development of a public-conscious, virtuoso style of composition through Berlioz, Liszt, Dvořák, Tchaikovsky, Strauss, Mahler, and a large number of assorted 'nationalists'; and on the *persona* of the new hero, the virtuoso conductor. In the nineteenth century the stock of the virtuoso performer declined as that of the conductor rose; and a number of the most eminent performers also undertook commissions as conductors. In a previous age they would have been composers.

PARIS

It was in Paris that particularly rapid development took place on most fronts at the same time. The Concerts du Conservatoire replaced the grand tradition of the Concert Spirituel, while at the other extreme the popularisation of music had been practised by Musard and Valentino. But before the middle of the century, in 1847, Habeneck's pupil Manera founded the concerts of the *Union musicale*, which, after being directed by Félicien David[1], passed into the hands of Berlioz. Between 1849 and 1854 the Société de Sainte-Cécile, using the same premises as the Union musicale, enjoyed a brief but colourful existence under François Seghers (1801–1881), a pupil of Baillot, and here Reber[2], Gouvy[3], Gounod, and Saint-Saëns found opportunity to exhibit the virtues of the new French orchestral style. And when the Société de Sainte-Cécile closed down the same

[1] 1810–76: an interesting study. David belonged to the Saint-Simonians, and after extensive travels in the East attempted, not without success, to write 'oriental' music. His chief work in this genre, *Le Désert* was represented at Habeneck's Conservatoire Concert on December 19, 1847, by the colourful, programmatic excerpts which were not without their effect on Reyer, Delibes, and Gounod, while Berlioz praised David's mastery of orchestration.

[2] Napoléon-Henri Reber (1807–80), pupil and later professor at the Conservatoire, composer of four symphonies, chamber music, and collaborator with Benoist in the ballet *Le Diable amoureux*.

[3] Louis Théodore Gouvy (1819–98), a self-taught composer of French birth who later lived in Germany. Among his works were seven symphonies.

composers transferred their scores to Pasdeloup's *Société des Jeunes Artistes du Conservatoire.*

Jules Pasdeloup (1819–1887), a pupil at the Conservatoire, based his career on a government appointment which came his way after the Revolution of 1848, as a result of which he found himself Governor of the Château of Saint-Cloud and in receipt of such handsome emoluments that he could invade the field of public music without much concern as to its financial return. Making an orchestra from students of the Conservatoire, Pasdeloup aimed at bringing new music to the notice of a not always enthusiastic public; in his aim he was supported 'par de hautes influences'[1]. Pasdeloup gave first hearings to Gounod, Lefébure-Wély[2], Saint-Saëns, the first Paris performance of Mozart's *Il Seraglio*, and fought for the music of Schumann and Wagner. In 1861 Pasdeloup, already engaged as conductor of concerts given under official sponsorship in the Hôtel-de-Ville and the Louvre, moved his concerts from the Salle Herz into the Cirque d'Hiver and, arranging them for Sunday afternoons to coincide with those of the Conservatoire, renamed them Concerts Populaires. Although these concerts suffered interruption during the Franco-Prussian War, they were afterwards resumed and aided by an annual grant from the government of twenty-five thousand francs. Through Pasdeloup the Parisian concert-going public—whose fickleness caused desertions to the Sunday matinées at the theatre and to the concerts of Colonne and Lamoureux—was given a broad view of music of all kinds, with a bias to modern French and German scores.

CHARLES LAMOUREUX

From the French orchestral concert tradition as by now established came the two names which, more than any other, still stand as the guarantee of French orchestral excellence: those of Charles Lamoureux (1834–1899) and Édouard Colonne (1838–1910). Lamoureux was a violin student at the Conservatoire where his teacher was Narcisse Girard, a friend of Berlioz and the first to conduct *Harold en Italie*. After playing for some time

---

[1] A. Elwart, *op. cit.*, p. 58.

[2] Louis Lefébure-Wély (1817–69), sometime organist of the Madeleine and of Saint-Sulpice.

in the orchestra of the Concert du Conservatoire, Lamoureux established chamber music concerts—one of his collaborators was Colonne—at which the music of Brahms of this order was presented for the first time in France. Impressed while in England and Germany by large-scale oratorio performances, Lamoureux, by now determined to specialise as a conductor, founded a Société de l'Harmonie Sacrée, on the model of the English Sacred Harmonic Society, and gave performances of *Messiah*, *Judas Maccabeus*, and the *St. Matthew Passion*, in 1874, that at least established the fact that there was in Paris a large public for this kind of music. But his interests were not limited by his antiquarian zeal, and in 1875 he gave the first performance of Massenet's as yet unpublished *Ève*. Occupying various posts, among which was the deputy conductorship of the Concerts du Conservatoire, Lamoureux took the plunge and became independent of public appointments in 1881, in which year he established the Nouveaux Concerts, or the Concerts Lamoureux. As a conductor he was precise in gesture, firm in intention, and capable of wielding an authority not attained by any previous conductor in Paris. Lamoureux, whose attention to detail was exemplary, was the ideal interpreter for Lalo, D'Indy, Chabrier, Franck, and Dukas, and his zeal for Wagner was considerable. Lamoureux became a conductor of international fame, and he appeared at the St. James's Hall for two concerts in 1881, at Queen's Hall in 1896, 1897, 1898 and 1899.

In this last year his orchestra, which had visited London in 1898, provided the main part of the London Musical Festival. 'Lamoureux had the French vision in art—that is to say, he was greatly preoccupied with order and design. The emotion was there, but simple and symmetrical, and kept strictly within bonds[1].' Lamoureux was succeeded by his son-in-law, Camille Chevillard (1859–1923), who maintained the disciplined tradition of Lamoureux but infused into it a greater degree of warmth. Chevillard, less enthusiastic about French contemporary composers (of whom he was one), was, however, a champion of modern Russian music, of which he was the first to make the Paris public aware. He was also a notable exponent of

[1] Rosa Newmarch, quoted in Henry J. Wood, *My Life of Music*, London, 1938, p. 127. Wood has much to say of Lamoureux, whom he respected most as a great orchestral trainer (see pp. 63, 98, 119, 172, 242).

237

Beethoven, and his interpretation of the Fifth Symphony in Berlin, in 1906, was a landmark in the tradition of orchestral music in that city.

ÉDOUARD COLONNE

Édouard Colonne also graduated as a violinist at the Conservatoire, and having conducted for Pasdeloup and, after 1871, the *Concerts du Grand Hôtel*, went into partnership with the publisher Hartmann and in 1873 and 1874 directed a series of concerts collectively entitled the *Concert National*. From this enterprise (which gave premières of Franck's *Rédemption* and Massenet's *Marie Magdalène*) stemmed the individual concerts eventually to be known as the *Concerts Colonne*. Colonne, intent on promoting the interests of Lalo, Dubois, Franck, and others of the contemporary French school, found it hard going against the well-established Concerts Populaires, but by 1880 his thoroughness in presenting all the orchestral and choral works of Berlioz in their entirety had established him in esteem, and thereafter he enjoyed a reputation equal to that of Lamoureux. Less magisterial than Lamoureux, Colonne had some fire in his temperament and a particular understanding of both the romantic virtues and the qualities of modern French orchestral élan. His especial claim to interpretative fame lay in his commanding advocacy of Berlioz.

TURIN

For one reason or other the later nineteenth century was an age of exhibitions—national, international, artistic, commercial, or in most cases a combination of these categories. An exhibition without a concert, or a series of concerts, was unthinkable, for thereby a kind of spirituality, in other ages confirmed by religious rites, was conferred. At the Paris Exhibition of 1878 the chief musical interest, so far as audience and critics were concerned, centred on the Turin orchestra which came to play under the direction of Carlo Pedrotti (1817–1892) and Luigi Mancinelli (1848–1921), the latter already known in France as the composer of the opera *Ero e Leandra*. The Italians, in some ways the most naturally musical people in Western Europe, were late starters in the field of orchestral music in the nineteenth century, preferring at all times the more exuberant and explicit opera. From this, of course, they supplied singers for all the opera houses in Europe, and most of the concerts. The popularisation of orchestral music *per se* was due in the first place to Pedrotti, who, having been appointed Director of the Conservatoire in Turin in 1867, inaugurated a Committee for Popular Concerts in 1872.

During the next ten years Pedrotti conducted some sixty popular concerts, focusing attention mainly on Beethoven, Rossini, Verdi, Mendelssohn, and Bizet. After Pedrotti's departure from Turin in 1882, concerts in Turin—the most memorable being for the International Exhibition of 1884— were conducted by Franco Faccio (1840–1891)[1], for whose benefit the wealthy Giuseppe Depanis assembled fine players from all over Italy and paid their fees and expenses. Depanis continued his patronage, and in 1898 Arturo Toscanini came to conduct the orchestra, now of more than a hundred players, for yet another exhibition in the city. Toscanini, one of the greatest of all conductors, exercised vast influence in the concert room as in the opera house, and it was largely due to him that the romantic-classical repertoire from Beethoven, through Mendels-sohn and Brahms, to Strauss became established in an initially somewhat reluctant Italy.

If Turin took the lead in orchestral concerts, the vogue was quick to spread, and series were established in Milan (conducted by Faccio), Naples (under Giuseppe Martucci (1856–1909)), Bologna (under Mancinelli), Parma (under Cleofante Campanini)[2], and Rome.

ROME—A LINK WITH THE RENAISSANCE

The concert life of Rome, revived as much for the foreign colonies in the city as for the natives, was under the aegis of the *Congregazione di Santa Cecilia*. This institution, founded as a particular kind of Academy in 1566, and given charters by Popes Gregory XIII and Sixtus V, was well endowed with

---

[1] Faccio conducted Verdi's *Aida* and *Otello* in Milan, in 1872 and 1887 respectively.

[2] Campanini (1860–1919) emigrated to the U.S.A. in 1883.

tradition. Palestrina had, indeed, been among its earliest members; but since that time its fortunes had waned with those of church music in general. In 1839 Gregory XIV gave to the *Congregazione* wider powers, and a School of Music was set up in connection with it by Ettore Pinelli and Giovanni Sgambati. In 1895 the erection of a concert hall made it possible for larger functions to take place, particularly oratorios. The orchestra of the Academy comprised seventy players, and in addition to being conducted by Sgambati also entertained foreign conductors of eminence. Sgambati himself had catholic interests and in his orchestral and chamber music concerts introduced the music of Brahms, Dvořák, Saint-Saëns, Franck, and Fauré.

BERLIN—FOUNDATION OF THE PHILHARMONIC ORCHESTRA

The pattern of concert-giving established in Berlin at the end of the eighteenth century continued until the middle of the nineteenth, with a multiplicity of separately organised events but with no central authority, and with pre-eminence in the orchestral field accorded to Leipzig. But the outcome of the Franco-Prussian War—which also affected the development of French music—and the capital dignity of the city, reflected in a plethora of architectural ventures, made it inevitable that orchestral music should be undertaken on a worthy scale. The possible director of a new enterprise—independent of the opera, whose orchestra from time to time gave public concerts[1]—was Benjamin Bilse (1816–1902). Bilse had represented Prussia at the Paris World Exhibition of 1867, and fortified by the success he there achieved established regular concerts in the Konzerthaus built in 1868. The programmes were popular, the prices cheap (from 40 Pfennigs to 1 Mark 75), and in the curtained recesses in the gallery it was usual to feed simultaneously both

---

[1] Undertakings by the Opera orchestra were, however, subject to the approval of the Intendant General, Georg von Hülsen. In January, 1873, von Hülsen rejected Wagner's application to give a concert in the Opera House. Thus Wagner, employing the orchestral players as individuals, was compelled to use the only available, but not adequate, Concert Hall. His performance, however, received royal patronage and he collected some eight thousand thalers in admission money.

body and soul. Bilse's concerts, ranging from fragments from *Parsifal* to cornet and harp solos by way of the obligatory classics, were, in fact, equivalent to Promenade Concerts. Nevertheless he built up the best orchestra (of seventy players) that Berlin had known, and his players, aware of their potential, looked to higher things. But Bilse lacked the right temperament. His strictness was uncongenial to his players, most of whom came from the more relaxed environments of Saxony and Thuringia, and they determined that they could best exist as a corporate body on their own.

Thus, known at first as the *Frühere Bilsesche Kapelle*, and then, tentatively, as a *Philharmonisches Orchester*, fifty-four musicians sallied forth independently. There was, however, one large impediment to progress: there was no convenient concert hall available other than the Konzerthaus, and that was too small. At first, then, the Philharmonic, keeping close to the popular style of programme initiated by Bilse, performed in the Flora, a garden in Charlottenburg. But in 1882 a change of fashion left the roller-skating rink in Bernburgstrasse vacant in the winter, and it was here that the Berlin Philharmonic Orchestra first set up its flag.

On October 17, 1882, the following programme inaugurated the tradition:

I

Overture, *Leonora 3*	Beethoven
Andante cantabile (String Quartet)	Tchaikovsky
Variations, *Non piu mesta*, for Violin	Paganini
Prelude, *Die Meistersinger*	Wagner

II

Overture, *König Manfred* (first performance)	Reinecke
Fantasia for Flute, *Le Carneval Russe*	Giardi
Nocturne, for 'Cello and Harp	Chopin
Slavonic Rhapsody No. 2 (first performance)	Dvořák

241

III

Overture, *William Tell*	Rossini
Swedish Dance for Strings	Gosson
Polonaise No. 2 (orch. Müller-Berghaus)	Liszt

The programme was directed by Professor von Brenner, but its pattern, comprehending music familiar in the beer-gardens with a certain amount of *avant-gardisme*, was what had been formerly established by Bilse[1]. But the popular character of this programme was offset by the sterner fare provided on the following evening, which was entirely dedicated to Beethoven. The Philharmonic Orchestra was, wrote Eugène d'Harcourt, proudly autonomous, a 'veritable republic' indeed, and it reserved to itself the right to decide who should conduct. Since the unhappy experiences with the authoritarian Bilse conductors of no great distinction came and went, but by 1884 it became clear that if the orchestra was to develop, as its supporters hoped, into one of world rank, some more inspiring and more specialist direction was required. It was hoped that Franz Wüllner, on the point of leaving Dresden, might be induced to take over the orchestra. But since he was offered the succession to Hiller at the Conservatorium and the Gürzenich Subscription Concerts in Köln, he could do no more than make occasional appearances. When he was not there either Joachim or Karl Klindworth (1830–1916) took over. Neither was, however, primarily a conductor. Joachim was, of course, the greatest violinist of his period, while Klindworth was a pianist, a teacher, and a scholar[2]. Both, however, brought wide experience and a generous understanding of music as a whole to the province of orchestral

[1] A Bilse programme quoted in F. Herzfeld, *Die Berliner Philharmoniker*, but undated, gives: Wagner's *Faust* Overture and *Festival March* composed for the Philadelphia Exposition in 1876; Raff's third symphony (*Im Walde*); a concerto by Spohr; Saint-Saëns's *Danse macabre*; the variations from the 'Emperor' Quartet of Haydn, but played by 34 performers; and a miscellany of Waltzes, Polkas, and a cornet solo. Cf. a letter from Hans von Bülow, of January 10, 1882, to his daughter Daniela: 'I am staying at the Park Hotel, near the Skating Rink (selected as a concert hall this time because of the popular character of the programme). Last week I chose the Hotel de Rome, as the six concerts took place in the Singakademie. With the exception of the fourth, a Mendelssohn evening, all of these were sold out so early that there was no box-office open at night.'

[2] As a teacher he counted Hans von Bülow and the American William Mason among his pupils.

interpretation, and helped to endow the Berlin Philharmonic with its distinctive quality of musical insight.

Klindworth, now best known for his reductions of Wagner's music-dramas to pianoforte scores, had a considerable experience of concert promotion in London, where he lived from 1854 to 1868. There, in addition to organising concerts on his own account, he took part in Ella's activities and also those of the New Philharmonic. It was at a New Philharmonic rehearsal on July 4, 1855, that an unusual incident occurred, creditable both to the London players and to Klindworth. Berlioz was conducting and Klindworth was the soloist in Adolf von Henselt's Concerto in F Minor:

> During the progress of the slow movement . . . Berlioz fell into a deep reverie, and, apparently forgetting all about the concerto, he stopped conducting. But the soloist and the orchestra went steadily on. At the end of the movement Berlioz was still entranced, and was only aroused when, at a sign from Klindworth, the orchestra began the last movement with an energetic attack of the opening passage[1].

Klindworth also made his mark in London as a champion of modern music, especially that of Wagner. He was responsible for the first London performance, in 1861, of Anton Rubinstein's 'Ocean' Symphony.

HANS VON BÜLOW AND ARTUR NIKISCH

Not having yet found the ideal conductor, the members of the Philharmonic were overjoyed when, in 1887, they found that Hans von Bülow (1830–1894) was willing to superintend their activities. He conducted his first Philharmonic concert on October 21, 1887, and his last on March 13, 1893, and in this period he gave to the orchestra the reputation that has remained with it. Von Bülow was a remarkable pianist, but his talent for conducting was in no way inferior. Indeed, it may be said that by applying his sensitive yet controlled intellect to the details as well as to the general properties of orchestral music as he did to piano music, and through an understanding of the human qualities of his colleagues, his two main functions were complementary. Before establishing himself in Berlin von Bülow

[1] *Musical Times*, August, 1898.

had made his mark as an orchestral director with the court orchestra of Meiningen[1].

This, for a time the most virtuoso orchestra in Germany, influenced orchestral playing generally, for it frequently went on tour[2]. The Berlin Orchestra now took as its manager Hermann Wolff (whose Viennese-born wife Louise exerted a strong influence on the orchestra's affairs through her talent for hospitality and diplomacy), and to him also went much credit for the strengthening of the tradition. Wolff, once secretary to Anton Rubinstein, left the conductor free to choose the programmes while he engaged the soloists and superintended the general business affairs. The character of the Philharmonic programmes was brought up-to-date by von Bülow, and the formerly ambivalent standards of selection were corrected. Tchaikovsky and Grieg were introduced to Philharmonic audiences, while with the Philharmonic Choir, trained since its inception in 1888 by Siegfried Ochs (1858–1929), performances were given of works by Wolff and Bruckner. Most important, the Philharmonic Hall was built in 1888.

The programme for the inaugural concert on October 5 included:

I

Organ Solo	
Overture, *Die Weihe des Hauses*	Beethoven
Spoken Prologue	
Prelude, *Die Meistersinger*	Wagner

II

Fantasia in C Major (Op. 80)	Beethoven
Pianoforte Solos	
'Hallelujah', *Messiah*	Handel

---

[1] This ducal orchestra, the last survivor of the grand aristocratic tradition, borrowed players from the theatre in Bayreuth and was, therefore closely associated with Wagner. But it also had associations with Brahms.

[2] E.g. 'On the 17th (February) our orchestral tour opens at Göttingen; 18th, 19th, Hamburg; 20th, Kiel; 21st, Lübeck; 22nd, 23rd, Bremen; 24th, Hamburg (matinee at the theatre); 25th to 29th, Berlin.' Von Bülow to Daniela, January, 1884.

On this occasion von Bülow was the pianist, the conducting being shared between his pupil and deputy, Kogel, and Ernest Rudorff, at that time conductor of Stern's Vocal Academy which provided the choral part of the programme.

After von Bülow's retirement in 1893 (he died during the next year) the Philharmonic carried on, principally under Kogel, while the search for a successor was conducted. Von Bülow had disciplined both orchestra and audience, the former to faultless intonation and rhythmic precision, the latter to punctuality and attentiveness. He had brought the orchestra to play modern music and the audiences to welcome it. What was now required was a director competent to maintain these standards, but in a more relaxed manner. Von Bülow was, it was considered after he had gone, somewhat pedagogic. Overtures were made to Richter, Felix Mottl, then conductor at Karlsruhe, Ernst Schuh, Wüllner's successor at Dresden, and Richard Strauss. But finally the appointment went to Artur Nikisch, conductor of the Gewandhaus after Reinecke. Nikisch thus became the most important conductor in Germany, with both the Leipzig and Berlin orchestras under his control. He remained in charge of both until his death in 1922.

AMSTERDAM—THE CONCERTGEBOUW

In the same year that the Berlin Philharmonic Orchestra was inaugurated, so also was the Concertgebouw in Amsterdam. Until that time and from the days of the eighteenth century Collegia Musica—the most celebrated institution of this kind in Amsterdam being that with the title Felix Meritis (1777)—the musical life of Holland had depended almost entirely on Germany, and when a renaissance took place it did indeed owe much to the German tradition. The principal of the Dutch revival was Johannes Verhulst (1816–1891), who as a student enjoyed a royal subsidy, which enabled him to go both to Köln and Leipzig. In the latter city he was highly considered by Mendelssohn and Schumann, with the result that he was entrusted with the direction of the Euterpe Concerts and remained in Germany between 1838 and 1842. On returning to Holland he controlled societies in The Hague, Rotterdam, and Amsterdam. During the period of Verhulst's activity as conductor further impetus came to orchestral music with the winter transformation of the home-guard bands (in the summer the players reverted to this function) at Groningen (1862) and Haarlem (1864)[1] into orchestras. In Amsterdam the principal orchestra was the Park Orkest, conducted by Willem Stumpff until 1883, when it was taken over by Willem Kes (1856–1934).

Encouraged by Verhulst's visits, which were responsible for introducing Liszt, von Bülow, and Brahms to Amsterdam, and by his high reputation both as conductor and composer, the Park Orkest—so named because its concerts originally took place in the Parkzaal—developed into an impressive body. In 1883 the major concerts were entrusted to a private body of subscribers called the Concertgebouw Gezelschap, but as in other cities a major impediment in the way of further progress was the lack of a suitable hall. In 1886, however, the erection of a new hall, designed by J. M. A. Rieke, was begun. Two years later it was ready for occupation, and the first programme to be given in the new Concertgebouw on April 11, 1888, was as follows:

I

'Entry of the Guests', *Tannhäuser*	Wagner
'Hallelujah', *Messiah*	Handel
Overture, Air, Gavotte, *Suite in D*	Bach
'Autumn', *The Seasons*	Haydn

II

Ninth Symphony	Beethoven

The soloists were Joseph Cramer (violin), Elise Harlaacher (soprano), Chr. Veltman (contralto), J. J. Rogmans (tenor), and J. M. Messchaert[2] (bass), the conductor Henri Viotta (1848–1933). Viotta, the son of a doctor turned musician, was an alumnus of the Köln Conservatorium and a keen Wagnerian. At Bayreuth in 1882 he had played the 'cello in the first performance of *Parsifal*, and thereafter he did his best to

---

[1] Similarly derived orchestras were formed in Arnhem (1889) and Utrecht (1894), while a municipal orchestra was established in Maastricht in 1883.

[2] Johannes Messchaert (1857–1922) was a singer of international reputation, and sang in Elgar's *Dream of Gerontius* in Düsseldorf in 1902. (See Elgar; *Letters to Nimrod* (ed. Young), London, 1965).

encourage the Wagnervereiniging, a Dutch society which played an important role in the promotion of new music for more than thirty years. On the other hand Viotta was aware of the forgotten tradition of the past (the inclusion of an item by Bach in the inaugural concert of the Concertgebouw being somewhat unusual at that time) and he was the first Dutchman to revive the music of Sweelinck. He conducted the Caecilia Concerts in Amsterdam from their inception in 1888, and eight years later moved to The Hague to succeed Willem Nicolai as Director of the Royal Conservatory. From the staff and pupils of this institution he was able, in 1913, to found The Hague Residentie Orchestra.

In the autumn of 1888 the first series of Philharmonic Subscription Concerts began in the Concertgebouw, under the direction of Kes, who remained their conductor until 1895. The programme of the opening concert of the series, on November 3rd, was of particular interest in that it contained a major work by a British composer: an unusual gesture, but prompted, no doubt, by the solidarity which might have been thought to exist among small nations inspired by a new sense of national pride. The complete programme otherwise showed affinities with others of the same sort already quoted:

I

Overture, *Die Weihe des Hauses*	Beethoven
Variations on a theme of Haydn	Brahms
Symphonic Poem, *Phaeton*	Saint-Saëns
Prelude, *Die Meistersinger*	Wagner

II

Symphony No. 3 ('Irish')	C. V. Stanford

The season having thus begun with progressive intention so continued. On November 22 Richard Strauss's first Horn Concerto (given first at Meiningen in 1885) received its first Dutch performance. In December Sarasate appeared in Holland for the first time, and in March Eugen d'Albert. In May there was a Wagner evening, the Wagnervereiniging combining with the orchestra of the Concertgebouw to present excerpts from *Lohengrin* and *Die Meistersinger*. In the spring of this season the orchestra established its claim to be the national

R   247

orchestra by playing for the Societät Harmonie in Rotterdam, and the Concert St. Caecilia in Arnhem. At this stage there were three magnificent music-making bodies in Amsterdam, the Concertgebouw, the Toonkunst organisation founded at the same time, and the Wagnervereiniging, and the strength of Amsterdam music lay in the co-operation of all three. On the foundation laid by Kes—who went to Glasgow in 1895 as conductor of the Scottish Orchestra[1], and to Moscow as conductor of the Philharmonic Society[2] in 1898—Willem Mengelberg (1871–1951) built; under his direction the Concertgebouw—by now firmly supported by State and Provincial Government subsidies rather than, as at first, by private subscribers—became world-famous. In an age when brilliance was rapidly becoming the quality most looked for, Mengelberg gave dazzling performances especially of Tchaikovsky, while his pioneer work on behalf of Mahler (the climax of which was the Mahler Festival of 1920) and his outstanding presentations of the *St. Matthew Passion* indicated a generous range of interest. Mengelberg made the Concertgebouw not only a national but also an international institution, so that Grieg, Brahms, Strauss, Rachmaninov, Debussy, Ravel, Respighi, Reger, Elgar, Kodály, Stravinsky, Schoenberg, and Berg, contributed to the programmes, while the practice of introducing famous foreign conductors—in the early days Siegfried Wagner, Artur Nikisch, Karl Muck, and Weingartner were the most outstanding visitors—has been consistently maintained. While Dutch composers have not been neglected by the Concertgebouw, the national character of the orchestra has depended less on narrow dogmas of nationalism than on an extension of the historic function of the country, as a focus for international thought and trade. The musical tradition of a country is, in the first place, the result of geographical circumstances.

CZECH PHILHARMONIC ORCHESTRA

In 1894 another great European orchestra was founded; that of the Czech Philharmonic Society. As in Russia, and Hungary,

[1] The result of the fusion of the Choral Union Orchestra (1874) and the Scottish Orchestra Co. Ltd. (1891) in 1894.

[2] An extension of the Conservatory founded in 1864 (Director, Nikolai Rubinstein).

and Italy, the first impulse towards musical emancipation from the hegemony of alien traditions, both cultural and political, came through opera. This medium understandably was explicit, and, on the whole, more immediately popular than that of 'abstract' music: or so it would appear. At the same time it was a concert in Pardubice, on September 4, 1862, which sparked off the Bohemian cultural revolution. This was a concert to celebrate the tenth anniversary of the death of the poet Turinský, at the conclusion of which the citizens collected outside Turinský's birthplace and sang the hymn (later the national anthem) *Kde domov můj*. This brought repressive action by the Austrian soldiery, the arrest of leading citizens, and impassioned protests against any prohibition of singing. In this year the National Theatre was instituted, providing the necessary incentive for Smetana to formulate a distinctively national form of opera, and also of instrumental music, of which the sequence *Ma Vlast* is the most familiar evidence. Like Erkel and Mosonyi in Hungary (the Budapest Philharmonic Society had been founded by the former in 1863) Smetana was, in the broad sense, an educator. Thus he established a school of music, but also reached out to a wider circle through choral music. It is notable that in the nineteenth century the deeper involvement of people in the more complex processes of musical experience was, in all countries, encouraged by commitment to music through choral performances: a condition which obtains less in the present age, with a consequent barrier being raised between contemporary music and audience. Smetana conducted the society formed by Karel Bendl (1838–1897) in 1865 and known as Hlahol. Thirteen years later a smaller Singverein was created. In the meantime symphony concerts in Prague were given either by the orchestra of the Conservatorium, or by the theatre orchestras. (In addition to the Czech National there was also a German National Theatre.)

In 1894 the members of the Czech Theatre orchestra, according to Viennese precedent, formed themselves into a separate concert-giving organisation, entitled the Czech Philharmonic Society. The first concert of the Society was given on January 4, 1896, Dvořák conducting a programme of his own works. Five years later the Society, its players withdrawing from their theatre commitments, was reorganised and conducted by

Ludvik Čelanský. Under Čelanský and his successor, Oskar Nedbal (viola player in the Bohemian Quartet), the Philharmonic Orchestra, despite the strains imposed by insecure financial backing, undertook missionary tours to Zagreb, Ljubljana, and Rijeka, and in 1902, with Jan Kubelik, the violinist, visited London. The Czech orchestra was conducted by Vilém Zemánek from 1903 to 1918, and during this period consolidated its position. Foreign virtuosi conductors, among them Nikisch, Siegfried Wagner, Safonov (who was exceptional in not using a baton), came to Prague, and on September 19, 1908, Mahler gave the first performance of his Seventh Symphony there. In 1919 Victor Talich, formerly leader of the Berlin Philharmonic, conductor of the Prague Amateur Orchestral Society, and of the Slovena Philharmonic Orchestra, was appointed chief conductor, and to him is due much of the credit for bringing the Czech Philharmonic, with a broad repertoire but also a comprehensive catalogue of Czech music, into the forefront of modern orchestras. In 1925 the Society was relieved of many of its material problems when subsidies were afforded by the Austrian and Bohemian governments, and by the city of Prague. Since the Second World War the orchestra has been guaranteed by the State.

The end of the nineteenth and beginning of the twentieth centuries saw an amazing proliferation of orchestras. Some developed from bourgeois self-esteem and some from nationalism, but these two sources tended to coalesce, and audiences remained constant in constitution, amiably middle-class; while frequent interchanges of orchestral personnel, virtuoso violinists and pianists, and conductors, and the increasing touring habit of whole orchestras, brought into being a predominantly international repertoire. Before the First World War the world suffered its divisions, but this was not apparent in the field of the orchestral concert. Programmes carried the classics, but also a fair representation of new music, and if programme-makers were conscious of local patriotisms they were frequently not reluctant to try at home what went abroad. The success of a particular beneficiary of this open-mindedness was Edward Elgar, whose foreign performances contradicted a view developed in ungenerous days that his music was a somewhat 'narrowly English' taste, and also stood as a reproach to the

more conservative among his fellow countrymen, whose acceptance of his stature on the whole succeeded foreign appreciation[1].

MUSIC IN WARSAW

The progress of music in Poland was similar to that in Bohemia
and Hungary, except that the weight of foreign oppression on
native culture was even heavier. In 1870, however, on the
initiative of certain leading musicians and amateurs, the Warsaw Musical Society was instituted to provide regular series of
symphony concerts, and in 1887 and 1906 choral societies (the
Lutnia and Harfa) of comparable standing to those in other
large cities were established. In 1901 the Warsaw Philharmonic
Society was founded, under the aegis of Prince Lubomirski and
Count Zamoyski, the first chief conductor being Aleksander
Rajchman, and the orchestral players being members of the
State Opera. After the Second World War, all musical activity
coming more directly under the control of the Ministry of
Culture, the Opera and Symphony Orchestras were separated,
thus enabling an expansion of educational concerts with which,
in fact, the Warsaw Philharmonic had been prominent between
the wars.

INTENSIFICATION OF GERMAN TRADITIONS
AND METHODS

In the last quarter of the nineteenth century and the first
decade of the twentieth the domination of the concert-hall, both
in Europe and America, was almost total. German players,
produced in even greater numbers than their own organisations
could absorb, were to be found almost everywhere, and so too
were German, or German-trained, conductors. During this
period the kind of organisation which stemmed from Mannheim

---

[1] One would have hardly expected Elgar's music to have carried into
Hungary, yet in the first years of the century the Budapest Philharmonic,
under István Kerner, played *In the South* (December 19, 1904), *Symphony
No. 1* (October 25, 1909), *Enigma Variations* (December 21, 1910), *Cockaigne*
(October 6, 1912), *Sea Pictures*—3 items (November 6, 1912); while under
Fritz Schalk the Vienna Philharmonic played *In the South* in 1905 (March
12th) and the *Variations* twice in 1906 (June 26, November 11). The whole
range of German appreciation of Elgar during this period is set out in his
Letters to Nimrod (1965).

—where virtuoso orchestra and school of music were inter-
dependent at an early stage—was, in revised form, general.
The so-called musical tradition of Germany was in some ways a
derivative from another tradition considered to be highly
developed in that country; that of organisation.

In Karlsruhe at the turn of the century the Conservatorium,
the Opera, and the Subscription Concerts (the latter self-
supporting and undertaken by the Opera musicians at their own
risk) were under grand ducal patronage. Of the conductors at
Karlsruhe, Michael Balling became conductor of the Hallé
Orchestra in succession to Richter, while Felix Mottl gained an
international reputation: both were disciples of the Wagner
tradition, and Mottl especially was ranked as one of the notable
exponents of Wagner. In Stuttgart also the Symphony Concerts
stemmed from the Opera, and both were supplied from royal,
State, and civic funds.

That the principle of separation between opera and symphony
orchestras was fundamental to an adequate concert life in a
German city was first properly understood by Franz Kaim, a
Stuttgart writer. In 1893 he established a Philharmonic Society
in Munich where he engaged an orchestra of seventy-five
players, controlling it in similar rigorous fashion to Major
Higginson in Boston. Among the early conductors of the Kaim
Orchestra were Hermann Zumpe, who later used his talents
throughout the German provinces, and Felix Weingartner, who
although Austrian by birth, was a conductor entirely trained in
Germany. During the season the Kaim Orchestra gave twelve
regular Philharmonic Concerts, to the rehearsals of which the
public were admitted; there were also twenty *Volks Symphonie-
Konzerte* (30 Pfennigs—1 Mark admission, as compared with
1–6 Mark for those in the first category), and fifty *Populäre
Konzerte* (1–1.50 Mark). These latter differed from the *Volks-
Konzerte* in that eating was allowed during the performance!
This arrangement stemmed from an older tradition (cf. Pleasure
Gardens) much respected by lower middle-class Germans and,
when widely applied, acted as a particular spur to a general,
unselfconscious, appreciation of music. The tradition had, of
course, been given a new lease of life by Bilse in Berlin, whose
'undress' concerts were widely imitated, most effectively,
perhaps, in Dresden where in winter one heard Willy-Olsen's

orchestra in the Gewerbehaussaal and in summer on the Royal Belvedere on the banks of the Elbe. The Kaim orchestra enjoyed a high reputation, not least on account of the variety of the programmes. In a season it was customary for forty or fifty new works (the most important premières were of Bruckner's Fifth and Ninth and Mahler's Sixth symphonies) to be presented—a state of affairs possible only when the conditions were as congenial as they were at Munich. In Hamburg the Conservatorium (f. 1873) was directed by Max Fiedler, who also conducted the concerts of the old-established Philharmonic Society until he went to America to conduct the Boston Symphony Orchestra (1908–1912). Returning from the United States, Fiedler became musical director in Essen and occasional conductor of the Berlin Philharmonic. In Hamburg there was also a *Verein Hamburgischer Musikfreunde* (1896) generously supported by the City Council, for some twenty years the New Philharmonic Concerts directed by von Bülow, and numerous other prosperous societies. In addition to the performances of these bodies there were also regular concerts by the Berlin Philharmonic Orchestra.

If music was thus disposed in the large German cities, as a legitimate public amenity, the smaller municipalities were not lacking in good intention put into practice. There were, for instance, municipal orchestras of between 40 and 70 players in Bielefeld, Bochum, Bremen, Brunswick, Chemnitz, Darmstadt, Dessau, Dortmund, Duisburg, Elberfeld, Erfurt, Essen, Freiburg, Gera, Görlitz, Gotha, Hagen, Halle, Heidelberg, Hildesheim, Kiel, Koblenz, Königsberg, Kottbus, Lübeck, Magdeburg, Mainz, Münster, Nürnberg, Rostock, Schwerin, Sondershausen, Stettin, Weimar, and Zwickau. Such disposition of public funds was and is only, perhaps, possible in a country where such investment had been commonplace since the Middle Ages, and where such expenditure could go through without overmuch philistine regret. But the fact remains that if music is to be built into the life of the community that is the only efficient way of doing it.

MORE AMERICAN ORCHESTRAS

The spirit of private enterprise, however, was indefatigable, especially in the United States, and permanent orchestras—

largely transatlantic repositories of superfluous German talent —were established in Cincinnati in 1895, Philadelphia in 1900, Minneapolis in 1903, St. Louis in 1907, San Francisco in 1910, Cleveland in 1918, and Los Angeles in 1919. The Cincinnati Symphony Orchestra was conducted in its first season by Frank van der Stucken[1], Anton Seidl[2], and Henry Schradieck[3], van Stucken being appointed permanent conductor and remaining as such for twelve years. The Philadelphia Orchestra developed from an amateur Symphony Society organised by Dr W. W. Gilchrist; a professional body was stimulated by the charity concerts given in 1900 for the benefit of those particularly afflicted by the Philippines War of that year, and Fritz Scheel, formerly assistant to von Bülow in Hamburg, became conductor. In 1907–1908 the Philadelphia Orchestra was conducted by Karl Pohlig, and from 1912 to 1938 by Leopold Stokowski. The first conductor of the Cleveland Orchestra was Nikolai Sokolov, a pupil of Rimsky-Korsakov.

In general these great American musical institutions have benefited from private munificence, sometimes on the grand scale, but they also succeeded in maintaining a representative body of middle-class support. They have, both directly and indirectly, given a great impetus to musical education, so that in every case the orchestra is balanced by a teaching institution which not only gives further employment to orchestral players but also guarantees a continuing supply of recruits.

HENRY WOOD AND PROMENADE CONCERTS

Of British musical institutions the most spectacular during this expansionist period was the Promenade Concert as reformed and developed by Henry Wood. The term Promenade Concerts

[1] 1858–1929: Texan, of Belgo-German parentage, van der Stucken studied in Antwerp and Leipzig. He was appointed conductor of the Arion Male Voice Choir in New York in 1884. He conducted works by American composers at the Paris Exhibition of 1889 and was the first conductor to sponsor all-American programmes.

[2] 1850–1898: Austro-Hungarian, conductor at the opera-houses in Leipzig and Bremen before emigrating. Seidl was conductor of the New York Metropolitan Opera (1885) and of the New York Philharmonic Society (1891). He gave the first performance of Dvořák's 'New World' Symphony.

[3] 1846–1918: leader of the Gewandhaus Orchestra. After a brief period in Cincinnati he returned to Germany, to lead the Hamburg Philharmonic Society Orchestra.

had been in sporadic use in England for more than half a century. That the principle had not been more consistently applied was largely due to the dearth of concert halls in London. By 1895, however, the Queen's Hall[1], in Langham Place, was fulfilling the need for a centrally situated auditorium. That concerts, similar to the older Promenade Concerts and to the popular concerts of the German cities (with food and drink available), should be given was the brain-child of Robert Newman, the impresario. But that the idea fructified was due to his perspicacity in engaging Henry Wood as conductor.

Wood came up the hard way. Born in 1869, the son of a 'cellist, his musical talents developed rapidly, so that at the age of thirteen he was giving pianoforte recitals and appearing as solo organist at the International Fisheries Exhibition. He became a church organist, and through a miscellany of accompanying commitments he graduated to the conductorship of various short-lived operatic concerts. During a season of opera at the New Olympic Theatre he conducted *Eugene Onegin*, gaining some reputation by so doing, for Tchaikovsky was then a composer unknown in London. A deep interest in singing led Wood to the Tredegar Choral Union in South Wales, for which he wrote his cantata *Joseph* in 1890, and a few years later he was appointed conductor of the Nottingham Sacred Harmonic Society. Thereafter he conducted many of the large English provincial choral societies. In 1893 he made his first appearance at Queen's Hall, as organist, at the opening concert on December 2. Shortly after this Newman broached the prospective Promenade Concerts, and with the financial and moral backing of a zealous medical practitioner, Dr George Cathcart, the scheme was launched on August 10, 1895.

The first programme was a familiar mixture of ballads, operatic excerpts from Wagner, Ambroise Thomas, Gounod, Bizet, Rossini, and miscellaneous pieces, for solo cornet, solo bassoon, and full orchestra. While the programme was, through Newman's intention to play safe, negligible, its presentation was not. The prices of admission ranged between one and five shillings; the programmes contained analytical notes by Edgar Jacques; there were a fountain and stalls for the sale of refreshments on the floor of the hall, and flowers. So far as the

[1] Destroyed in an air raid, May 11, 1941.

music was concerned this programme inaugurated the new Philharmonic pitch[1], which 'Mr Newman is glad to say . . . will also be adopted . . . by the Philharmonic Society, the Bach Choir, the London Symphony, Mottl, and Nikisch Concerts, and in concerts under [Newman's] direction: i.e. the Queen's Hall Choir, and the Sunday Afternoon Concerts which begin on October 6'[2].

Newman's ambition, shared by Wood, was to 'educate a new public'—an ambition frequently stated but seldom fulfilled. Wood succeeded in realisation of this aim, more, perhaps, than any other conductor of the first half of the twentieth century. That he did so was because of his blend of commonplace qualities (his taste, according to the highest canons far from impeccable, was a good guide to that of his audience) with enthusiasm for new music of all kinds, method in rehearsal, success in abolishing the 'deputy' system[3] which had long flourished among orchestral players, and ebullience of personality. He was also incredibly energetic. The record of Wood's activity is best summarised in the list of 'novelties' introduced at Promenade Concerts between 1895 and 1937 and detailed in Wood's autobiography[4]. His career lasted until his fiftieth season of Promenade Concerts, by which time, available to millions rather than thousands through the medium of radio, they were accepted not only for their own musical content but also as some kind of symbol of British virtue. Disrupted by war, with their home ultimately in ruins, they were kept going, in due course to be handed to the safe-keeping of the British

[1] In England pitch had tended to rise rather than fall during the nineteenth century, and Wagner complained in 1877 of the strain placed on his singers. There were two main reasons: the pre-eminence of the organ, with its high pitch, in musical affairs; and the contention of woodwind instrument-makers that higher pitch ensured the better tone. At the Viennese International Conference of 1885, which helped to stabilise low pitch on the Continent, Britain was not represented. But there were those who argued that Britain should come into line. Newman's insistence on the new tuning for the Queen's Hall organ was, in the end, decisive. It was resolved on July 11, 1895, 'that henceforth the Philharmonic Society will adopt the French Diapason Normal Pitch'.

[2] From programme of first Promenade Concert.

[3] When Wood finally won his point in 1904 some forty players, objecting, seceded from the Queen's Hall Orchestra to found their own. This was the London Symphony Orchestra, which was based, like the Berlin Philharmonic which had started in much the same way, on a co-operative principle.

[4] *My Life of Music*, London, 1938, pp. 353 ff.

Broadcasting Corporation and Sir Malcolm Sargent, whose credentials in versatile musicianship and public relations well qualified him to continue and expand the established tradition.

AUDIENCE AND CONDUCTOR

In the seventeenth and eighteenth centuries the concert may be said to have been controlled by the audience, in that the function was more social than ritual. During that period it may be taken for granted that performances came within the category of *Unterhaltungsmusik*—that is, music to accompany conversation—or merely recreational. At the early Gewandhaus concerts the Chairman would often indicate the need for greater attention by hitting a chord on the pianoforte when conditions threatened to grow out of hand: on the whole the present attitude of piety on the part of audiences was unknown. On the credit side there was no general aversion from music that was contemporary. This aversion began to show during the nineteenth century as a by-product of backward-glancing Romanticism, but the rapid growth and appreciation of technical standards of orchestras at that time—which caught up with the problems of adequately interpreting chiefly Beethoven (but also Haydn and Mozart)—also provided composers with opportunities to exploit a new range of timbres in such a way that the general aesthetic and philosophic principles of the age were exposed in a compelling manner. Thus in programmes up to the First World War there was, in general, a fair balance between the old and the new. Between Spohr's seventh symphony, *Irdisches und Göttliches im Menschenleben*, and Mahler's eighth, there were not many tracts of intellectual speculation, or historical or biographical circumstances, that had not been treated in musical form. It has, in fact, taken a good deal of the twentieth century to come to terms with the nineteenth—which is one reason (among others) why so much music of that era is to be found in present-day programmes. First of all, decisions had to be made as to what was worthy of preservation and what was not. Secondly, performers had to grow up to the music. This matter of catching up started after the so-called classical era; it is likely to continue into the foreseeable future.

The extension of orchestral virtuosity entailed a further change. In the eighteenth and early nineteenth centuries the solo singer (indispensable at a symphony concert until the beginning of this century) or the pianist, or the violinist, commanded individual attention. In the case of solo pianist or principal violinist (and either might also be a composer) the status was higher in that in one or other or both reposed a great deal, if not all, of the responsibility for the whole performance. When the directorial function was removed to the conductor the latter naturally became a figure of dignity. By the end of the century he was supreme: often a dictator, so far as the subordinate players were concerned; an arbiter in the matter of composers' intentions (so long as the composer was either dead or absent), and interpretation; a kind of semi-deity to audiences which by now had acquired a docile reverence not known in days when audiences were to a large extent made up of active amateurs able themselves to cope with all but the severest demands of the music of their own generation. A number of the major conductors of the era of development have been mentioned. The greatest, perhaps, was Nikisch, conductor of the Gewandhaus and Berlin Philharmonic Orchestras in Germany, of the Boston Symphony Orchestra in America, and of the concerts which went by his name in London and in many parts of Europe. 'He was,' said Wood, 'certainly the greatest master of emotional expression I ever met[1].' Since Nikisch two generations of conductors have grown to maturity and carrying the heroic properties of the office into the twentieth century, have successfully maintained the primacy in the public field of music. While the virtuoso qualities of conductors have maintained a *status quo* (though smaller ensembles like the Netherlands Chamber Orchestra have reverted for Baroque music to a Baroque disposition of direction by a performing Konzertmeister) those of the major orchestras have contributed to the general revolution in musical thought that has produced what is generically termed 'modern music'. An intellectual revulsion against programmatic music (not necessarily shared by audiences), a discontinuance of former methods of design, both stemming from the temper of the times, have much responsibility for the character of *avant-garde* idioms; but not all.

[1] *Op. cit.*, pp. 160–1.

The orchestral works of Stravinsky, Messaien, Henze, and Nono, as well as those of a somewhat different approach, of say, Malcolm Arnold, are all as much due to recognition of high orchestral talent as were those of Berlioz a century ago.

Compared with a century ago, however, there is this difference; that the gap between composer and audience has widened. The resistance to living music by audiences is stronger than it was at any time. There are two interpretations of this situation, each being the result of dogmas which are applied to music (and the arts in general) from without. Where the freedom of the composer to express his personality (whatever that may mean) is a paramount consideration the audience is to blame, or to be pitied for its collective stupidity; where, on the other hand, the cultural requirements of the audience, defined in rather general terms, came first, the fault is with the composer. This brings us back to the question of patronage.

OFFICIAL LINES

In a narrow sense music may, no doubt, be said to exist *per se*, seeking no justification other than that of existing. Anyone is at liberty to compose, or to perform, or to listen. But where the three factors are brought together a whole lot of new ones emerge, which have been indicated throughout this book. The central one is financial. The provision of music is more or less expensive. The underwriting of the necessary expenses could once, in a narrow sense, be treated as a private responsibility; but even when it was, considerations of prestige emerged. And at this point diplomatic and political issues became apparent. There is no dynasty which has appeared in the role of patron of the arts which has not collected from the judgments of history a sizeable credit balance to set against whatever sins of omission or commission may show in other fields. Frederick the Great is certainly remembered more for his hospitality to Sebastian Bach than for his aggressions against Maria Theresa. In the changed circumstances of the later twentieth century communal and official attitudes to music stem from the past, and music itself is no less conditioned by extra-musical considerations.

In general terms music is regarded, somewhat vaguely, as a good thing. As a good thing it falls into one of two categories, those of luxury and necessity; or it falls between these two into the classification of past-luxury-present-necessity. In the English-speaking countries, for the most part, bourgeois standards are still dominant. Concerts are mainly organised for a middle section of society according to the principles of taste which are acceptable to the dogmas of classical capitalism. They should be self-supporting; better still, profit-making. This being so the promoters must play safe, and in thinking of their receipts admit only what is commercially viable. Thus in a period in which virtuoso achievement is venerated to a greater extent than ever before, emphasis must lie on brilliance of execution rather than on the intrinsic properties of musical works. The result is that too many orchestras pursue too few works, with a disastrously compressing effect on the public which, in any case, is held responsible for such contraction.

At this juncture education comes into the picture again, and we are back with practically every missionary since the end of the eighteenth century, and ambitious to educate a new public. Concerts for schools—once promoted in America by Theodore Thomas, launched on a generous scale by Robert Mayer in England in 1923, and subsequently sponsored by some few education authorities in Britain; concerts for 'workers', the latter few, half-hearted, and tainted with the idea of charity. While official policy in Britain is philistine (finding any generous endowment of the arts from public funds some kind of restriction on freedom, or a distasteful inconvenience) it is also ambivalent. The partial subsidisation of certain activities, mainly opera and the symphony orchestras, is undertaken by the semi-official Arts Council. But the inadequacy of the gesture is reflected in the working lives of the orchestral players, and the dearth of any kind of concert-life in all but a handful of large cities. All British orchestras have too many concerts (with too few rehearsals) to give, with their members additionally dependent on private engagements of one kind or another in order to maintain themselves.

In many parts of Europe on the other hand the conditions created in the nineteenth century have remained, with generous State and civic contributions. In Eastern Europe the matter is simpler. The principal orchestras are publicly owned, in the sense that their members are State (or municipal) employees. Where there are Ministries of Culture, working on the principle that what formerly was a bourgeois preserve must now be a general amenity wherever possible, there is a good deal of vigorous direction of activity. Concerts in schools, for youth organisations, and in factories are a regular part of the social framework. The extent to which people are thus made receptive is arguable. Probably it is not a point to be laboured in any case, since the issue of improvement (of morals, or imagination) of people is an irrelevance. What matters is the enrichment of experience and the extension of the doctrine that such enrichment comes in its own way through opportunity. There is also something to be said for the principle of equality of opportunity.

The concert began as an entertainment for princes. It escaped from the aristocratic environment to become a symbol of middle-class pride. Another social revolution has left it half in the old and half in the new order. It is inevitable that in due course it will undergo further adaptation; and so too will music.

BIBLIOGRAPHY

ALFIERI, P. *Accademia di Santa Cecilia di Roma*, Rome 1845

ANON. *A Succinct Account of the Person, the Way of Living, and of the Court of the King of Prussia, translated from a curious manuscript in the French Found in the Cabinet of the late Field Marshall Keith*, London, 1759

ANON. *Concert Strictures revived*, Dublin, 1805

ASOW, H. and MUELLER, E. H. VON *Collected Correspondence of C. W. Gluck*, London, 1962

ARNOLD, DENIS 'Orphans and Ladies: the Venetian Conservatoires (1680–1790)' in *PRMA*, 1962–3 p. 31 *et seq.*

BAGENALL, HOPE 'Musical Taste and Concert Hall Design', in *PRMA*, 1951–2, p. 11 *et seq.*

BECKFORD, WILLIAM *The Travel Diaries*, Cambridge, 1928

BENNETT, JOSEPH *A Story of Ten Hundred Concerts, 1859–87* (History of Monday and Saturday Popular Concerts to the 1000th concert), London 1896

BLAINVILLE, C. H. DE *Histoire générale critique et philologique de la Musique*, Paris, 1767

BLOESCH, HANS *Bernische Musikgesellschaft, 1815–1915* (with earlier history), Berne, 1915

BRENET, M. *Les Concerts en France sous l'ancien Régime*, Paris, 1900

BRIDGMAN, NANIE 'Fêtes italiennes de plein air au Quattrocento', in *Hans Albrecht Gedenkschrift*, Kassel, 1962

BROSSES, CHARLES DE *Lettres familières sur l'Italie*, Paris, 1931

BURGH, A. *Anecdotes of Music*, London, 1814

CARSE, ADAM *The Orchestra in the Eighteenth Century*, Cambridge, 1940

CASTIGLIONE, BALDASSARE *Il Cortegiano*, tr. T. Hoby, London, 1561

CUDWORTH, CHARLES 'Vivaldi and the Symphony', in *Ricordiana*, Vol. 8, No. 1, 1963, p. 1 *et seq.*

Deakin MSS, Vol. 20, Birmingham City Library, 255235

DEAS, STEWART; 'Arcangelo Corelli', in *Music and Letters*, XXXIV, p. 1 *et seq.*

DIBDIN, CHARLES *Musical Tour, 1787–88*, London 1788

DIDIER, LIMOJON DE ST. *The City and Republick of Venice*, London, 1699

Dittersdorf, The Autobiography of Karl von (dictated to his son), trs. A. D. Coleridge, London, 1896

DOERFELL, ALFRED *Geschichte der Gewandhauskonzerte zu Leipzig*, Leipzig, 1884

EINSTEIN, ALFRED (ed.) *Lebensläufe deutscher Musiker von ihnen selbst erzählt*, I. Johann Adam Hiller (1728–1804), Leipzig, [1915]

ELLA, JOHN *First Annual Record of the musical winter evenings*, London, 1852

——*Record of the Musical Union*, 1845 etc., London, 1845–52

ELWART, A. *Histoire des concerts populaires*, Paris, 1864

——*Histoire de la Société des Concerts du Conservatoire Impérial de Musique*, Paris, 1860

ERSKINE, JOHN *The Philharmonic Symphony Society of New York, Its First Hundred Years*, New York, 1943

Evelyn, Memoirs of John, ed. William Bray, 2 vol., London, 1819

FARMER, H. G. 'Music in 18th Century Scotland', in *Scottish Art and Letters*, No. 2, Glasgow, 1946

——*Music Making in the Olden Days*, London, 1950

——*The Royal Artillery Concerts (1810–1911)*, London [n.d.]

FÉDOROV, VLADIMIR 'Des Russes au concile de Florence, 1438–9', in *Hans Albrecht Gedenkschrift*, Kassel, 1962

FELLER, MARILYN 'The New Style of Giulio Caccini, Member of the Florentine Camerata', in *Bericht über den siebenten internationalen musikwissenschaftlichen Kongress, Köln 1958*, Kassel, 1959

GANZ, A. W. *Berlioz in London*, London, 1950

GENEST, J. *Some Account of the English Stage*, London, 1832

GRADENWITZ, PETER *Johann Stamitz*, Prague, 1936

GROVE, SIR GEORGE *Analytical Notes in Book Form*, London, 1896

——*Life and Letters*, London, 1904

HALLÉ, SIR CHARLES *Life and Letters* (ed. C. E. and M. Hallé), London, 1896

HANSLICK, E. *Geschichte des Concertwesens in Wien*, 2 vol., Vienna, 1869–70

HARCOURT, E. D', I *La Musique actuelle en Italie:* II *La Musique actuelle en Allemagne et Austriche-Hongrie*, Paris, 1908

HARRIS, D. H. *Saint Cecilia's Hall in the Niddry Wynd*, Edinburgh, 1911

HELM, E. E. *Music at the Court of Frederick the Great*, Oklahoma, 1960

HERZFELD, FRIEDRICH *Berliner Philharmoniker*, Berlin, 1960

HILLER, J. A. *Wöchentliche Nachrichten und Anmerkungen die Musik betreffend*, Leipzig, 1766–70

HOGARTH, GEORGE *Musical History, Biography and Criticism*, 2 vol., London, 1838

HOWE, M. A. DE WOLFE *The Boston Symphony Orchestra*, Boston and New York, 1931

ISRAEL, K. *Frankfurter Konzertchronik*, Frankfurt, 1876

JOHNSON, H. EARLE *Musical Interludes in Boston*, 1795–1830, New York, 1943

KIRKPATRICK, RALPH *Domenico Scarlatti*, Princeton, 1953

KLOB, K. M. *Drei musikalische Biedermänner*, Ulm, 1911

KOBALD, KARL *Klassische Musikstätten*, Vienna, 1929

KREHBEIL, H. E. *The Philharmonic Society of New York*, New York and London, 1892

KRÜGER, WALTHER *Die authentische Klangform des primitiven Organum*, Kassel, 1958

LANDON, H. C. ROBBINS *The Collected Correspondence and London Notebooks of Joseph Haydn*, London, 1959

MADEIRA, LOUIS C. *Annals of Music in Philadelphia and History of the Musical Fund Society*, Philadelphia, 1896

MELLERS, WILFRID *François Couperin*, London, 1950

Miscellaneous

——*Concertgebouw/Concertgebouworkest:* Jubileennummer Preludium, Amsterdam, Sept 1962

——*Czech Philharmonic, The*, Prague, 1956

——*Denkschrift zur Feier des fünfzigjährigen ununterbrochenen Bestandes der Philharmonischen Konzerte in Wien, 1860–1910*, Vienna and Leipzig, 1910

——*Festschrift zum 175 Jährigen Bestehen der Gewandhauskonzerte*, Leipzig, 1956

——'La Jeunesse de Mme de la Pouplinière', in *Revue des Deux Mondes*, Feb. 1917

——*Liverpool Philharmonic Society, Programme and Rules*, 1840–

——*Musical Directory of the Royal Academy of Music*, London, 1853

——*Reid Concert Programmes*, 1867–74, Edinburgh

——*St. James's Hall: Monday Popular Concerts*—Programmes and Analytical Remarks, 1859–1904

——*St. James's Hall Concerts, Analytical programmes of the* (with notes by Grove and others), 1879–1904

——*Worcestershire Philharmonic Society, Programmes of the* (with notes by Sir Edward Elgar), 1898–1904

——*Zur Geschichte der Sing-Akademie in Berlin*, Berlin 1843

——*Zürichs musikalische Vergangenheit im Bild*: Neujahrsblatt der Allgemeinen Musikgesellschaft Zürich, CXXXIII/CXXXIV, 1945–6

——*50 Jaar Concertgebouw, 1888–1938*, Amsterdam, 1938

MITTAG, ERWIN *The Vienna Philharmonic*, Vienna, 1950

MUELLER, JOHN H. *The American Symphony Orchestra*, Indiana, 1951

NETTEL, R. *The Englishman Makes Music*, London, 1952
——*The Orchestra in England*, London, 1946
PARKE, W. T. *Musical Memoirs*, 2 vol., London, 1830
PEACHAM, HENRY *The Compleat Gentleman*, London, 1622
PINCHERLE, MARC *Corelli*, Paris, 1933
PISCHNER, HANS *Musik und Musikerziehung in der Geschichte Weimars*, Weimar, 1954
PINTHUS, GERHARD *Das Konzertleben in Deutschland*, Strassburg, 1932
PREUSSNER, E. *Die bürgerliche Musikkultur*, Hamburg, 1935, Kassel, 1950
REDWAY, V. L. 'A New York Concert in 1736', in *Musical Quarterly*, 1936, p. 170 *et seq.*
REICHARDT, J. F. *Briefen eines aufmerksamen Reisenden*, Frankfurt, 1776
——*Schreiben über die Berlinische Musik*, Hamburg, 1773
RIESS, KARL *Musikgeschichte der Stadt Eger in 16 Jahrhundert*, Brno/Prague, 1935
ROLLAND, ROMAIN *A Musical Tour through the land of the past* (trs. Bernard Miall) London, 1922
SADIE, STANLEY 'Concert Life in Eighteenth Century England' in *PRMA*, 1959, p. 17 *et seq.*
Samuel Scheidt Festschrift, Wolfenbüttel, 1937
SCOTT, H. A. 'London's earliest public concerts', in *Musical Quarterly*, 1936, p. 446 *et seq.*
SERAUKY, W. *Musik der Stadt Halle*, Halle, 1939
SERAUKY, W., SASSE, K., SIEGMUND-SCHULTZE, W. *Halle als Musikstadt*, Halle, 1954
SITTARD, JOSEF *Zur Geschichte der Musik und des Concertwesens in Hamburg*, Leipzig, 1890
SMITH, J. SUTCLIFFE *The Story of Music in Birmingham*, Birmingham, 1945
SONNECK, O. *Early Concert Life in America*, New York, 1949
Spohr, Louis, The Musical Journeyings of, ed. and trs. H. Pleasants, Oklahoma, 1961
STRAETEN, E. VAN DER *The Romance of the Fiddle*, London, 1911
STRUNK, OLIVER *Source Readings in Musical History*, London, 1952
Telemann, Georg Philipp, Autobiography of, trs. Stanley Godman, in *The Consort*, 1953, p. 20 *et seq.*
TILMOUTH, MICHAEL 'Some early London concerts and Music Clubs, 1670–1720', in *PRMA*, 1957–8, p. 13 *et seq.*
TWINING, REV THOMAS *A Country Clergyman of the Eighteenth Century* (A selection from his correspondence), London, 1882

Uffenbach, Die musikalische Reisen des Herrn von, ed. E. Preussner, Kassel, 1949

WALTER, F. (ed.) *Archiv und Bibliothek des Grossh. Hof- und National-theaters in Mannheim, 1779–1839*, 2 vol., Leipzig, 1899

WERNER, ARNO, *Freie Musikgemeinschaften alter Zeit im Mittel-deutschen Raum*, Wolfenbüttel and Berlin, 1940

——*Städtische und Fürstliche Musikpflege in Weissenfels*, Leipzig, 1911

——*Städtische und Fürstliche Musikpflege in Zeitz*, Bückeburg, Leipzig, 1922

WESLEY, SAMUEL and CHARLES, Accounts of the Subscription Concerts of 1779–83 BM, Add. Ms. 35017

WOOD, HENRY J. *My Life of Music*, London, 1938

WYNDHAM, H. SAXE *August Manns and the Saturday Concerts*, London, 1909

Index